PRAISE FOR

"My frien[...] [...] onfidence in the Lo[...] true 'steel magnolia.[...] , when to console and when to confront, how to be both a peacemaker and a warrior. Mary is the right kind of strong. I can't think of anyone better to help you navigate the challenge of living in a world that celebrates and promotes a very different kind of strength. The seven strength-building habits Mary unpacks from God's Word are foundational. This book will not leave you unchanged. I wholeheartedly commend it."

—NANCY DEMOSS WOLGEMUTH,
AUTHOR; FOUNDER AND TEACHER
OF REVIVE OUR HEARTS

"Mary Kassian's *The Right Kind of Strong* is the right kind of book for the culture we, as Jesus-adoring Christians, have been placed in. Around us are a plethora of voices, images, tweets, blogs, and influencers appealing to that nagging mumble inside of us all that tells us not to be weak. Naturally, we rarely silence this voice with humility before God and submission to His Word that would then lead us to discover the kind of strength that He delights in. And it's for that reason alone that Mary's book is the theological compass for our lost and drifting girls, women, mothers, daughters, sisters, and friends. Mary's words have theological depth, humor, and cultural relevance. By reading and receiving them, we will have more women who have found their strength in a Savior who's really good at making the weak strong."

—JACKIE HILL PERRY, SPEAKER, POET,
AND ARTIST; AUTHOR OF *GAY GIRL,*
GOOD GOD: THE STORY OF WHO I WAS,
AND WHO GOD HAS ALWAYS BEEN

"Compelling. Radical. Beautiful. Mary did an excellent job of showing us why a strong woman isn't built on power and hustle, but on humbly acknowledging our need for Christ and embracing His strength in our lives. We pray this book inspires many generations of Christian women to rise up and become the right kind of strong women for God's glory!"

— KRISTEN CLARK AND BETHANY
BEAL, FOUNDERS OF GIRL DEFINED
MINISTRIES, AUTHORS, AND YOUTUBERS

"I needed this book! It gave me permission to be strong but invited me to a holy weakness that allows God's strength to shine in me. For every woman who is walking well with God and thinks she may be spiritually strong, Mary challenges you to examine the vestiges of weakness to which you may be blinded, and invites you to a new revival of Truth."

—DANNAH GRESH, FOUNDER
OF TRUE GIRL AND AUTHOR
OF LIES GIRLS BELIEVE

"In a society that is increasingly obsessed with empowering women for all the wrong reasons, this book is a refreshing challenge to be strong in the Lord. In her typical no-nonsense style, Mary A. Kassian gives us a clear punch list of seven habits to develop as we swim against the cultural tide and avoid at all costs the behavior of weak-willed women found in 2 Timothy 3. Mary's wise biblical instruction coupled with down-to-earth illustrations are a winning combination. This book will be a valuable addition to the library of women in all ages and stages who are truly seeking to be spiritually strong to God's glory."

—MARY K. MOHLER, AUTHOR OF
GROWING IN GRATITUDE; PRESIDENT'S
WIFE AND DIRECTOR OF SEMINARY
WIVES INSTITUTE, THE SOUTHERN
BAPTIST THEOLOGICAL SEMINARY

"Mary Kassian has given a gift to Christian women by reclaiming the word *strong* from a culture that has distorted what God meant for women today. Building upon 2 Timothy 3, Mary paints a much needed, clear picture of a strong woman who is a follower of Christ. A must-read for women, especially leaders, today."

—TERRI STOVALL, DEAN OF WOMEN'S
PROGRAMS AND PROFESSOR OF
WOMEN'S MINISTRY, SOUTHWESTERN
BAPTIST THEOLOGICAL SEMINARY

"Mary Kassian has written a timely book in our era of overturning the historical wrongs done to women. We definitely need more strong women in every generation! But Mary's book shows us that this is not a new trend. God has always wanted His daughters to be strong—'in the strength of His might' (Eph. 6:10). Mary flips your expectations in this book. If you are expecting girly fluff, you won't find it. If you are expecting self-centered girl power, you won't find that, either. Instead, you will be challenged to develop the kind of discernment, wisdom, and spiritual habits that will ensure that you are truly a strong woman to the end. A great resource for discipling women of all ages!"

—CAROLYN MCCULLEY, AUTHOR
OF *THE MEASURE OF SUCCESS*
AND *RADICAL WOMANHOOD*

"My twenty-something-year-old fierce self could've desperately used this, but even now, my fifty-something-year-old self is deeply encouraged and challenged by these truths. I love this book. Mary's insight into the right kind of strength provides women with a worthy pursuit: being courageous enough to live for God's glory, no matter the cost. This is a thorough work that provides women with spine-strengthening theology plus practical help! I want every woman I know to have this resource. (I'll be buying a lot of copies! It's a great investment.)"

—KIMBERLY WAGNER, AUTHOR
OF *FIERCE WOMEN*

"I was the eighth-grade girls wrestling champion. Now, decades later, I want to know how to demonstrate strength as a wife, a mother, a daughter, a friend, and an ambassador for the gospel, while walking with the humility Christ calls me to. That's why I'm grateful for this book. In the wise style we've come to expect from her, Mary Kassian discredits cultural messages about strong womanhood while pointing us to the source of true strength, God's Word."

—ERIN DAVIS, AUTHOR, BLOGGER,
BIBLE TEACHER, (AND GIRLS
WRESTLING CHAMPION)

"In a time when women-empowerment messages are at an all-time high, I couldn't imagine a more needed message than the one found in *The Right Kind of Strong*. By unpacking the scripture in relatable and refreshing ways, Mary Kassian exposes how surprisingly flimsy the 'strength' being peddled by the world is. In this book you'll find an experienced guide and trusted friend in Mary, as she graciously leads you to discover what makes for a truly strong woman."

—KELLY NEEDHAM, AUTHOR OF *FRIEND-
ISH: RECLAIMING REAL FRIENDSHIP
IN A CULTURE OF CONFUSION*

THE RIGHT KIND OF STRONG

THE RIGHT
KIND OF
strong

SURPRISINGLY SIMPLE HABITS
OF A SPIRITUALLY STRONG WOMAN

MARY A. KASSIAN

NELSON
BOOKS

An Imprint of Thomas Nelson

Published in Nashville, Tennessee, by Nelson Books, an imprint of Thomas Nelson. Nelson Books and Thomas Nelson are registered trademarks of HarperCollins Christian Publishing, Inc.

Published in association with the literary agency of Wolgemuth & Associates, Inc.

Thomas Nelson titles may be purchased in bulk for educational, business, fund-raising, or sales promotional use. For information, please e-mail SpecialMarkets@ThomasNelson.com.

Any Internet addresses, phone numbers, or company or product information printed in this book are offered as a resource and are not intended in any way to be or to imply an endorsement by Thomas Nelson, nor does Thomas Nelson vouch for the existence, content, or services of these sites, phone numbers, companies, or products beyond the life of this book.

Unless otherwise noted, Scripture quotations are taken from the ESV* Bible (The Holy Bible, English Standard Version*), copyright © 2001 by Crossway, a publishing ministry of Good News Publishers. Used by permission. All rights reserved.

Scripture quotations marked GNT are taken from the Good News Translation in Today's English Version—Second Edition. Copyright 1992 by American Bible Society. Used by permission.

Scripture quotations marked HCSB are taken from the Holman Christian Standard Bible*, copyright © 1999, 2000, 2002, 2003, 2009 by Holman Bible Publishers. Used by permission. HCSB* is a federally registered treademarks of Holman Bible Publishers.

Scripture quotations marked KJV are taken from the King James Version.

Scripture quotations marked THE MESSAGE are taken from The Message. Copyright © by Eugene H. Peterson 1993, 1994, 1995, 1996, 2000, 2001, 2002. Used by permission of Tyndale House Publishers, Inc.

Scripture quotations marked NASB are taken from the New American Standard Bible*, Copyright © 1960, 1962, 1963, 1968, 1971, 1972, 1973, 1975, 1977, 1995 by The Lockman Foundation. Used by permission. (www.Lockman.org)

Scripture quotations marked NIV are taken the Holy Bible, New International Version*, NIV*. Copyright © 1973, 1978, 1984, 2011 by Biblica, Inc.™ Used by permission of Zondervan. All rights reserved worldwide. www.zondervan.com. The "NIV" and "New International Verion" are trademarks registered in the United States Patent and Trademark Office by Biblica, Inc.™

ISBN 978–1–4002–0984–2 (eBook)

Library of Congress Cataloging-in-Publication Data

Names: Kassian, Mary A., author.
Title: The right kind of strong : surprisingly simple habits of a
spiritually strong woman / Mary A. Kassian.
Description: Nashville : Thomas Nelson, 2019. | Includes bibliographical
references.
Identifiers: LCCN 2018054926 | ISBN 9781400209835 (pbk.)
Subjects: LCSH: Christian women--Religious life.
Classification: LCC BV4527 .K375 2019 | DDC 248.8/43--dc23 LC record available at https://lccn.loc.
gov/2018054926

Printed in the United States of America

19 20 21 22 23   LSC   10 9 8 7 6 5 4 3 2 1

*To my mother
and to
Pearl, June, Marigold, Sarah, and Dorothy—
Strong Women
of the little pink church on the corner*

CONTENTS

No Weak Girls Here

She dresses herself with strength and
makes her arms strong. . . .
Strength and dignity are her clothing.

—Proverbs 31:17, 25

I was good at arm wrestling.

And proud of it.

I could defeat all the girls at my middle school and many of the boys too.

As the only girl in a household of six kids, I was bent on proving that I was just as strong as my brothers. Anything they could do I could do better. Hitting a baseball? Performing a daredevil balancing act across the train trestle? Building a woodworking masterpiece in Dad's garage? Scuttling up a tree? Collecting a handful of slugs? No problem. I could do it.

Independent. Capable. Confident. Fearless. Strong.

That was me.

My can-do attitude was bolstered by the rise of second-wave feminism. During my childhood the airwaves were filled with Girl Power anthems. I knew most of the lyrics by heart and often hummed them under my breath as I went through my day. Nancy Sinatra's "These Boots Are Made for Walkin'" convinced me that a strong woman crushes any man who dares cross her. Look out, guys . . . one of these days my boots might just walk all over you!

Aretha Franklin's catchy tune empowered me to demand boldly that my five brothers (and all the other males in my life) *respect* me. And then there was Helen Reddy's "I Am Woman," which reinforced that I ought to be strong . . . invincible even.[1]

Yup.

I was sure that being strong and invincible was what womanhood was all about. Little patience did I have for girls who didn't grasp this fundamental concept.

The other girls were content to enroll in the obligatory home economics course. Not me. I lobbied my principal to let me take mechanics/shop and drafting with the boys instead, and I think I got the best mark in the class. I was a go-getter. A leader. I started a small business. I started a rock band. I was president of the Christian club.

After I finished high school at age sixteen, I convinced a major department store manager to hire me as a night janitor—a physically demanding position that had, up until then, only been filled by burly males. The salary was four times higher than what I could have earned as a sales clerk or secretary. In the interview I pushed for the opportunity to prove that I could do the job as well as any man. I knew when they probationally hired me that I would need to do it even better.

I saved up enough money from that job to spend almost a year in Europe and to support myself through college. Of all my six siblings, I'm the only one who earned a professional degree and an opportunity to climb the corporate ladder. These were lofty achievements for a child of a family of poor immigrants, and especially for a girl.

I was a strong woman.

That is, I was strong in all the ways the world admired.

But as the years passed, I began to suspect that I wasn't nearly as strong as I made myself out to be. The more I read the Bible, the more it challenged my idea about what it truly meant to be strong. I realized that bending my will to do what God wanted me to do required a strength I did not possess. I was strong enough to demand my rights, yet not strong enough to relinquish them. I reluctantly concluded that what I extolled as strength was often little more than stubbornness, insolence, self-sufficiency, and prideful self-promotion.

And then there was Pearl Purdie.

That was her name.

For real.

Pearl attended the church I grew up in, the little pink church on the corner. In my teens and early twenties, Pearl invited me over to her home from time to time to sip Orange Pekoe tea and play some rousing games of shuffleboard.

Pearl was old. Very old. She had tiny blue veins. Blue hair. Dentures. Coke-bottle glasses that made her right eye look bigger than her left. She stood at four foot ten—maybe. And that was with her sensible Aerosoles Mary Jane pumps on. Pearl was so frail that a high wind could have snapped her in half.

She didn't have a college degree.

She hadn't climbed up any corporate ladder.

She didn't have the assertive, self-confident swagger of all the power-house female achievers I normally hung out with.

But as I got to know her, I discovered that she was a truly strong woman.

Curiously, she seemed even stronger than the strong women I admired and tried to emulate.

Pearl didn't exhibit the brash, sassy, self-serving, demanding kind of strong that the women's movement had cultivated in me and many of my peers. Hers was a different kind of strong. It was far kinder. Far more beautiful. Far more certain. Far more genuine. Far more profound.

And far more powerful.

Pearl's strength was accompanied by a quiet and gentle spirit. The kind of womanly spirit that the Bible informs us is exceedingly precious to God (1 Peter 3:4). She was a woman of faith with deep, unshakable convictions. This sweet, gentle woman was fearless. Resolute. Passionate. Bold. An eighty-something, four-foot-ten, Orange-Pekoe-tea-sipping, shuffleboard-playing spiritual-giant slayer. A force to be reckoned with.

I learned from Pearl that godly strength has a far different texture to it than worldly strength. I also learned that strength can come in all sorts of shapes and sizes.

Pearl was Pearl. She didn't need to get a professional degree, climb the corporate ladder, or adopt a different set of personality traits to be a strong woman. She didn't need to be young, sexually attractive, and full of energy either. When Pearl's eyesight failed and she was no longer able to strap on her Mary Janes, play shuffleboard, or make the perfect pot of tea, her inner strength continued to shine through—and even brighter—right to the end.

Pearl was my hero.

She was a woman who had made a lifelong habit of clothing herself with the right kind of strength.

Our heavenly Father wants all his girls to be strong. He wants all of us to clothe ourselves with strength and dignity and make our arms strong.

You may be an introvert or extravert. Love pink or hate it. Work as a CEO or a waitress. Know your way around the kitchen or around the racetrack. You may be the type of girl who lists perfume on her Christmas wish list, or the type who'd rather receive a power tool.

(Brent, if you're reading this, I'd like a Bosch or Makita power planer, please.)

Regardless of our varied personalities and interests and gifts, we can all become strong, godly women.

I suspect the reason you picked up this book is that you want to be strong. Maybe you've had a Pearl in your life who has inspired you with a vision of spiritual strength, a godly older woman who has modeled it well. Or perhaps you suspect that the popular formula for what it means to be a strong woman is lacking and misses the mark. Maybe you feel weak and inadequate. Maybe you're tired of merely pretending to be strong.

Whatever your motivation, rest assured that your desire to grow stronger is in line with what God wants for you.

He does not want women to be weak and wimpy.

He wants us to be the right kind of strong.

SHE DRESSES HERSELF WITH STRENGTH

How do we become the right kind of strong?

The Bible tells us that it starts with believing in Jesus Christ. When we do that, we are filled with *his* strength. The Holy Spirit makes us strong in the Lord. Done deal. We are strong because God makes us strong. He does the work. It's part of the gift we receive at the time of our salvation.

But the Bible also says that we have a responsibility to learn how to *put on* the strength that God provides. A godly woman "dresses herself with strength and makes her arms strong" (Proverbs 31:17). Both metaphors imply that strength requires ongoing action on our part.

Dressing ourselves is something we do every day—multiple times a day. Gym clothes. Work clothes. Dress clothes. Comfortable clothes.

Night clothes. Accessories. Coats and jackets. Shoes. Flip-flops. Snow boots. Slippers.

Making our arms strong also indicates ongoing action. It likens the process of building spiritual strength to the process of building physical strength. Our arms won't grow strong if we only go to the gym once a year to exercise our muscles on the shiny bench press machine. No. We make our arms strong by making a habit of lifting weights on a regular basis.

Proverbs 31:17 shows us that a woman grows spiritually stronger by incorporating strength-building habits into her life.

Habits are such small, seemingly insignificant things. The actions, in the moment, don't seem like much. The changes they produce are so subtle they're almost imperceptible. So it's easy to minimize the importance of them.

What difference does it make if I miss getting exercise today? Or if I enjoy a soft drink? Not much. But if I consistently fail to exercise and continue to consume a soda each day, a year from now my body will seize up like an old, rusty bike and I will have put on an extra fifteen pounds.

The individual choices may be small, but they certainly aren't inconsequential. Little choices compound over time. Small things done consistently produce big results.

A series of small, negative choices will lead to significant negative results. A series of small, positive choices will lead to significant positive results. It's the consistency of the habit over time rather than the magnitude of each individual action that makes the difference.

This book is about the surprisingly simple habits of a spiritually strong woman. It's about the little things we can do on an ongoing basis to strengthen our spiritual core. I'm going to tell it to you straight, though: There is no secret formula, quick fix, or magic pill. There are no shortcuts. Becoming a strong woman doesn't just happen overnight. It takes years of consistent habits, thousands of small, seemingly insignificant steps of obedience.

These small steps, taken consistently over time, will make a radical difference in our lives. Godly habits are what will turn us into strong godly women.

I debated whether I should subtitle this book *Secrets of a Spiritually Strong Woman* instead of *Habits of a Spiritually Strong Woman*. *Secrets* might have made for a better sell. *Habits* are just so mundane. Unremarkable. Tedious. Humdrum. *Secrets* sounds much more mysterious, intriguing, and tantalizing. I thought women would be excited about some brand-new secrets and questioned whether they'd be as eager to be reminded of all the small, routine, day-to-day choices they need to make consistently in order to become strong.

We live in a secret-formula, quick-fix world. So we often lose sight of the simple but profound fundamental truth that steady, consistent effort over time is the best way to make progress.

Is there a secret formula for becoming strong?

No, there is not.

There's just the age-old wisdom that lays out the habits that are necessary to build spiritual strength.

Do these habits take effort?

Yes, they definitely do.

But they are not prohibitive or complicated. They're simple. So simple, in fact, that it's easy to overlook them.

In this book, you will find seven surprisingly simple habits. These habits would likely not top the list if we were to ask women to think of the ones that are important for building spiritual strength. The basic habits of Bible reading, prayer, memorization, church attendance, and Christian fellowship likely would, as they are vital disciplines for a healthy spiritual life. It almost goes without saying that you would benefit from consistently doing these things.

The habits in this book are just as important though. They're not meant to replace disciplines like Bible reading and prayer but to accompany and build on them. The list is not comprehensive. There are undoubtedly other habits that could be added. So, why then, you may ask, did I pick these particular habits?

It's because they specifically counter the strength-sapping habits of a group of women the apostle Paul characterized as weak. These habits would have prevented these women from becoming weak and made them spiritually strong.

The seven strength-building habits we're going to talk about in this book are not big, sweeping changes that will take huge amounts of time and effort. They aren't difficult tasks you'll need to add to your daily to-do list. Some may require greater follow-through, but mostly they're just small correctives to attitudes and ways of thinking that won't take much energy to implement. They're simple, little things you can do all the time.

But women who do these things consistently will grow stronger, while women who just think about doing them, or only do them from time to time, won't.

WEE, TINY, WEAK WOMEN

Some women in the church of Ephesus were weak. Paul warned Timothy about ungodly people who would "creep into households and capture weak women" (2 Timothy 3:6).

I don't know about you, but if a prominent male pastor publicly called me weak, I'd feel insulted. Given the connotation of the Greek word Paul used, the women in Timothy's church likely felt that way too. Let me explain why.

The Greek word for *woman* is the feminine noun *gynaikes*, but Paul called these women *gynaikarion*. *Karion* is a diminutive, which is an ending added onto a word to indicate a smaller version or slighter degree than its root. It can refer to someone or something that's smaller in size or quality, younger, or cuter.

Musicians know that the word *diminuendo* means they should decrease the loudness or intensity with which they are singing or playing.

We don't have many diminutive endings in English, and the ones we do have usually only refer to size, without the other connotations. Like the suffix *-let* in *piglet* or *booklet*, for example. But many other languages, such as Greek, Latin, French, and Polish, apply grammatical diminutives to nouns.

German, which was my first language, is another. It often uses the diminutive ending *-chen*. *Brot* is a loaf of bread; *brötchen* is bread rolls. *Katze* is a cat; *kätzchen* is a kitten. *Punkt* is a dot; *pünktchen* is a tiny dot. You get the idea.

Sometimes diminutives can be used to convey a sense of affection. They're frequently used when speaking to small children (Tiny Tim), when expressing tenderness and intimacy (sweetie, kitten, little bear), or in nicknames (calling Michael "Mikey").

But in other contexts diminutives are used to denote that someone or something is weak or childish. For example, one of the last of the Western Roman emperors was named Romulus Augustus, after the legendary first king of Rome, Romulus, and its glorious first emperor, Augustus. But the public added a diminutive *ulus* to his name, dubbing him *Romulus Augustulus*, to convey that he was far less than these great leaders and to ridicule the young emperor's ineptitude. Augustulus didn't even last a year before being deposed.

When Paul called women in Ephesus *gynaikarion*, he wasn't using the diminutive in a positive way. He wasn't commenting that they looked cute in their funky shoes. He wasn't employing an affectionate term of endearment. No. What he said was akin to name-calling. It was a put-down. Paul was literally calling them "little women" or "wee tiny women."

And he wasn't talking about their height.

Gynaikarion contains the idea of being small, underdeveloped, and insufficient. Translating the word into English isn't an easy task.

Different versions of the Bible use "weak" (ESV), "gullible" (NIV), "idle" (HCSB), and "silly" (KJV).

The important thing, the concept I want you to take away from all this talk about diminutives, is that these women were less than they ought to have been. They were stunted versions of true womanhood. They were weak in a way that diminished them. They weren't mature, beautiful examples of what strong, godly women should be.

They were just wee, tiny, and weak.

STRONG FEMALE FRIENDS

Was Paul a chauvinist? A woman-hater? A casualty of the patriarchal ideology of his time?

Many modern women take offense at the fact that Paul labeled these women weak. If a male pastor or blogger were to use that label for women today, the Twitterverse would explode with rage. He'd be denounced as a vile, sexist misogynist. At the very least he'd be viewed as a politically incorrect boor in severe need of some gender-sensitivity training.

Based on this derogatory label Paul used for the women in Ephesus, and some other things he wrote about women, many conclude that he was a chauvinist who didn't view women as equals. But I don't think this conclusion is justified. Paul had a lot of close friends who were strong women. His letters mention twelve women by name—strong females who worked with him in gospel ministry.

There was Chloe, whose people brought Paul news of division within the Corinthian church (1 Corinthians 1:11); Nympha, the woman who hosted the house church in Laodicea (Colossians 4:15); Apphia, hostess to the Colossian church (Philemon v. 2); Lydia, a wealthy businesswoman who engaged in the lucrative trade of purple cloth, whose home became operation-central for Paul and Silas's ministry in Philippi (Acts 16:14, 40).

And there was Phoebe, who carried and delivered Paul's letter to the Romans. Paul described this strong female coworker as a minister (deaconess) of the church in Cencrea and as a patron. Being a patron (or sponsor) was an influential public role that wealthy women held in the first-century Greco-Roman world (Romans 16:1–2).

There was also Mary, Tryphaena, Tryphosa, and Persis—strong women whom Paul lauded for working very hard to forward the gospel (vv. 6, 12).

And then there was Euodia and Syntyche. These two women were such strong forces that they constantly clashed. Paul encouraged them to work out their issues and get along (Philippians 4:2–3).

But outshining Paul's many strong female friends was his special friend Priscilla, the female half of the ministry powerhouse couple Priscilla and Aquilla.

Like Paul, Priscilla and Aquilla were tentmakers by trade. They initially met Paul in Corinth, where they invited him to live with them and join them in their tentmaking business. While in Corinth, the three friends also worked together to establish a church (Acts 18:2). Later, Priscilla and Aquilla accompanied Paul on his evangelistic journey as far as Ephesus (Acts 18:18–19).

In Ephesus, Priscilla and Aquilla instructed Apollos in the Christian faith (vv. 24–26). As the number of believers grew, they hosted the church in their home (1 Corinthians 16:19). Their ministry in Ephesus was so impactful that Paul told his friends that all the churches of the Gentiles owed them a huge debt of gratitude (Romans 16:3–5).

Priscilla and Aquilla were mentioned six times in Paul's letters, and four of the six times Priscilla's name comes first. In ancient times, the order of names often indicated priority or importance. The fact that Paul mentioned Priscilla first might suggest that she was from an influential Roman family, or that, of the two, she was stronger in ministry and more of a go-getter. Regardless, it's undeniable that

Priscilla (who was sometimes nicknamed Prisca) was a woman whose strength Paul respected and admired.

She was a strong woman.

As I mentioned before, she was an integral part of the church in Ephesus. So maybe that was the reason why Paul called those women in the Ephesian congregation to account for being weak. The difference between them and Priscilla was just so glaring.

When Paul disparagingly called them wee, tiny, weak women, his point was that they ought not to have been weak. He wanted them to be *strong* women. The irony is they likely thought they were. But, unfortunately, their concept of what made a woman truly strong was not in line with the Lord's.

They were caught up in bad habits that diminished their spiritual strength.

Perhaps they were mimicking their culture's ideal of what it meant for a woman to be strong.

WOMEN IN ANCIENT EPHESUS

To get a better idea of why the women in Timothy's church likely viewed themselves as strong, let's take a brief tour of ancient Ephesus.

When you think of Ephesus, don't think of a small, dusty town with dirt streets and a few camels and donkeys tied up here and there. Think of a metropolitan city, one of the biggest in the world, with a bustling harbor and the pace, architecture, and infrastructure of a large, commercial cosmopolitan center. Think Chicago, Toronto, or Los Angeles. That will get you closer to the mark.

Ephesus was a busy urban Greco-Roman port.[2] In the Romans' time it was called "the first and greatest metropolis of Asia."[3] At its height some 250,000 people lived there. It was exceeded in population only by Rome and Alexandria.

A theater mentioned in Acts 19:29 was the largest in the world. It accommodated twenty-four thousand people on three tiers. The doors of the spectacular theater opened onto the great marble main street, which was flanked on either side by tall marble columns. The street was bordered by lovely fountains, civic buildings, houses, shops, a library, baths, and a great marketplace. This cosmopolitan center also boasted a centrally located brothel and casino.

Ephesus was a wealthy city. The multistory residences of its upper-middle class rested on the north terraces of a mountain. They boasted amazing opulence and split-level construction, with floor space often exceeding ten thousand square feet. Some homes had elaborate mosaic floors and marble walls. Many had hot and cold running water and heated bathrooms. They were mansions, even by today's standards.

Of the metropolitan population, at least a third were slaves. The majority were employed in domestic service in households and could expect an easier life than rural free folk. Many slaves earned money. Some had slaves of their own. It's important to understand that slavery in that day was markedly different from the type witnessed in our eighteenth- and nineteenth-century Western world. In Paul's day people sometimes sold themselves as slaves, knowing they could have a higher standard of living than if they had to fend for themselves.

According to legend Ephesus was founded by the Amazons, great female warriors, so it comes as no surprise that its people believed that a female deity watched over the city. The goddess Artemis was depicted as a virgin "tomboy huntress . . . with her quiver and bow and dogs by her side."[4] The Temple of Artemis (also known as the Temple of Diana), just north of the city, was one of the Seven Wonders of the Ancient World. As big as a soccer field and three to four times as large as the Parthenon in Athens, it was the largest and grandest building in the world at the time. One historian testified that it was more marvelous than any of the other six Wonders of the Ancient World.[5]

This state-run temple was famous not only for its great size but also for the magnificent works of art it contained. It was the primary banking and real-estate holding institution of Asia Minor, holding in deposit the money of wealthy locals and even foreign states and kings. It also promoted a profitable tourist industry. Silversmiths, such as Demetrius (Acts 19:24, 38), the leader of the Silversmiths Guild, made their fortunes by peddling souvenirs of the temple and the goddess Artemis to the city's many tourists (vv. 25–28).

The state-sponsored religious cult was also responsible for the city's many cultural activities. Besides daily public sacrifices, the Temple of Artemis hosted feasts, festivals, banquets, processions, contests of athletes, actors, and musicians, and other sacred games in the virgin goddess's honor. A plethora of other gods and goddesses were also worshiped.

Most women in Ephesus were educated. Roman and Greek culture valued education, so both boys and girls were schooled up to about the age of twelve, learning to read, write, and do basic mathematics. Some older boys, whose families could afford it, would go to more advanced schools where they studied public speaking and the writings of the great intellects. Ephesus was home to a renowned center for philosophical and rhetorical studies, though few people advanced in their formal education to that degree. This elite graduate school was not open to women. But that doesn't mean that women didn't pursue advanced education.

Upper-class women were educated by private tutors. The fact that they read and wrote literature and poetry during this period is illustrated by several tributes and poetic epigrams, proving that females were among the known devotees of literature.[6] The most famous female philosopher of ancient times, Hypatia of Alexandria, wrote several treatises and became head of a school of philosophy. While the men in Ephesus routinely gathered in public halls to listen to philosophers' debates and lectures, upper-class women did so in private settings, frequently attending lectures in home parlors and salons.

The lore that Ephesus was founded by great Amazon female warriors and was watched over by a female deity indicates that women played a significant role in that society. What's more, Roman law guaranteed women many rights and freedoms.

Male and female offspring had equal inheritance rights, so women inherited property. Furthermore, the law stipulated that a wife's property be kept separate from her husband's (except the dowry) and that her money could be reclaimed following a divorce. A married woman could keep her maiden name or use her husband's name. Divorce was easily achieved by either party and was a common occurrence.

There were many independently wealthy women. Although they legally needed permission from the head of the family for legal transactions, this was apparently not hard to come by. Women routinely owned property and businesses and had their own money.

Women of that day couldn't vote or hold office, but that doesn't mean they weren't involved in political life. In 42 BC a wealthy woman named Hortensia gave a famous speech in Rome's forum to oppose a proposed bill that would tax the wealth of Rome's richest women to fund the war against Caesar's assassins.

She wasn't the only woman who wielded significant political influence. A woman named Livia was highly influential in politics—so much so that she was given the illustrious title Mother of the Fatherland. Like many independently wealthy women, Livia was also a noted patron of the arts, literature, and philosophy.

The early church relied on the wealth of these types of women. They hosted churches in their homes and provided financial support for the ministry.

In Ephesus, women could work in just about every profession. A woman couldn't be a soldier or a Roman senator, but pretty much everything else was fair game. She could be a shopkeeper, vendor, or jewelry maker, or work in the craft or textile industry. According to historical records, at least one woman was a blacksmith. Priscilla was a tentmaker. Whether or not a woman worked had more to do with her economic and social status than anything else. As I already mentioned, a third of the population in Ephesus worked as slaves, serving the upper class. Many middle-class women worked in trades with their husbands. And many middle- and upper-class women owned businesses. So, it appears that the majority of women in Ephesus were "gainfully employed" in work that extended beyond their roles as wives and mothers.

The vibe of ancient Ephesus was surprisingly much like our own.

The population had a passionate devotion to fitness. Athletes, musicians, and actors were wildly popular and achieved considerable fame and fortune.

Shopping and consumerism were rampant. Women tried to copy the latest clothing and hairstyles of the Roman aristocrats.

Moral beliefs were diverse.

The gossip on the street blazed with the sexual scandals of high-profile women like Messalina, the powerful and influential wife of the Roman emperor Claudius; she welcomed a string of lovers through her bed. And Poppaea Sabina, a commoner who shunned her husband, seduced a senator, and eventually became mistress (and then wife) to the ruthless emperor Nero. Prostitution was legal, public, and widespread. No moral censure was directed at the man who engaged in sex acts with boys.

Ephesus was extremely pluralistic, including Greek, Roman, and various other ethnic and cultural backgrounds. The culture embraced religious diversity, celebrated moral freedom, and encouraged tolerance and inclusion. Anyone claiming to have the right religion, the only god, or a corner on truth was bound to face social marginalization and even persecution.

It's safe to assume that many of the females in Timothy's church were literate. The elaborate hairstyles, jewelry, and clothing mentioned in 1 Timothy 2:9 and the warning to the rich in 1 Timothy 6:17–18 prove that there were wealthy women in the congregation. More than a few would have owned their own businesses. At least some of them were privately educated, being tutored by teachers like Hymenaeus and Philetus (2 Timothy 2:17–18). A few, conceivably, were highly accomplished in poetry and philosophy.

Given the historical and cultural backdrop, I suspect that the women in Timothy's church would not have considered themselves to be weak. They would have viewed themselves as strong. They were successful, independent, and self-sufficient. Some probably packed a sassy, brazen attitude to go along with their privileged positions and stylish purses. By contemporary Roman standards, and probably by our standards, too, they would have been upheld and extolled as models of strength.

But Paul didn't base his assessment on the community standard. He based it on a spiritual one.

These women weren't nearly as high and capable as they thought themselves to be. Instead, they were small, underdeveloped, and insufficient. They weren't strong like Paul's friend Priscilla.

They were just weak little women.

Why?

LITTLE GIRL PROBLEMS

I can't recall anyone ever calling me *little*. Standing at nearly six feet tall, the comment I usually get is, "Wow. You're tall. Do you play basketball?"

Depending on my mood, I sometimes need to bite my tongue to keep from retorting, "Wow. You're short. Do you ride ponies?" Sigh. #TallGirlProblems.

As we discussed earlier, Paul used the diminutive *gynaikarion*, which means "little women," to refer to that group of women in Timothy's church, and the label had nothing to do with their physical height. These women were spiritually shorter than they should have been. They were spiritual Lilliputians—shrunken, stunted versions of godly, strong women.

Why? What is it that diminished them?

SEVEN STRENGTH-SAPPING HABITS

Second Timothy 3:6–7 is extremely enlightening: "Among them are those who creep into households and capture weak women, burdened with sins and led astray by various passions, always learning and never able to arrive at a knowledge of the truth." If we break this down into clauses, we can discover seven unhealthy habits that shrunk those fine-feathered Ephesian women down into tiny spiritual minikins. #LittleWomanProblems.

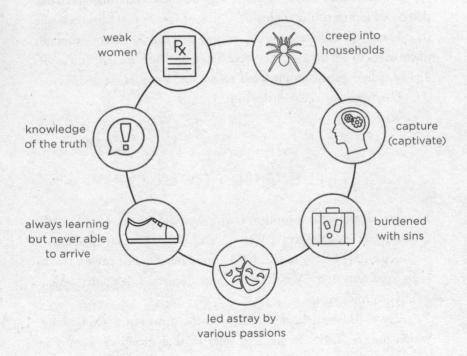

1. She tolerates creeps ("creep into households").
2. She fails to guard her mind ("capture").
3. She lets things pile up ("burdened with sins").
4. She's governed by emotions ("led astray by various passions").

5. She doesn't apply what she learns ("always learning and never able to arrive").
6. She doesn't have solid convictions ("knowledge of the truth").
7. She embraces the wrong kind of strong ("weak women").

There you have it.

Seven clauses. Seven strength-sapping habits that diminished the Christian women in Ephesus. Seven bad habits that you'll want to avoid if you want to become a strong woman.

Every bad habit has a good counterpart. If smoking is a bad habit, then not smoking is a good habit. In this book you will learn to avoid the habits that make women weak by embracing the ones that make them strong.

If you consistently do the following, you will become strong:

- Catch the creeps.
- Master your mind.
- Ditch the baggage.
- Engage your emotions.
- Walk the talk.
- Stand your ground.
- Admit your need.

As I said before, these aren't the only habits that will strengthen a woman's spiritual core. But they certainly are some critical ones.

BRAVE. BOLD. STRONG.

This generation has been raised with the idea that *strength* is the most important trait for women. Hollywood resolutely marches out a parade of capable female heroines to show us what it means to be strong. There's been an explosion of campaigns and initiatives by the government, nonprofits, corporations, and educators whose express purpose is to promote female empowerment. Billions of dollars have been spent on this mission.

Girl Power propaganda is reinforced by celebrities, by the media, and in our schools. A crop of Girl Power anthems fills the airwaves to rally our hearts to the cause. Like Beyoncé's "Run the World (Girls)," Destiny's Child's "Independent Women," Demi Lovato's "Confident," Rachel Platten's "Fight Song," Sara Bareilles's "Brave," Britney Spears's "Stronger," and Alicia Keys's "Girl on Fire."[7] What better way to infuse the idea into the subconsciousness of girls than to have them constantly singing lyrics about women taking charge?

We are literally bombarded with the message that women should be bold. Brave. Strong.

Weakness must be avoided at all costs.

But if you're at all familiar with the Bible, you'll know that being weak isn't necessarily a bad thing. In 2 Corinthians 12:10, for example, Paul told his friends that he delighted in weakness: "For when I am weak, then I am strong." Paul's frailties and sufferings presented him with the opportunity to rely on Christ's power, so he viewed them in a positive light. As a girlfriend of mine frequently reminds me, "Anything that increases our dependence on Jesus is a good thing!"

Paul felt the same way. There's no doubt that he would have encouraged (and not scolded) women who felt inadequate and lacking in strength. But when Paul called out the women in Timothy's church for being weak, he obviously didn't have the when-I-am-weak-then-I am-strong kind of weakness in mind. That kind of weakness is a positive trait.

And there's the rub.

The Bible's concept of weak and strong doesn't line up with culture's. This is especially the case when it comes to ideas about womanhood.

All too often women think that being strong means foregoing their femininity and denying the most integral and beautiful aspects of who they are as women. Sadly, a woman who thinks she is strong may just be headstrong. A woman who thinks she is brave may just be rash. A woman who thinks she is bold may just be aggressive. A woman who thinks she is confident may just be arrogant. A woman who thinks she is independent may just be standoffish. A woman who thinks she is smart may just be foolish.

Many women have embraced the wrong kind of strong. Christian women aren't immune to having a skewed image of what constitutes a strong woman.

We've all sipped the cultural Kool-Aid.

If we read the Bible, it's undeniable that God wants his girls to be strong—but strong in the right kind of way. Because the wrong kind of strong simply makes women weak—weak in the wrong kind of way.

Thankfully, Scripture makes the difference between the right kind and the wrong kind of strong abundantly clear. That's why we're going to rely on the Bible to help us figure it out.

If you like, you can read through Paul's second letter to Timothy before we get started. It's only four chapters long. It's the book of the Bible that contains the passage about weak women. That's where we're going to park and spend a lot of time. If you're ambitious, you can also read Paul's first letter to Timothy. And if you're super ambitious, you can add the book of Ephesians. All three of these letters were written for the congregation in Ephesus. Reading them will give you a richer understanding of what was going on there. (Ha ha! And I said I wasn't going to add any big to-dos to your list.)

God does not want you to be a weakling. He wants you to be a steel magnolia: a soft, feminine woman with fire in your belly, courage in your heart, and steel in your spine. He wants you to have the strength to say no to what's wrong and yes to what's right and to live your life for the glory of Christ.

Imagine what it would be like to be a genuinely strong woman.

I'm not talking about the brash, worldly kind of strength that relies on your own capacities—the kind of strength that's brittle and fragile and shatters when tested—but a soft, quiet, confident strength that relies on the power of the Holy Spirit. The kind that makes you bold to stand for truth and brave to navigate through any kind of storm.

Are you ready to get started?

These surprisingly simple habits offer you more than Girl Power ever could. You only need to take a series of tiny steps, consistently, over time, to strengthen your spiritual core radically. Just think: you can become bolder, braver, and stronger than ever before—and best of all, it will be the right kind of strong.

HABIT 1

Catch the Creeps

Sin does not advance by leaps, it advances
by creeps—one tiny compromise at a time.

Would you lock yourself in a container with five
thousand deadly scorpions? A Thai woman dubbed the Scorpion
Queen did. And for thirty-three days at that! Onlookers grimaced as the
clicking, writhing, black blanket of curvy-tailed arachnids completely
obscured her face. To claim yet another Guinness World Record, she
held a large, pincered, poisonous, eight-legged creature in her mouth for
a staggering three minutes and twenty-eight seconds.[1] Yikes!

The Scorpion Queen is an oddity. Most people hate creeping
things. Just the thought of spiders, tarantulas, crickets, grasshoppers,
snakes, or any other type of creepy-crawly is enough to make us cringe.

Even though I'm not particularly frightened by them, I don't tol-
erate their existence either. Whenever I encounter a spider scuttling

across my floor, I view it as an unwelcome intruder and quickly snuff out its life.

Sometimes our feelings about creeping things go deeper than disgust. They border on terror. I'm convinced that a guest at a barbeque I hosted in my backyard last summer had a full-blown phobia.

There are always insects buzzing and crawling around my outdoor patio, and most of the time, people simply swat them away in annoyance. Not this time. When a spider slid down a silky thread and nimbly landed on this guest's shoulder, her reaction could not have been more extreme. With a bloodcurdling scream, she jumped up onto the chaise.

Her plate of food went flying in all directions. A slice of tomato slathered in mayonnaise landed on my head. Startled, the dogs began running in circles, barking, and knocking glasses off the coffee table. Some guests grabbed their plates and took cover. Others just stared wide-eyed.

The woman continued to screech and howl, whacking invisible assailants from her hair, swatting at every inch of her body, and hopping back and forth—foot to foot—faster than a football player on an agility ladder.

I froze in confusion when I noticed the horrible red streak on her leg. Had one of the dogs viciously attacked? It took a moment for me to realize that the streak was ketchup. And that her torment (and squealing) would not end until someone got rid of the teeny tiny spider lounging at her feet.

What is this strange, terrifying power of creepy-crawlies?

We shriek when they land on our skin, give them prominent roles in our horror movies, hire exterminators to vanquish them from our homes, and conscript chivalrous males to chase them away.

Fear of creatures like spiders and snakes is right at the top of the list of the world's most common phobias, affecting women four times more than men. Nearly half of all women feel anxious, nervous, or extremely frightened when confronted with one.[2] There's just something alarming and despicable about a creature that creeps.

It's bad enough when we spot a little intruder and can see that it doesn't pose any threat. But it's far worse when we ignore the danger (the Scorpion Queen *willingly* put poisonous scorpions in her mouth?) or when we aren't even aware that intruders have crept in and are causing damage.

Our family has an old cabin at a lake in northern Alberta, Canada. One day I noticed a small pile of sawdust on the ledge of the front window. I quickly brushed it off and didn't give it another thought. The following spring when we opened up the cabin, there was a much, much bigger pile of sawdust sitting on the ledge of the window. On closer examination I discovered why.

Carpenter ants!

That's bad. Not quite as bad as termites; carpenter ants are more like their ant cousins. They typically seek out wood that has been softened by moisture or decay. They don't like to chew wood that's too hard. Nevertheless, these intruders can still cause significant damage and weaken the supporting structure of a building. The infestation can get so severe that the walls start rustling like crinkling cellophane, and large winged ants start to emerge from every crevice.

Thankfully we were able to fix the damage and exterminate them before things got that bad.

CREEPS THEN AND NOW

The first habit of a spiritually strong woman is that she is always on the lookout for creeps. The women in Ephesus had a bad habit of letting them enter into their households.

Some women welcomed the creeps. Like the Scorpion Queen, they didn't seem to think they posed any danger. Others probably had no idea that they were encroaching. Like the situation at our cabin, they didn't pay attention to the early warning signs and were unaware that intruders had crept in and were causing significant damage.

Apparently, some prominent members of Timothy's congregation were promoting ideas that "swerved from the truth" (2 Timothy 2:18). Their bad theology was spreading "like gangrene" (v. 17). It was whipping up "foolish, ignorant controversies" (v. 23), breeding "quarrels" (v. 23), and "upsetting the faith of some" (v. 18).

Paul noted that these charlatans were finding disproportionate success among the women. Why?

Because in Paul's assessment, these women were not strong enough to resist them. Instead of slamming the door on these rogue teachers and their novel ideas, they were allowing them to walk right in.

The verb that Paul used to describe the actions of these men is *enduno*, which means to enter through devious means or pretense. It can also be translated as "worm their way in, sneak into, infiltrate, or enter on the sly."[3] It's a derogatory term that paints these guys as sinister and treacherous tricksters.

To creep is to move slowly or gradually, to advance with subtlety and almost imperceptibly. It's making persistent progress a teeny little bit at a time.

Like the women in Ephesus, many modern women let the wrong kind of guys come into their lives. I constantly get letters from women who were swept off their feet by a Mr. McDreamy only to discover that he was actually Mr. McDreadful in disguise.

I think of Emily, a middle-aged woman who was widowed when her husband of twenty-seven years died of a sudden heart attack. About a year later Emily met Harvey. He introduced himself to her in the church parking lot just before the service. They sat together in church that Sunday. Harvey was charming. He asked her out for lunch. Within two weeks, they were seeing each other on a daily basis. The grief of mourning her husband's death finally lifted.

Emily felt like a schoolgirl again.

She shrugged off the probing questions from her adult children about Harvey's past. He didn't like to talk about it. Besides, what did it matter? She also shrugged off their suggestion that things were moving a bit too fast. So what? Harvey was perfect. He was funny and attentive and affectionate (very affectionate!). Emily was smitten.

Harvey took Emily on a romantic trip to Mexico. They spent a lot of time alone together in her condo. So much time that it seemed to her children that Harvey practically lived there. Emily bristled when her kids pointed out that she was breaking all the dating rules she had demanded they follow. And she grew extremely defensive when her daughter confronted her about Harvey being there at breakfast one morning when she happened to drop by.

"What does Harvey even do?" her kids demanded. Emily couldn't exactly say. Something to do with business investing. He definitely spent a lot of time on the computer.

Four months after meeting, Emily and Harvey got married. But it didn't turn out to be the happily-ever-after fairy-tale ending Emily had hoped for.

Not even close.

Harvey abandoned her soon after their first wedding anniversary. But not before hoodwinking her into signing over her car. And not before cleaning out all her bank accounts, including most of the money she had received from her late husband's estate.

You may wonder how Emily could have been so blind to Harvey's true intentions. But creeps are notoriously clever and sneaky. They know exactly what to say and do to beguile their prey. They know how to exploit a woman's vulnerabilities and gain her trust.

There's something sinister about creeps.

They come in and infringe. And supplant. And take over. But they do it so gradually and incrementally that a woman is often left scratching her head and wondering, *How on earth did this happen to me? How did I get from there to here? How did I get myself into such a mess? How?*

I'm sure these are the kind of questions Eve asked herself when she realized what a mess she had gotten herself into, after falling for the sales pitch of that clever old Creep in the garden.

THE BIGGEST CREEP OF ALL

Creeps are nothing new. Since the dawn of time, women have been susceptible to tricksters worming their way in. It all started with that wily old talking serpent in the garden of Eden.

The Bible tells us that he was "more crafty" than any other animal (Genesis 3:1). One translation states he "was the most cunning of all" (HCSB). When it came to creeps, he was the worst. He was evil, shrewd, and exceptionally skilled in deception.

The serpent slid into Eve's idyllic life and engaged her in friendly conversation. To Eve, their banter seemed innocent enough. Little did she know that he was a smooth, calculating trickster. As they talked he bent the truth just a teeny tiny bit. What he proposed sounded right and good and reasonable to Eve. I'm sure she was convinced that he was just trying to be helpful. But he really wasn't.

He had a much more sinister goal in mind.

He was like a slick used-car salesman making a lemon out to be a Lincoln. Using a series of small lies, he duped her into falling for his underhanded pitch. He "deceived Eve by his cunning" (2 Corinthians 11:3).

If she could have imagined the ugly, painful, deadly consequences of her choice, do you think she would have listened to the serpent's lies and disobeyed God? Probably not.

You know the rest of the tragic story. Eve ate the forbidden fruit and gave it to Adam, who also took a bite. Their eyes were opened, and they were ashamed and horrified by their own nakedness. They tried to stitch together some big fig leaves to cover up their private parts. And when God came to see them later that evening, they hid.

The first thing God did after asking Adam and Eve to explain their behavior was to curse the serpent. He condemned it to slither with its belly and mouth on the ground forever, eating dirt, which is a posture of extreme humiliation. (Before this, serpents apparently had limbs and didn't slither.) The Lord warned that conflict between the woman and the serpent would intensify and continue. But, amazingly, he hinted that a Deliverer would eventually crush and defeat this powerful foe. "The LORD God said to the serpent: Because you have done this, . . . you will move on your belly and eat dust all the days of your life. I will put hostility between you and the woman, and between your seed and her seed. He will strike your head, and you will strike his heel" (Genesis 3:14–15 HCSB).

Eve had no idea what all this meant.

She didn't know that the serpent was the archenemy of God. She didn't know that the "he" who would strike the serpent's head was Jesus. Before humanity ever sinned, God already had a plan in place to defeat the serpent and conquer sin (Romans 16:20; Revelation 12:9).

I'm sure that Eve listened intently to the curse God pronounced on the one who had crafted her downfall, and to the bad-news/good-news scenario his words contained. God used the word *hostility* to describe the perpetual strife that would exist between the woman and the Creep. In Hebrew this forceful word describes loathing and a murderous level of animosity for a wartime foe. It implies a fierce conflict of life-and-death proportions. This was the type of battle Eve was up against.

This part of God's pronouncement was definitely bad news. Though Eve couldn't have fully understood the good-news part of the message—the part about someone striking the serpent's head—I think she must have caught the glimmer of hope.

Eve called the fraudster who had deceived her "the serpent" (Genesis 3:13). She really didn't know much about him. It wasn't until later that God revealed more about this Creep and his tactics. Now we know that the serpent has many names. We often refer to him as the Devil. He is also known as Belial, Beelzebul, the Adversary, the Dragon, the Enemy, the Tempter, the Accuser, and the Wicked One.

Satan is the supreme evil being who is God's enemy and the powerful ruler of the world (Luke 4:6; John 14:30; Acts 26:18; 2 Corinthians 4:4). He relentlessly opposes God and his people. He is intent on stealing, killing, and destroying everything and everyone who belongs to God (John 10:10).

He commands a host of fallen angels, better known as demons, to carry out his will (Matthew 25:41). He governs over a host of unseen dark evil forces, including "authorities, . . . cosmic powers," and "spiritual forces of evil" (Ephesians 6:12). He enslaves everyone who does not call on the name of Jesus, conscripting each one to obey him and join him in his cosmic rebellion (John 8:34, 44).

There are a few more things that you should know about this highly intelligent, evil Creep. First, his chief weapon is deception, and he uses it effectively.

Very effectively.

Jesus said this about him: "He was a murderer from the beginning, and does not stand in the truth, because there is no truth in him. When he lies, he speaks out of his own character, for he is a liar and the father of lies" (v. 44).

Second, he is the master pretender. He always hides his true nature and intentions. He "disguises himself as an angel of light" (2 Corinthians 11:14). This means that he portrays himself as good, wholesome, and even righteous and holy, though his character is the exact opposite of this. The fact that he hides behind a mask of goodness makes him tough to spot.

Third, he is extremely patient. Scripture says he "prowls around like a roaring lion," looking to destroy people's lives (1 Peter 5:8).

The word *prowl* contains the same sort of idea as the word *creep*. It means to lurk, skulk, slink, or sneak. Like a lion, Satan uses stealth and strategy. He takes his time closing in for the kill. He is willing to wait for an opportune time. He's in the battle for the long haul, so he's content to advance just a little at a time.

Fourth, Satan is relentless. He does not give up. Ever.

He is constantly trying to sneak in. When one approach fails, he tries another. If there is one thing you can be sure of, it is that he's *always* trying to make inroads into your life.

Finally, it's important for you to realize that Satan is the Übercreep. *Über* comes from the German language, meaning "over" or "above." Satan is over all other creeps. He is over the fallen angels (demons), principalities, authorities, cosmic powers, and all forces of evil. He is also over everyone who does not serve God and who, therefore—by default—serves Satan instead. He is the father of creeps.

Why is this important for you to know?

Because when you encounter a destructive fraud in your life, you can be sure Satan is ultimately behind it. What's more, this gives you insight into the nature and tactics of the fraud. As the old adage goes, "Like father, like son."

Creeps are all made from the same cut of cloth. They wear disguises and pretend to be righteous, just as Satan does. "Such men are false apostles, deceitful workmen, disguising themselves as apostles of Christ. And no wonder, for even Satan disguises himself as an angel of light. So it is no surprise if his servants, also, disguise themselves as servants of righteousness" (2 Corinthians 11:13–15).

Creeps are deceptive. They masquerade as something they are not. They encroach slowly yet persistently. And they are out to do you great harm.

Scripture warns us, "Be sober-minded; be watchful" (1 Peter 5:8).

31

The fact that we have a powerful and murderous Enemy who is out to harm us is not a point we should minimize or overlook. C. S. Lewis suggests that the two mistakes people make in talking about Satan are either taking him too seriously or not seriously enough.[4]

According to this verse, neither of these is an option. Satan is not a little cartoon man wearing a red suit and horns who you can easily flick off your shoulder. You need to realize that you are engaged in a life-and-death battle with a daunting and cunning foe. To resist his schemes effectively, you need to know your Enemy and his characteristics and tactics.

Because, just as there are tricksters targeting people on Facebook, he and his demons are currently targeting you. They're tracking your movements, making note of your habits, your friends and family, your conversations, and your weaknesses. Even now, they are formulating a sinister plan to worm their way into your life and destroy you.

That's what creeps do.

QUALITIES OF A CREEP

As I said earlier, the weak women in Ephesus had a bad habit of tolerating intruders. Some didn't recognize them as intruders; others didn't think that they were a problem or that they posed any kind of threat.

If we want to be strong, and not weak as they were, we need to take the threat of creeps seriously. Instead of ignoring or shrugging off the danger, we need to make a habit of catching the imposters who are trying to make inroads into our lives. But since they're so good at impersonation, how can we figure out who's who?

We can find a detailed list of the qualities of creeps in the five verses that come right before our weak women passage. "In the last days there will come times of difficulty. For people will be lovers of self, lovers of money, proud, arrogant, abusive, disobedient to their parents, ungrateful, unholy, heartless, unappeasable, slanderous, without self-control, brutal, not loving good, treacherous, reckless, swollen with conceit, lovers of pleasure rather than lovers of God, having the appearance of godliness, but denying its power" (2 Timothy 3:1–5).

Notice that these vices are characteristics of the false teachers who were worming their way into the households of weak women. Creeps try to hide these negative traits, but if we're on the lookout, we'll probably see these bad attitudes peeking out from under their good-looking veneer. If you think carefully about this passage, you can learn to spot the fakes.

To make it even easier, I've put together a checklist of those qualities to help you determine whether a creep is making a move on you. A creep is:

- ❑ self-centered: self-serving, narcissistic, self-absorbed, looking out for number one
- ❑ materialistic: loves money, greedy, covetous, possessive, stingy
- ❑ self-promoting: boasting, bragging, swaggering, showboating
- ❑ contemptuous: haughty, condescending, snobbish, disdainful
- ❑ berating: abusing, insulting, reviling, criticizing, castigating
- ❑ insolent: rebellious, defiant, disobedient (especially to parents)
- ❑ ungrateful: thankless, unappreciative, entitled, demanding
- ❑ irreverent: coarse, crass, profane, vulgar, crude
- ❑ callous: heartless, unloving, cold, unsympathetic
- ❑ resentful: unforgiving, irreconcilable, implacable, grudge-holding
- ❑ defaming: slandering, falsely accusing, bad-mouthing, disparaging
- ❑ undisciplined: intemperate, unrestrained, lacking self-control
- ❑ malicious: brutal, savage, fierce, venomous, vicious, cutthroat, cruel
- ❑ cynical: despising, mocking, derisive, scornful of good things/people
- ❑ backstabbing: treacherous, betraying, double-crossing, two-timing

- ❑ impulsive: impetuous, reckless, rash, wild, headstrong
- ❑ self-important: conceited, lofty, puffed up, high-minded
- ❑ self-indulgent: hedonistic, self-gratifying, licentious, wanton
- ❑ hypocritical: deceitful, fraudulent, two-faced, posing

Having *one* of these qualities may not automatically mean a person is a creep. But if there are a lot of checkmarks as you go down the list, or if the attitude is severe, sirens should go off in your mind. Don't ignore these red flags!

Too many women ignore these early warning signs in men who are pursuing them. They think that he'll change or that he's just having a bad day. Or they find his impulsive, undisciplined, and insolent bad-boy behavior exciting. Or they rationalize that they're supposed to be salt and light and forgiving of people's sins. Right? Yes, but does God really want you hanging out with a creep?

No. He does not.

The list of nineteen vices ends with the stern command: "Avoid such people!" (v. 5).

The problem with hanging out with creeps is that their attitudes and behaviors tend to rub off. Scripture warns, "Do not be deceived: 'Bad company ruins good morals'" (1 Corinthians 15:33). It also advises, "Whoever walks with the wise becomes wise, but the companion of fools will suffer harm" (Proverbs 13:20).

Pretty much everyone has heard this kind of warning from their parents at some point and for good reason—the advice stands the test of time. The Bible stresses the importance of good friends. The people we allow into our innermost circle will become key parts of our story for decades to come. Depending on their character, they will either help or harm us.

It's not always easy to spot creeps. They can be smart, charming, funny, and likable. But if we carefully observe them, we can usually discern their dark side. We can spot many of the qualities Paul listed.

A weak woman ignores the warning signs. A strong woman is aware of the danger and stays alert to the threat.

ALL SORTS OF CREEPS

A false teacher, or a controlling, obnoxious boor, is not the only type of creep you need to be aware of. There are lots of other types.

A creep might worm its way into your attitude or wriggle its way into your behavior. It might inch into your habits or intrude on your time. It might influence you to compromise your morals, or it might make inroads into your ideas.

A creep is *any* negative influence that enters into your life.

ATTITUDE CREEPS

All of us experience negative thoughts from time to time. But if we allow these thoughts to creep in on a regular basis and fail to restrain them, they'll start to become part of our mind-sets.

The most common attitude creep is negativity—negativity toward oneself, toward others, and toward one's circumstances. Having a melancholic, glass-is-half-empty type of personality myself, I've often had to contend with this one.

Negativity is a key characteristic of the Übercreep, Satan. He spends a lot of time condemning and accusing people. The Bible calls him "the accuser of our brothers . . . , who accuses them day and night before our God" (Revelation 12:10). So it's no wonder, really, that he likes to see this negative attitude make its way into our lives.

Satan condemns us all the time, so it's a win for him when we buy into the deception and start to condemn ourselves. Satan also wins when we exhibit a negative, critical attitude toward others. Scripture tells us there is "*no condemnation* for those who are in Christ Jesus" (Romans 8:1, emphasis added). If we have a critical and condemning attitude toward ourselves or toward others, we are going against God.

We are letting the Creep in.

Scripture also says to "do all things without grumbling or disputing" (Philippians 2:14) and to "give thanks in all circumstances; for this is the will of God in Christ Jesus for you" (1 Thessalonians 5:18). So when we negatively grumble and complain about our circumstances, we're also letting the Creep in.

What about you? Are you having an increasingly critical attitude toward your husband? Your kids? Your in-laws? Your church? Your boss? Your neighbor? Your circumstances?

You can stop an attitude creep of negativity by intentionally being grateful and by speaking words of blessing instead.

We've talked about the creep of negativity, but there are many other types of attitude creeps, such as unforgiveness, resentment, envy, selfishness, thoughtlessness, impatience, or blame. Whenever one of these shows up, we have a choice to make. We can intentionally catch the creep and shut it out, the way God wants us to, or we can passively allow it to worm its way in.

BEHAVIORAL CREEPS

An attitude creep is a gradual negative change in our *attitude*, whereas a behavioral creep is a gradual negative change in our *behavior*. The two are often connected. Jesus said, "A good man brings good things out of the good stored up in his heart, and an evil man brings evil things out of the evil stored up in his heart. For the mouth speaks what the heart is full of" (Luke 6:45 NIV).

If we harbor ill will, ungratefulness, bitterness, and discontentment in our hearts, it's bound to show up in our words and actions. Perhaps you berate your coworker and repeatedly slander her behind her back. Maybe you make snide, hurtful comments. Have you become increasingly rude and caustic toward your husband? Are you using more crass and foul language?

Or maybe you claim sick days when you're really not sick. What about cheating your employer by doing personal things on work time? Asking for cash payments so you can avoid paying taxes? Maybe you tell lies to prevent being embarrassed. Do you have different versions of the truth for different people? Break your word and your budget by buying something you planned not to buy? Or fail to follow through on what you promised?

Whether we find ourselves making more excuses, developing a shorter fuse, becoming lazier, more reckless, or more disrespectful, any incremental negative change demonstrates that we are the victim of a behavioral creep.

TIME CREEPS

"There is a time for everything, and a season for every activity under the heavens," said Solomon (Ecclesiastes 3:1 NIV). There is a time to work. A time to serve. A time to rest. And a time to play. Unfortunately one category can bleed past its margin and steal time from another. We can play when we ought to be working. Or work when we ought to be resting. Or rest when we ought to be serving. What's more, we can procrastinate and waste time with meaningless activities.

Time is our most precious commodity. The Bible challenges us to make the best use of our time (Ephesians 5:16). Even the fiercely agnostic Charles Darwin admitted, "A man who dares to waste one hour of time has not discovered the value of life."[5]

In 2016 the marketing agency Mediakix put together an infographic depicting how much time, on average, people spend on social media and other daily activities across a lifetime. They concluded that the average person will spend seven years and eight months watching TV and five years and four months on social media, compared with one year and three months socializing with friends and six months doing laundry.[6]

Just think: by the time you reach the end of your life, you will have probably spent thirteen solid years watching TV and engaging with social media.

Cutting out the social media alone would have given you the time to climb Mount Everest thirty-two times or to walk the entire length of the Great Wall of China three and a half times. That's astonishing!

And it's even more astonishing when you consider that the amount of time people spend on these activities has risen since 2016 and continues to rise.

I think of these statistics whenever I find myself saying, "I don't have the time to . . ." It's usually not true that I don't have the time. The truth is, I often choose to spend my time on things that have relatively little value instead of disciplining myself to use my time wisely.

All those minutes we waste or spend procrastinating add up.

Satan likes to keep us busy with unproductive activities. He likes to distract us from what's important and occupy us with the unimportant. Are you alert to the time creeps that constantly try to worm their way into your life? Are you doing something to stop them from moving in?

HABIT CREEPS

A habit creep is a negative behavior pattern, and it is often tied to a lack of self-discipline. It starts out as a seemingly harmless behavior, but over time it becomes a negative habit—something we customarily do or don't do.

We know we need to get up early, but instead we sleep in and then race around like a madwoman to get out the door on time.

Or we say we are trying to lose weight, but we eat that second piece of dessert anyway (says the woman who just ate handfuls of Halloween chocolate set aside to give to costumed kids). We tell ourselves we'll fit in an extra workout session. But we don't do that either. We have plenty of time to watch Netflix and no time for exercise.

Perhaps quiet time with the Lord somehow gets neglected, and our friends don't see us at Bible study. Our excuses seem rational and good. Then we skip going to church. We have a good reason, but then it happens again. Then three times. Before we know it, our habit of going to church has been replaced with the habit of missing church.

Sometimes this lax attitude about commitment to our convictions spills into areas of vice too. An occasional bad habit turns into an addiction.

Time on our smartphones can lead to a social media addiction. The thrill of making a new purchase can lead to a shopping addiction. An occasional glass of wine can lead to an alcohol addiction. The purchase of lottery cards can lead to a gambling addiction. Frequent exposure to R-rated scenes can lead to a sex addiction. The use of painkillers can lead to a drug addiction. Casual partying can become an increasingly regular way of life.

Small bad habits often lead to bigger, more destructive habits. Watch out for these types of creeps!

IDEOLOGICAL CREEPS

Another kind of creep is an ideological one. It encroaches on our ideas and opinions and worms its way into our thinking. It influences us to accept a worldly point of view rather than a godly one.

The things we watch, read, and hear all impact the way we think. Paul warned his protégé, "O Timothy, guard what has been entrusted to you, avoiding worldly and empty chatter and the opposing arguments of what is falsely called 'knowledge'—which some have professed and thus gone astray from the faith" (1 Timothy 6:20–21 NASB).

We only need to check our social media feeds to see that there's a lot of empty chatter going on. And that a lot of people are getting caught up in it.

Ideas have a lot of power. They can lead us astray. What's worse, they can even "shipwreck" our faith (1:19). We'll talk about false ideas more in later chapters, but for now I just want you to be aware that some of the most relentless creeps you will face are the ones that constantly try to worm their way into your mind.

MORAL CREEPS

And then there are those powerful moral creeps. They are present whenever we compromise God's standards for moral purity.

One tiny compromise leads to another and then another.

The sex scenes we would have refused to watch years ago become our new tolerated entertainment norm. What was once outrageous doesn't seem so outrageous anymore. The pull to indulge becomes stronger. The attraction to spicy, scandalous shows or porn becomes more potent. Images get raunchier. Self-pleasuring becomes more frequent. Lust grows. Fantasies and daydreams increase. Sexual standards slip.

We go farther than we'd wanted to, and then we go even farther than that. We end up doing what we never would have conceived of doing a few years ago.

Maybe you end up sleeping with your boyfriend before marriage, or you end up moving in with him. Perhaps you end up having a series of one-night stands. You start picking up guys in bars. Start experimenting. Maybe your sexual behavior gets increasingly kinky and perverted. Maybe you're married, and you make excuses like, "It's just lunch," or "We're just friends." Instead of fleeing temptation you entertain it. Slowly you become entangled. Lunch with the good-looking married executive becomes a regular thing. The emotional affair leads to a physical affair.

Next thing you know, your life is a mess.

None of the women I talk to who have gotten themselves into a moral predicament ever planned to do that. When they realize how far they've fallen, they incredulously ask themselves, *How on earth did this happen to me? How did I get from there to here? How did I get myself into such a mess? How?*

By now I hope you know the answer. Sin does not advance by leaps; it advances by small steps, one tiny compromise at a time.

The compromises, in the moment, don't seem like much. The changes they produce are so subtle they're almost imperceptible. So it's easy to minimize the significance or importance of them. But Satan knows that a series of small negative choices will lead to significant negative results. He loves to prey on weak women who make tiny little compromises.

Positive or negative, it's the consistency of the habit over time rather than the magnitude of each individual action that makes the difference.

It is how we become enslaved or become stronger.

A strong woman evaluates whether her morals are moving in a positive or negative direction. If she sees them slipping, she immediately acts to stop the creep.

IS IT REALLY A CREEP?

There are so many different types of creeps and ways we can be led astray. There are too many for us to cover them all. The thing is, if we let one type of destructive influence into our lives, we open the door for others to follow. An attitude creep becomes a behavior creep. An ideological creep becomes a moral creep. And there are so many more.

How can we know if something is a destructive influence? Well, they all share the same characteristics. To qualify as a creep, it must be something that:

- *slowly encroaches*—Just like a lion, a creep advances and pushes in slowly, subtly, and almost imperceptibly. It patiently and ever so persistently keeps moving its way into our lives. It steadily encroaches, but only a little bit at a time.

- *exhibits the qualities of the Übercreep*—A creep is cut from the cloth of the Übercreep, so it will have one or more underlying characteristics of the father of all creeps. Remember the checklist of nineteen qualities? All creeps are of the same nature and have these qualities, usually many of them.

- *influences us to move in a negative direction*—A creep nudges us over. It pushes us and causes us to shift position slightly. The shift is so small that we usually don't perceive it as significant. We take small steps in a negative direction. We make compromises, rationalize, and start to have a different attitude about things. Often it takes some time before we, or the people around us, notice that things in our lives are sliding downhill.

- *gains power over us*—As a creep's influence continues, we give increasingly more power away and adopt its behavior. As this happens *we* become increasingly self-centered, materialistic, self-promoting, contemptuous, berating, insolent, ungrateful, irreverent, callous, resentful, defaming, undisciplined, malicious, cynical, backstabbing, impulsive, self-important, self-indulgent, and hypocritical.

Lisa could clearly remember the day she clicked on that first link. Her husband had tickets to the hockey game and was out for the evening. Bored, Lisa surfed the Web. She was reading the entertainment news when the sexy link popped up. At first, she hovered her cursor over the *x* to shut it down. She hesitated for a brief moment. Then, on impulse, she moved her mouse over an inch or two.

And clicked.

The pornographic images shocked her. Aghast at the lewdness, she shut the site down after a few minutes. But she couldn't rid herself of the images she had seen. They haunted her thoughts and dreams.

Over the next few weeks, Lisa revisited the porn site and a few related ones too. Her initial shock morphed into a dark, tantalizing fascination. On a whim she ordered some sex toys to be delivered to her house in an unmarked package. Alone in her locked bedroom, she tried them out but kept that secret from her husband.

And then there was that other link—the one that offered chatting instead of viewing. She saw it several times before she finally summoned up the nerve.

Click.

The conversations with the man she met online were hot and steamy. *All in good fun,* Lisa rationalized. She certainly didn't ever plan on meeting him or following through on their exchange. She planned to remain anonymous. No harm done. She was certain things would fizzle out after a couple of weeks. But they didn't.

Lisa couldn't remember whether he shared his cell phone number first or she did. But at some point the virtual flirting moved from their computers to their phones. And then the sexting started.

She wasn't planning on having an affair. She really wasn't. She planned to meet up with him in a restaurant in a nearby town to call things off. But the sexual attraction was too strong. The novelty was too alluring.

The affair lasted three months. Her husband never knew.

Afterward Lisa's discontentment with her marriage grew. It wasn't long before she was involved in yet another affair. This time, she didn't manage to keep it secret. Her teenage daughter was the one who got suspicious and had her dad start snooping around. Lisa's husband tried to get her to join him for marital counseling, but her heart wasn't in it.

She had changed. Her attitudes had changed. And so had her behavior, habits, morals, and ideas. Two years after she first clicked on that link and allowed that one little sneak in, Lisa walked away from her husband, her children, church, and everything she had once held dear.

THE DANGER OF CREEPS

What's the big deal about little creeps, like clicking on a link or lingering to talk to a coworker? Those don't seem all that bad. You may say to yourself, *I'm just curious.* Or *A little flirting is harmless. It's not like I'm sleeping with him.*

The thing is, the danger isn't always obvious at first. And the first time the compromise happens, you may not even realize that it's a creep trying to get into your life. It may seem innocent and random, just an everyday sort of slipup.

Maybe.

But then it happens again.

And again.

And again.

You've likely heard of the parable of the frog in the kettle. In the late 1800s researchers did a series of experiments with frogs. They found that when they dropped a frog into a pan of hot water, the frog quickly jumped out. But when they put the frog into a pan of cool water and gradually increased the temperature, the frog didn't perceive the danger. If the increase in heat was slow enough, the frog would just sit there until it cooked to death.

While modern-day scientists question the results of this experiment, it's still a good metaphor for how you can be damaged by seemingly harmless new attitudes, behaviors, or people in your life. Too often you can naively let these things in a little bit at a time and not recognize the danger until it's too late. It's not until sometime later that you notice how drastically the situation has changed.

Has there been a slow, negative change in your attitudes, behaviors, habits, morals, ideas, or ways of spending time? Can you identify any areas where you've been a weak woman and tolerated a creep?

Here are some possibilities:

- a website you shouldn't be viewing
- a book you shouldn't be reading
- a show you shouldn't be watching
- music lyrics you shouldn't be singing
- a secret text or e-mail exchange you shouldn't be pursuing
- a lunch meeting with a married guy you shouldn't be having
- a daydream or scenario you shouldn't be envisioning
- a place you shouldn't be going
- an activity you shouldn't be involved in
- a friend you shouldn't be seeing
- an excuse to skip church you shouldn't be making
- a bitter resentment you shouldn't be nursing
- a marital affection you shouldn't be withholding
- gossip you shouldn't be spreading

Don't rationalize and justify these things by saying, "It won't affect me," "I'm strong enough to handle it," "It's really not a big deal!" or, "That won't happen to me."

You're right, it's probably not a *big* deal—of course it's not, it's a creep! It's one in a series of *little* deals that are taking you off course.

A strong woman knows that it's not the *big* compromise that poses the biggest threat to her well-being; it's all those *little* ones.

It's the little things that have the power to bring about the greatest change. Neglecting the small stuff can lead to great disaster; taking care of the small stuff ensures the greatest success.

I think the apostle Paul would agree. In 2 Timothy 3:5, after spelling out the nineteen negative characteristics of a creep, he warned his friends to avoid them. That word *avoid* is a present direct imperative. Literally it means to constantly turn yourself away from something. Avoiding the destructive influence usually only requires a small effort, but that effort must be consistent and continuous.

The trouble with the weak women of Ephesus is that they were naive to the danger, and they were passive. They didn't see how these little choices, which were developing into attitudes and habits day by day, were a problem. They tolerated false teachers, they tolerated the drift, they tolerated the creeps. And little by little they lost their way.

We can, too, if we don't take creeps seriously.

CURTAIL THE CREEPS

Peter gave us some clues about not only curtailing creeps but also defeating them. Remember what he said about the prowling lion? "Be sober-minded; be watchful. Your adversary the devil prowls around like a roaring lion, seeking someone to devour. Resist him, firm in your faith" (1 Peter 5:8–9). I mentioned this verse earlier. It not only describes the Devil's activities but also offers the antidote to being weak.

Take another look.

Peter mentioned four necessities for warding off the roaring lion. First, a strong woman is aware of the danger ("sober-minded"). To be sober means to have a serious, no-nonsense attitude toward creeps. It means to be well-composed in your mind, clearheaded, and not deluded. A strong woman knows that she has a wily Enemy that is always lurking—always wanting to steal, kill, and destroy. Another translation of 1 Peter 5:8 reads, "Be serious!" (HCSB). She takes the threat seriously.

Second, a strong woman stays alert to ways creeps might be making a move on her ("watchful"). Being watchful means being vigilant and staying awake and attentive. Spiritually, she does not doze off.

She is like a watchman in a tower guarding a city, keeping watch for the enemy. She stands guard over her own heart and household. She is constantly on the lookout for creeps. She doesn't let them sneak up on her and catch her off guard.

Third, a strong woman actively pushes back ("resist"). She follows the teaching of James 4:7: "Submit to God. But resist the Devil, and he will flee from you" (HCSB).

A strong woman doesn't passively wait for the creep to make a move. She actively and intentionally counteracts its advance. Maybe she puts a smut filter on her Internet. Maybe she gets an app to put time restrictions on her social media.

Strong women don't let life happen to them. They are active. Intentional. Decisive. They take a stand and make a point to resist creeps. They stop negative influences and little encroachments before they can gain a foothold.

Finally, she stays anchored in Jesus ("firm in your faith"). To defeat the Creep, our convictions and all of our actions must be secured to an unshakable foundation. If Jesus is not our anchor, we will not be able to prevent the drift. We will be blown and tossed this way and that (1:6). When the tides of popular opinion change, our standards will change too. A strong woman's convictions are based on the unchanging standard of the Word of God, not political correctness, feelings, or popular opinion.

So many of us women nowadays think we're strong, but we're actually not.

We're weaklings.

Hapless victims of the drift.

But if we do what Scripture advises us to do—if we remain aware, alert, active, and anchored in Christ—we will be strong enough to resist the power of those sneaky creeps.

THERE'S A CREEP IN MY HOUSE

There's something else I want you to notice in 2 Timothy 3:6, and that's the phrase "into households." The false teachers were creeping into the households of weak women. Their activities affected not only the women themselves but also the people around them. The creeps were messing up entire families!

Another one of Paul's protégés, Titus, faced the same situation in Crete as Timothy faced in Ephesus. False teachers were creeping in and destroying households. "They must be silenced, since they are upsetting whole families by teaching for shameful gain what they ought not to teach" (Titus 1:11).

Creeps are dangerous because they aim to take down as many people as possible. When the Creep in the garden went after Eve, his plan was to leverage her influence to bring Adam down too. He was gunning for their whole household—indeed, for the entire human family.

As a woman I have a unique responsibility to watch out for creeps that are making a move on my household.

But what about men? Don't husbands and fathers have that responsibility too?

Yes, they undoubtedly do. But by design, God has wired women to be different from men. Most women have been given this amazing internal how-is-everyone-doing barometer. When it comes to people and relationships, we often see things that men don't naturally see, clues they might miss. We usually pick up on subtle indicators that something is not quite right.

Mama Bear is the perceiver, the watcher, the snoop, the detective, the cheerleader, the weeper, the burden-carrier, the pray-er, the checker-outer of girlfriends and boyfriends and best friends. That's the way we're wired. As nurturers and guardians of the home, we can't afford to be lackadaisical or inattentive in this role and foolishly allow things to creep in on our loved ones. I can't even begin to count the times I've intervened to prevent creeps from encroaching on my children, my husband, my marriage, my household.

Incidentally, I believe God gives *every* woman a household—a sphere of people—to look after. Psalm 113:9 says, "He gives the childless woman a household, making her the joyful mother of children" (HCSB). You don't have to have a husband and kids to be the mama of a household. Your household may be your volleyball team, Sunday school class, sorority, coworkers, the women in your recovery group or your nursing home. It may be your nieces and nephews or your neighbors.

Think carefully about the people in your life who you have some influence over. God wants you to take up your mantle of Mama Bear and start looking after your household. Watch out for the creeps in their lives. Be a strong woman. Do what you can to protect and warn and persuade them about the danger.

The Bible says that a strong woman "looks well to the ways of her household" (Proverbs 31:27). "The wisest of women builds her house, but folly with her own hands tears it down" (14:1).

How does this happen?

Either way—whether she builds or destroys—it happens one brick at a time.

JUST A LITTLE BIT AT A TIME

What creeps can you see worming their way into your life? I hope you're eager to get rid of them and that you will act just as swiftly and decisively as you would if it were an ugly, black creepy-crawly inching its way across your kitchen floor.

Don't be a spiritual Scorpion Queen—don't let poisonous intruders crawl all over you. And don't ignore the telltale signs that creeps are encroaching and causing damage. Don't be like me when I brushed that pile of sawdust left by carpenter ants off the windowsill at our cabin.

The weak women in Ephesus shrugged off and denied the danger of creeps. They didn't take the threat seriously.

I hope you won't make that same mistake.

I told you earlier that this book wouldn't add a lot of difficult, burdensome tasks to your to-do list. Catching the creep isn't complicated; it just takes a bit of consistent attention. We need to be aware that we have a mortal Enemy who is *always* trying to encroach. Because of this, we *always* need to be alert and on the lookout for creeps.

If we want to be strong and not weak, catching a creep is one of the most important things we can do.

HABIT 2

Master Your Mind

In your struggle against sin, the
victory will be won or lost on the
battlefield of your mind.

"The party has just begun!" hollered escaped convict
Jan-Erik Olsson, as he peppered the ceiling of the bank with bullets.[1]
On August 23, 1973, Olsson entered the *Kreditbanken*, one of the
largest banks in Stockholm, Sweden. As he approached the till, he
pulled a submachine gun from underneath the folded jacket he carried. Unbeknownst to him, one teller had the presence of mind to press
a silent alarm before she dove for cover.

When two police officers arrived on the scene, Olsson panicked. The heist was not going as planned. He fired at the officers
and retreated into the vault, forcing four bank employees—one man
and three women—in with him. Olsson strapped dynamite to their

chests and threatened to blow them to pieces if police did not meet his stipulations.

His first demand was the release of his prison cellmate, Clark Olafsson, a notorious criminal serving time for armed robbery. Olsson also wanted a substantial sum of money and a getaway car. Within hours police delivered the cellmate, the ransom, and a vehicle. The police insisted the duo take the money and leave the hostages behind. But the gunmen refused. To assure their own safe passage, they wouldn't leave the bank without at least one hostage in tow.

For the next five days, the criminals remained holed up inside the cramped bank vault in a standoff with police. Snipers stood in position on top of adjacent buildings. Dozens of news crews camped out nearby. However, while the outside world worried that the hostages would be mistreated and killed, something quite odd was happening inside the vault. The hostages were forming a strong emotional bond with their captors.

Police listening devices indicated that the mood inside the vault was surprisingly good. The criminals told stories from their past as the hostages roared in laughter. When they allowed the police commissioner to come check on the hostages' condition, the hostages seemed hostile toward the commissioner but relaxed with the gunmen—with whom they joked, bantered, and interacted on a first-name basis.

As the drama unfolded, the hostages demonstrated more and more empathy for their captors and became less cooperative with police attempts to rescue them.

One hostage phoned the prime minister and pleaded that he allow the gunmen to take her with them in the escape car, as she fully trusted the gunmen to keep her safe. A day or two later, two hostages were presented with a golden opportunity to escape. The gunmen had allowed them to leave the vault to go use the washroom. Out of sight, they spotted crouching policemen. But instead of running to freedom, they chose to return to their captors.

On the sixth day, police felt they had no choice but to pump tear gas into the vault. The criminals surrendered almost immediately. In the doorway of the vault, the hostages and convicts kissed, embraced, and shook hands before the police hauled the convicts away.

Even after being threatened and abused and fearing for their lives for almost six days, the freed hostages continued to exhibit a shocking attitude of loyalty toward their captors. In media interviews, it was clear that they supported their captors and distrusted the law enforcement personnel who had come to their rescue.

All four hostages refused to testify at court proceedings. Not only that, they worked to raise money for the convicts' legal defense and, afterward, visited them in jail. According to some reports, one hostage even got engaged to one of the convicts.

The hostages' seemingly irrational attachment to their abductors baffled the police and public alike. But psychologists chalked it up to a cognitive syndrome related to brainwashing. The phenomenon of victims coming to identify and sympathize with their captors—displaying compassion, loyalty, and affection toward them—subsequently came to be known as Stockholm syndrome, named after the city where this infamous bank robbery took place.[2]

Given the right conditions, captors can exert an astonishing amount of influence over their victims and extract total allegiance from them. The victims end up supporting, loving, and defending their abusers and controllers, and are reluctant to engage in behaviors that may assist in their detachment or release. What's more, they believe their allegiance is totally voluntary and often deny that they are, in fact, being held captive against their will.

They can't think straight, because little by little the captors have brainwashed them.

STOCKHOLM SYNDROME
HITS EPHESUS

Women in Timothy's church were suffering from a spiritual type of Stockholm syndrome. The false teachers had captured them. Your translation of the Bible may say "gain control over," "make captives of," or "captivate." The Greek word is a military term that indicates these women were held captive like prisoners of war. But there's more. The reason some translations use the word *captivate* is that the word includes an element of psychological domination. It means to gain influence or control over the mind.

These women weren't just taken captive; they were captivated. To captivate is to attract and hold the attention or interest of. A person who is captivated is enthralled, charmed, enchanted, bewitched, fascinated, entranced, enraptured, delighted, dazzled, mesmerized, allured, beguiled.

The weak women in Timothy's church were ensnared by ideas that were not in line with truth. False teachers had charmed and beguiled them to think and act the wrong way. They were dazzled with the new ideas and oblivious to the fact that they'd been taken hostage. They'd been brainwashed to embrace their captivity.

The creeps had messed with their minds.

These women were victims, to be sure. But Paul indicated that they were party to their own imprisonment.

Paul presented the same idea in the previous chapter when he argued that people must "escape from the snare of the devil, after being captured by him to do his will" (2 Timothy 2:26). The image here is not of a prisoner who resists captivity but of a Stockholm syndrome–type of hostage who embraces her captivity, becomes sympathetic to the captor's agenda, and begins to cooperate and work with him to achieve his goals.

It's like the story of Patty Hearst, a nineteen-year-old heiress, who was kidnapped at gunpoint in 1974 by the SLA (Symbionese Liberation Army). The domestic terrorist organization abducted her to garner a hefty ransom from her wealthy family. In a bizarre turn of events, Hearst joined their cause.

Two months after she was taken hostage, a bank security camera recorded her wielding a semiautomatic rifle during a heist. Over the next seventeen months, Hearst actively participated in SLA-led criminal activity in California, including extorting an estimated $2 million from her father.[3] By the time of her arrest, she was a fugitive wanted for serious crimes.

What happened to Hearst is like what happened to the women of Ephesus and what happens to us on a spiritual level when we are ensnared by the Devil. He captivates—charms, dazzles, mesmerizes, allures, fascinates, bewitches—us and convinces us to do what he wants us to do.

How does he get us to cooperate?

By attacking our minds.

He gets us to *think* the wrong way. Little by little he encroaches on our thoughts and takes us captive to do his will.

WHAT WERE YOU THINKING?

Though Satan mentally entraps and imprisons us, the Bible says it's possible to break free. People can "come to their senses and escape from the snare of the devil" (2 Timothy 2:26).

According to this verse, what we need to do to escape the snare of the Devil is to come to our senses and start thinking the right way—God's way. The Greek word translated "come to their senses" is *ananepho*. It means to return to a proper state of mind or to one's right senses, to again think right or no longer think wrong thoughts.[4]

Ananepho involves a change of mind, from sinful, wacky,

destructive, irrational, wrong thinking to righteous, sane, sober, sensible, wise, healthful, right thinking.

Have you ever been enticed into doing something wrong and afterward wondered, *Why did I do that? What was I thinking? Was I out of my mind?*

Chances are, you were *not* thinking right and were *not* in a proper state of mind. Why? Because sin makes us stupid. It makes us think silly thoughts and do foolish things.

Over the years I've listened to many heart-wrenching stories from women ensnared in moral failures, affairs, addictions, betrayals, deceptions, self-harm, and all sorts of other sins. And often as they finish telling me their tales, they hang their heads in shame, eyes spilling with tears, and whisper the reproaching question, "What was I thinking?"

Carla approached me at a women's conference and asked if I could pray that the Lord would make a way for her and her son and her son's father to be united as a family. It sounded like a noble request. That is, until I got the details.

Carla had been married for fifteen years. For fourteen of those years, she had carried on an affair with her husband's only brother. The man whom her twelve-year-old son called *uncle* was, in fact, the boy's father. Her husband and the rest of his close-knit Italian family had no inkling of the long-standing affair. Carla wanted to divorce her husband and wed his brother. What's more, she hoped her son, her in-laws, and the rest of the family would be okay with that.

"So can you pray that God would make a way for me to marry my true love?" she inquired after she finished sharing the sordid details.

"Umm . . . no. I can't pray that."

I wanted to slap my palm to my forehead and loudly exclaim, "You slept with your husband's brother? Are you out of your mind? *What were you thinking?*"

What was Carla thinking? She was probably thinking:

- *He's my husband's brother; it's good that I feel close to him.*
- *What's the harm in flirting?*
- *It's just a little kiss. Not a big deal.*
- *How can this be wrong when it feels so right?*
- *I can't help that I'm in love with my brother-in-law.*
- *It's my husband's fault. He drove me to it.*
- *I guess I married the wrong brother.*
- *It's better that my husband doesn't know he's not my son's father.*
- *God wants me to be happy, and I won't be happy until I'm married to my lover.*
- *My son and I deserve to be together as a family with his real father.*

The twisted train wreck of a predicament Carla found herself in didn't just happen overnight. It happened incrementally. What's more, each small compromise in behavior was preceded by a compromise in her mind.

Someone once said that every sin we commit, we commit twice— once in our thoughts and once again when we act on those thoughts.

Carla was not thinking straight. Had she "come to her senses" early on and started thinking the right way, she likely could have gotten back on track. But with each faulty thought and rationalization and compromise in behavior, she became increasingly entrapped, and it became more and more difficult to discern a way out.

Carla asked me to pray because she realized she was caught up in a terrible mess. But I could see that she still hadn't come to her senses. She was still thinking the wrong way. It was obvious that Carla did not view adultery, lying, and betrayal the way God viewed it. She was not yet thinking the way the Lord wanted her to think. Satan, the Creep, was still messing with her mind.

Contrary to what she believed, Carla's biggest need wasn't figuring out how to divorce her husband, marry her lover, and somehow get her son, in-laws, and extended family on board. What she needed was to be renewed in the spirit of her mind.

She needed to break free from the Devil's snare.

She needed to come to her senses. No longer think wrong thoughts. Think right thoughts instead.

The good news for Carla—and for us—is, that's exactly what the gospel of Jesus Christ gives us the power to do.

BATTLEFIELD FROM THE BEGINNING

Our minds have been a battlefield from the very beginning of time. Our foremother, Eve, was captivated by Satan's lies, and the tendency to fall for them has plagued women ever since.

The problem with Eve wasn't one of willful disobedience. She didn't obstinately defy the Lord. She loved God! Satan wouldn't have even suggested that she betray him. No. He knew that a direct approach wouldn't work. So he used a much subtler strategy. He just crept in and insidiously introduced her to some new ways of thinking. Satan knew exactly what to say to push Eve's thoughts in the direction he wanted them to go (Genesis 3:1–6).

He suggested that God was holding out on her, that God's ways were too restrictive. He suggested that she should focus on her own self-interests and implied that she wouldn't suffer any negative consequences by doing so. On the contrary, she'd experience amazing benefits.

Oh, he didn't come right out and say these things. He merely hinted at them. He twisted the truth ever so slightly and implanted cunning distortions and questions in her mind. He knew that if he could get her to think the wrong way, he could get her to feel and act the wrong way.

Once Eve began to dwell on the false ideas, they infected her thoughts. It wasn't long before the problem snowballed:

She began to doubt the motives of God.

She began to doubt the goodness of God.

She began to doubt the wisdom of God.

She began to think that she knew better.

She began to dwell on her own right to choose.

She began to feel slighted, resentful, and entitled.

She bit into the forbidden apple.

Satan knew that if he could topple the first domino, Eve's *thinking*, that her *feeling* and *acting* dominos would topple too.

Scripture tells us that the Devil's key tactic is to defeat our thinking. "The god of this world [Satan] has blinded the minds of the unbelievers, to keep them from seeing the light of the gospel" (2 Corinthians 4:4). And just as the Devil goes after the minds of unbelievers to keep them from understanding the gospel, he also relentlessly seeks to mess with the minds of those of us who trust in Jesus, to try to keep us from thinking the way the Lord wants us to think.

Satan is the master manipulator. He's a slimy, double-dealing, duplicitous, treacherous, street-smart hustler who "masquerades as an angel of light" and constantly tries to sell us a bill of goods (11:14 NIV).

He's like a real-estate con man with movie-star good looks who deals in Florida swampland.

Or like charismatic George C. Parker, the infamous New York swindler who twice a week for thirty years convinced people to buy the Brooklyn Bridge.

Or like a clever cybercriminal who extorts people with his sophisticated Internet phishing schemes.

Time and time again Scripture teaches that God's ways are for our good and our protection and that obedience brings blessing and freedom. But the Devil plays mind games with us, just as he did with Eve. He introduces the idea that God's ways are unreasonable and unfair, that if we obey him we'll be miserable and miss out. He constantly tries to deceive and defeat us by leading our thoughts away from truth.

He messes with my mind.

He messes with yours.

Paul was worried that this might happen to his friends too. "I am afraid that as the serpent deceived Eve by his cunning, your thoughts will be led astray from a sincere and pure devotion to Christ" (2 Corinthians 11:3).

All of us are vulnerable to the Creep messing with our minds. Satan knows how to outwit. Outplay. Outlast. But Scripture makes us wise to his tactics and game plan so that we will "not be outwitted by" him (2:11). Though our Enemy is crafty and relentless, we can—with God's help—win the battle for our minds.

THE WAY YOU THINK IS THE WAY YOU WALK

How many thoughts would you guess go through your mind each day? Maybe one thousand? Five thousand? Ten thousand?

According to the Laboratory of Neuro Imaging at the University of Southern California, the average person thinks about 48.6 thoughts per minute. That adds up to a staggering total of seventy thousand thoughts per day.[5] Some of these thoughts are conscious and intentional, but many come uninvited and pass through our minds at lightning speed.

This mental chatter starts the moment we wake up and continues throughout our waking day. The chatter goes on in the background as we shower, get dressed, eat, talk, read the news, check our social media feeds, work, walk, drive, or even make love. It goes on when we are alone and when we are with others. It's like a fly that constantly flits from one place to another, a background buzz that's exceedingly difficult to turn off.

Researchers say that, of all the thoughts that pass through the average person's mind each day, about 95 percent are the same repetitive thoughts the person had the day before, and about 80 percent are negative in nature.[6] That's a lot of negative mental chatter! Deep down, people are much more self-condemning, insecure, pessimistic, and fearful than their sunny social media updates lead us to believe.

Negative thoughts usually fall into one of the following categories:

- regret, guilt, shame, and blame
- lack of love, approval, or worth
- inferiority, insecurity, and lack of ability
- lack of control or desire for control
- anxiety, apprehension, and fear

And it's the *repetitive nature* of this constant, underlying negative mental chatter that causes the most damage both to ourselves and to others.

The process is similar to what happened in the backyard of my house one year. It is positioned back-to-back against the backyard of a house from an adjacent neighborhood. A retaining wall and a six-foot-high fence separate the two properties. This high barrier made it difficult for my sons to play with their friend Jesse, who lived on the other side of the fence.

To get to his house, they had to hike out of our neighborhood, around the corner, and back through his neighborhood. Even though our yards are right next to each other, it took more than ten minutes to get there. To avoid this trek I often stood tiptoe on a garden chair and heaved my boys over the fence. When I fell and badly twisted an ankle while trying to do so, my husband and I decided we needed an alternate solution. We built a small gate in the back fence.

The boys were thrilled. That summer they played with Jesse nearly every day.

It wasn't until fall, when school started, that I noticed a problem. There was a path worn into the grass stretching from the back gate diagonally across our whole lawn. Over the next few weeks, the path got wider, and the grass along the path disappeared completely, leaving only hard-packed dirt, which turned to mud whenever it rained.

One morning, sitting at my kitchen table in my nightgown, I spotted a couple of unfamiliar teenagers sheepishly sneaking through my backyard. That's when it dawned on me. The kids from Jesse's neighborhood were using my yard as a shortcut to get to school. It was ruining my lawn. Each time they walked on that path, it got harder and more entrenched and less hospitable to growing grass. We had to lock the gate to stop the constant flow of traffic. Even so, it took more than a year for the path to fade and the grass to grow back.

The same sort of thing happens with a repetitive negative thought. It wears a path into our minds. As the path gets harder, deeper, and more pronounced, the recurrent negative thought turns into an unhealthy mind-set. It becomes the way we habitually think. It becomes part of our belief system, part of how we view and interact with the world.

Part of who we are.

Ten-year-old Bethany brings home a report card from school. She's an excellent student—the card is filled with Bs, As, and even a few A-pluses. The only subject in which she got less than a B was PE (physical education), for which she got a C-plus and a "needs improvement" comment. Bethany isn't much of an athlete, unlike her younger sister, Baily, who lives in gym clothes and sneakers and is the star of both her soccer and volleyball teams.

As Bethany's dad reviews the report card, his eyes stop to rest on the C-plus. Amused, he tussles her hair and teases, "I guess we'll have to get your sister to put you through some ball drills."

Bethany's heart sinks. A dark thought crosses her young mind: *I'm not good enough. I'm a failure. My dad loves my sister more than me.* She dwells on the thought. Replays it. And replays it. *I'm not good enough. I'm a failure. My dad loves my sister more than me.*

By the time she turns seventeen, the thought has become a stronghold in her life. Bethany struggles with her weight. She seeks affirmation from boys. In college she loses her virginity to the first creep who knows how to capitalize on her insecurities. Guilty and shame-filled thoughts are added to her loop of self-talk. *I'm not good enough. I'm a failure. I've disappointed God. I'm damaged goods. No one will love me.*

Bethany's insecurities follow her into marriage. Her husband quickly tires of her nagging and needy attempts to control him. He becomes distant. She turns to food, erotic romance novels, and deep glasses of red wine for comfort. She's steeped in feelings of self-loathing and self-pity. At work and in relationships, she adopts a victim mentality. Her loop of self-talk becomes a self-fulfilling prophecy.

I'm not good enough. I'm a failure. No one loves me. Everyone is against me. Things never go my way.

Satan uses circumstances and faulty thinking patterns to build strongholds in our lives. He's extremely patient. He knows that if he can sidetrack our thoughts, he'll eventually sidetrack our lives.

Bethany is at a critical point. Her thoughts have led her to a place where she's emotionally fragile and highly susceptible to sin. She's already carrying around significant resentment toward her father, sister, and husband. She's cranky, snippy, and irritable. Presented with the right set of circumstances, she's ripe for having an affair, abusing alcohol or drugs, getting hooked on porn, or other self-destructive types of behavior.

But her misery also presents an opportunity for self-evaluation and change. Though it would take some effort, she could seize the opportunity to lock the gate to the destructive thoughts that are wearing an ugly, hard-packed path across the backyard of her mind.

WWJT

Psychologists tell us that negative self-chatter is a common problem that can be countered with various positivity and self-affirmation techniques. They'd encourage people like Bethany to cultivate the habit of countering negative thoughts with positive ones. And that might help a bit. In the short-term.

But Scripture has a different analysis of the problem and the solution. It informs us that without Jesus, we are doomed to unhealthy thinking patterns. There is a futility of thinking that exists in the lives of those who do not know him. Paul referred to it as "ignorance" and said that people in this state have been "darkened in their understanding" (Ephesians 4:17–18).

According to Paul, we don't need more positive thinking. What we need is a completely different kind of thinking. We need to think the way Jesus thinks. We need the mind of Christ (1 Corinthians 2:16).

Have you ever seen a bracelet or wristband bearing the letters *WWJD*? It's an acronym for the phrase "What Would Jesus Do?"

The question dates back hundreds of years. It was originally posed by Thomas à Kempis in the 1400s in his book *The Imitation of Christ*. In 1891 Charles Spurgeon, a well-known evangelist in London, asked the same question several times in a sermon. A few years later Charles M. Sheldon wrote a book entitled *In His Steps: What Would Jesus Do?* The novel sold 30 million copies worldwide, becoming one of the top fifty bestselling novels of all time.

In the early 1990s Sheldon's great-grandson, Garrett W. Sheldon, and Deborah Morris published a contemporary retelling of the classic novel *What Would Jesus Do?* This launched a grassroots movement among Christian youth, who wore bracelets bearing the initials WWJD as a reminder to ask themselves this vital question constantly.[7]

All actions start out as thoughts. If we don't think the right thoughts, we won't do the right things. So, arguably, a question that's even more important than "What Would Jesus *Do?*" is "What Would Jesus *Think?*" (WWJT). Maybe we should start a new trend and wear WWJT bracelets to remind ourselves how essential it is to check that our thoughts are in line with Christ's. According to the Bible, there are really only two directions our thoughts can go: we can think *carnal* thoughts or *spiritual* ones.

The carnal mind is nonspiritual, worldly, according to the flesh, merely human. Remember the Stockholm syndrome? Like a hostage in love with her captor, this kind of thinking blindly follows the course of this world, which is controlled by Satan, the convict who holds his hostage (Ephesians 2:2).

The carnal mind isn't really interested in what Jesus would think. It won't (and essentially can't) submit to God's truth (Romans 8:7). Carnal thinking is the common, popular way to think. It depends on human wisdom. It's the kind of thinking that often gets us into trouble. With a carnal mind-set, I focus on myself—my ability, my worth, my value, my capability. I leave God out of the picture.

The second type of mind is spiritual, which focuses on what the Spirit of God desires (v. 5). Spiritual thoughts are otherworldly, supernatural, divine in origin. They focus on Jesus Christ—his ability, his worth, his value, his capability. The spiritual mind is also called the "mind of Christ" (1 Corinthians 2:16). It's the mind-set we receive when we come to faith in Jesus and the Holy Spirit comes to dwell in our hearts. It's a WWJT way of thinking.

So what do the two types of mind-sets say about how to handle all my negative mental chatter?

HOW DO I DEAL WITH THOUGHTS RELATING TO REGRET, GUILT, SHAME, AND BLAME?

Popular thinking tells me to recognize that everyone has faults and to forgive myself and others. WWJT thinking reminds me that if I repent and accept God's lavish grace, my sins will be blotted out, and I will experience times of refreshing in the presence of the Lord (Acts 3:19–20). I can be confident that there is no condemnation for me because I am united with Christ Jesus (Romans 8:1). What's more, because the Lord forgave me, I now have the power to forgive others (Colossians 3:13).

HOW DO I DEAL WITH THOUGHTS RELATING TO LACK OF LOVE, APPROVAL, OR WORTH?

Popular thinking says to appreciate myself more, stop comparing myself to others, stop seeking approval, and cultivate higher self-esteem. WWJT thinking reminds me that I am chosen by God, a holy and dearly loved daughter of the Creator of the Universe, who has blessed me in Christ with every spiritual blessing in the heavens (2 Corinthians 6:18; Ephesians 1:3–4; Colossians 3:12).

HOW DO I DEAL WITH THOUGHTS RELATING TO INFERIORITY, INSECURITY, AND LACK OF ABILITY?

Popular thinking says that with grit and determination, I can muster up enough strength to do anything I set my mind to. WWJT thinking says I can tap into "the immeasurable greatness of [God's] power toward us who believe, according to the working of his great might" (Ephesians 1:19). "I can do all things through him who strengthens me" (Philippians 4:13).

HOW DO I DEAL WITH THOUGHTS RELATING TO LACK OF CONTROL OR DESIRE FOR CONTROL?

Popular thinking says to recognize that I can only control what I can control and to take small positive steps to reclaim my life. WWJT thinking says that I can be confident that God is in control. "Whatever the LORD pleases, he does, in heaven and on earth, in the seas and all deeps" (Psalm 135:6). All things *will* work together for good for me, because I love God and am called according to his purpose (Romans

8:28). I can be confident that he who began a good work in me will surely bring it to completion at the day of Jesus Christ (Philippians 1:6).

HOW DO I DEAL WITH THOUGHTS RELATING TO ANXIETY, APPREHENSION, AND FEAR?

Popular thinking says to breathe deeply, face my fears, relax, and talk myself through it. WWJT thinking says, "Do not be anxious about anything, but in everything by prayer and supplication with thanksgiving let your requests be made known to God. And the peace of God, which surpasses all understanding, will guard your hearts and your minds in Christ Jesus" (Philippians 4:6–7). I can overcome fear because Christ has overcome the world (1 John 4:4; 5:4).

Do you see the difference between the two types of thinking?

Popular thinking is *androcentric*—it relies on my own human wisdom and strength. WWJT thinking is *Christocentric*—it relies on the divine wisdom and strength of Jesus Christ.

Scripture tells us that the former is guided by the Spirit of deceit and the latter by the Spirit of truth (John 14:17; John 8:44).

The way you think makes a profound difference in the way you live. The more you change your thoughts for the better, the more your life will change for the better. But it all starts with embracing the mind that is yours in Christ Jesus (Philippians 2:5).

FROM A CATERPILLAR TO A BUTTERFLY

I grew up across the street from a forested gully called the Mill Creek Ravine. During the warm, languid days of summer, my mom and dad would often take us into the ravine for a Sunday afternoon walk. Whenever we spotted a common milkweed plant, we'd examine the leaves for caterpillars and for the jade-green podlike chrysalides that turned them into monarch butterflies. (Fun fact: if it's a fuzzy cocoon, it probably belongs to a moth, not a butterfly.)

I was fascinated that a creepy-crawly caterpillar could transform into an exquisite butterfly. Once, I spotted a monarch struggling hard to emerge from its shiny chrysalis. I wanted to crack open the casing to make it easier for it to get out. But my dad warned me that this would hurt rather than help. If I released the butterfly, I'd cripple it for life.

It's the struggle of trying to get out of the chrysalis that pumps blood into a new butterfly's tiny, crumpled, wet wings. The difficult task of breaking free is what brings fitness to its body and strengthens and enlarges its wings so it can fly.

When you put your faith in Jesus, the Lord changed you into a new creation (2 Corinthians 5:17). He replaced your futile, carnal mind with the mind of Christ (Ephesians 4:17–24). You underwent a complete metamorphosis. It's as if you changed from a caterpillar into a butterfly. You used to have a caterpillar brain, and now you have a butterfly brain.

Your carnal mind has been replaced with the mind of Christ.

The transformation is complete.

Done deal.

That doesn't mean, however, that your old ways of thinking are gone. It's as though you're still stuck in the chrysalis. God gave you wings, but it's up to you to fight your way out of your old, restrictive, caterpillar-mode of existence.

In one sense, the metamorphosis from a caterpillar into a butterfly is complete when the caterpillar dies in its green casket and turns into caterpillar soup, and then nature refashions the sludge into a butterfly. But, in another sense, the metamorphosis isn't complete until the butterfly breaks out of the chrysalis, starts behaving like a butterfly, and completely leaves all remnants of its caterpillar life behind.

The process of butterfly metamorphosis can help you understand the difference between God's act of *regeneration*, wherein he changes you into a new creation, and the process of *sanctification*, wherein you must cooperate with the Holy Spirit and put in the daily effort to know and live out your new identity.

That crusty old jacket that encases you serves a useful purpose. As you push against it, your wings will strengthen and mature. One day you'll break free from the chrysalis, spread your wings, and fly.

The problem with the weak-willed women in Ephesus—and the problem with many of us—is that we're not thinking the right way. We're monarch butterflies who still think and act like caterpillars. We're not working to strengthen our wings and leave creepy-crawly ways behind. Some of us aren't aware that we even have wings! We're comfortable snoozing in our crusty old caterpillar shroud. We're not spreading our wings and soaring in the sunlight.

Caterpillar thoughts are keeping us down.

KEYS TO MASTERING YOUR MIND

How can you master your mind so that you are thinking God's thoughts instead of worldly ones? How can you break free from old ways of thinking? I have some suggestions that may help.

1. ASK GOD TO RENEW THE SPIRIT OF YOUR MIND.

Paul said, "Do not be conformed to this world, but be transformed by the renewal of your mind" (Romans 12:2). The word *transformed* in this verse is the Greek *metamorphoo*, from which we get the word *metamorphosis*.

Isn't it interesting that the Bible uses butterfly-type language here?

Figuratively speaking, you can be transformed from an immature, entangled, weak baby butterfly into a mature, beautiful, regal specimen who flies far and wide and lives up to the monarch's reputation as King of the Butterflies.

How?

Through the renewal of your mind.

Let that sink in for a moment. It's a profound truth: *you will grow strong through the renewal of your mind.*

Thinking the right thoughts will increase your strength. It will get the blood pumping through your baby wings. Caterpillar thoughts won't do. You need to think butterfly thoughts to grow strong enough to break free of that stubborn old casing that's keeping you down.

There's another word I want to draw your attention to. It's the word *renewal*. To renew means to be restored to a former state; to become new or as if new again. Being renewed in our minds means that our thinking gets aligned with God's.

Again . . . And again . . . And again.

The ongoing, repetitive nature of the renewal is evident in the verb Paul used. For the benefit of those of you who are linguistic geeks, he used a present passive imperative: *be* renewed, *be* transformed. The present tense means that it reflects a current and ongoing action. The passive aspect means we are the object of the action rather than the cause of the action. In other words, the constant renewal of our minds is not something we do as much as it is something that is done in us. The Holy Spirit is the one who does all the heavy lifting. The imperative part means that it's a must-do command, like *Go!* or *Stop!*

Now, you might be scratching your head. This involves an action we receive and an action we must take? Yes, it's both. But it's not as tricky as it might seem at first.

The word *renewal* in Romans 12:2 is also used in Titus 3:5, where Paul wrote, "[God] saved us, not because of works done by us in righteousness, but according to his own mercy, by the washing of regeneration and renewal of the Holy Spirit."

Ongoing renewal is what is necessary for the transformation of our minds, and this is the work of the Holy Spirit. We are radically dependent on him to make it happen. The renewal happens because of God's amazing grace—"Not a result of works, so that no one may boast" (Ephesians 2:9).

But there is something vital we need to do—we need to *ask*! "If any of you lacks wisdom, let him ask God, who gives generously to all without reproach, and it will be given him" (James 1:5).

Don't lose the battle for your mind because you're too self-sufficient to ask for help.

Don't let it be said of you, "You do not have, because you do not ask" (4:2). Jesus promised, "Ask, and it will be given to you; seek, and you will find; knock, and it will be opened to you" (Matthew 7:7).

So, ask! Ask God for help and ask often. Ask daily, and even a hundred times a day. Asking the Lord to help you think correctly is the first and most important key to mastering your mind.

2. EXAMINE YOUR THOUGHTS.

The second key to mastering your mind is to make a habit of examining your thoughts. "Who knows a person's thoughts except the spirit of that person, which is in him?" (1 Corinthians 2:11). No one except you can know with certainty exactly what you are thinking. The best others can do is guess at your motives and thought processes. Yet with the constant stream of chatter running through our minds, it's easy for us to stop paying attention.

David, the psalmist, made a habit of asking the Lord to help him with the process of self-examination. "Test me, LORD, and try me; examine my heart and mind" (Psalm 26:2 HCSB). "Search me, O God. . . . Try me and know my thoughts!" (139:23). David wanted to make sure he was thinking the right way. He wanted his thinking to align with God's. So he regularly examined his thoughts to make sure he was thinking the right way.

Failing to align our thinking with God's is at the root of most of the difficulties we encounter in life. If we want to change the way we act, we must change the way we think. To get to the root of the problem, we can't start with the action. We've got to start with the thought (Mark 7:21–23).

Behind every sin we commit hides a lie we believe. Many of us are believing lies: Lies about God, such as, "God's ways are too restrictive." Lies about ourselves, such as, "I shouldn't have to live with unfulfilled longings." Lies about sin, such as, "This sin isn't really that bad." Lies about circumstances, such as, "My bad circumstances are responsible for my bad attitude." Lies about our priorities, sexuality, marriage, children, about who we are and how we ought to behave. Lies. Lies. Lies. Satan is the father of lies. His aim is to get us thinking, feeling, and acting the wrong way.

And I said earlier, it's the *thinking* domino that's usually the first to fall.

Sometimes we focus too much on trying to change or stop our undesirable behaviors when what we need to do is go back and find out what kind of faulty thinking produced that behavior in the first place. It's much easier to fix the *what* if we understand the *why*.

Why did you lash out at your mother?
"Because she made a cutting, sarcastic comment."

No. What happened is that the situation revealed your faulty thinking. You believe you have the right to retaliate for past hurts, to return them tit for tat.

Why did you say bad things about your friend behind her back?
"Because they were true."

No. What happened is that the situation revealed your faulty thinking. You believe that making her look bad is going to make you look good.

Why did you indulge too much last night?
"Because I had such a tough week and just needed to unwind."

No. What happened is that the situation revealed your faulty thinking. You believe that life should be easy and that it's your right to self-indulge.

'I'he reason you can't control your actions is that you're not fighting to control your thoughts. Chances are you haven't even taken the time to identify where your thinking is out of line. It's tough to correct faulty thinking if you're not paying attention to the chatter going on in your head.

The solution is to do what David did. Make a habit of examining your thoughts. This is especially important when you notice your behavior is off. That's the time to ask yourself, *What was I thinking?* and to ask the Lord to help you figure it out. When you trace the behavior back to the faulty thought that caused it, you'll be far more successful at pulling that sin out by its root. And the sooner the better! The longer you fail to deal with a faulty thought pattern, the more it will entrench an ugly path across the backyard of your mind.

Evaluate your thoughts constantly.

As you go through each day, make a habit of attentively checking: *What am I thinking? What would Jesus think? Are my thoughts in line with his?*

3. PREPARE YOUR MIND FOR ACTION.

It isn't possible to know if our thoughts align with the Lord's if we are uninformed about the way he thinks. Paul told his friends to stop thinking like those who were "darkened in their understanding, alienated from the life of God," because of their "ignorance" (Ephesians 4:17–18). Peter echoed these sentiments, telling believers to prepare their minds for action. He also said, "Do not be conformed to the passions of your former ignorance" (1 Peter 1:13–14).

These verses indicate that it's possible for those of us who know Jesus and have received the mind of Christ to walk in ignorance, just as we did before we knew him. The solution? To prepare our minds for action by equipping them with truth.

A woman of strength equips her mind. She seeks to overcome her ignorance. She regularly reads and studies Scripture so she can train her mind to think the way Jesus thinks. This is where the discipline of Bible reading comes into play. As R. C. Sproul once said, "God gives us the revelation of sacred Scripture in order for us to have our minds changed so we begin to think like Jesus. Sanctification and spiritual growth is all about this. If you just have it in your mind and you don't have it in your heart, you don't have it. But you can't have it in your heart without first having it in your mind. We want to have a mind informed by the Word of God."[8]

Do you know how the FBI trains secret service agents to identify counterfeit money? It makes them spend countless hours handling, examining, and intensely studying real money. The agents are so familiar with the real thing that when a counterfeit is presented, its flaws are obvious to them. They can immediately tell that the texture, feel, and look aren't quite right.

The Lord wants us to follow the same sort of training technique. He wants us to soak in the truth of his Word and become so familiar with truth that we can immediately discern that something is off when we encounter a counterfeit thought or idea.

I was in high school in the late 1970s, during the peak of the second-wave feminist movement. I remember wondering what my spiritual mentor, Diane, thought about all the new ideas. Diane, who was in her midtwenties, was the adult sponsor of the Christian club I helped colead. She was a go-getter—extremely gifted, capable, articulate, and intelligent. I expected she'd enthusiastically support a movement that pushed for the equality of women.

When I asked for her opinion, Diane thoughtfully paused, and then said something like this: "Well . . . I can't say I know much about it, but from what I've heard, something seems *off*. While I sympathize with some of the concerns, the clamoring for personal rights and the inciting of anger just doesn't sit right with me. It doesn't fit with the character of Jesus."

Diane resisted immediately embracing ideas that appealed to a lot of other women. Because she had prepared her mind for action, she was in a good position to evaluate whether the concepts lined up with God's Word.

The thing about a lie is that it normally contains enough truth to make it compelling. It's just a little bit *off*. Otherwise we wouldn't fall for it.

I fear that many of today's Christian women are being taken captive by popular ideas that are full of empty deceit and in line with human wisdom (Colossians 2:8), just like the weak women in Paul's day were. The reason we're being duped is that we're spending far more time listening to those ideas than we're spending in the Word of God.

If we don't work at becoming intimately familiar with the truth of God, we'll be left ignorant, weak, and vulnerable to deception.

4. DEFEND AND PROTECT YOUR MIND.

If we want to master our minds, we must not only fill them with truth but also defend and protect them from lies. We need to guard them.

The *putting on* of light needs to be accompanied by the *putting off* of darkness (Romans 13:12). The *putting on* of the new self needs to be accompanied by the *putting off* of the old self (Colossians 3:9–10). The *putting on* of truth needs to be accompanied by the *putting off* of falsehood (Ephesians 4:22–25).

Yes, the truth will set us free. But we'll have a tough time discerning what's true if we spend all our time being exposed to garbage and lies.

Garbage in, garbage out.

God's Word tells us that sex outside of marriage is a shameful violation of the true meaning of covenant faithfulness. But that popular TV show glorifies sex outside of marriage and tells us that it's our ticket to happiness and fulfillment. Let me ask you this: Which message are you spending more time stuffing into your brain? Are you giving truth or lies more access?

Scripture warns, "Be on your guard, so that your minds are not *dulled*" (Luke 21:34 HCSB). "Be on your guard, so that you are not led away by the error of lawless people and fall from your own stability" (2 Peter 3:17 HCSB).

Are we exposing ourselves to things that will dull our minds? You see, our minds are always moving in one of two directions. They are either being *transformed* to think like Jesus, or they are being *conformed* to think like the world (Romans 12:2). It's like the difference between being pulled down a slippery, snow-covered slope, or being towed up.

This past winter, my Texan daughter-in-law, Amanda, went for her first skiing lesson in the Canadian Rockies, where she was exposed to one of the basic laws of nature. When you're on a snowy mountain, movement in a downward direction is virtually inevitable. Gravity makes sure of that. Whether standing on skis, flailing head over heels, or sliding on your back end, one way or the other skiers eventually end up at the bottom of the hill.

Amanda also discovered that it's not as easy to move *up* a slippery slope on skis. In fact, without help it's nearly impossible. To get to the top of the run, she had to hitch a ride up the magic carpet, the conveyor belt by the bunny hills. And later in the day, as her skill improved, she used the T-bar, chairlift, and gondola.

Like a skier's momentum down the side of a slippery mountain, the pull to conform is exceptionally strong. Being *conformed* to the world doesn't take any effort. It's a downward slide that just naturally happens.

But if you want to be *transformed* and move upward, it will take some effort and intentionality. You'll need to drive your ski poles into the ground, resist the downward pull of gravity, and reach out for something that has enough power to move you in the opposite direction.

I've often caught my thoughts sliding in the wrong direction. Not intentionally sliding, of course, but sliding nonetheless. This usually happens when I've carelessly allowed myself to be exposed to enticing ideas masquerading as entertainment. As pastor Tim Challies has observed, we "are most often conformed to the world by carelessness, by neglecting to consider the allure of the world and by failing to guard against its encroachment."[9]

Sadly, many Christians remain unaware of the powerful pull of conformity. They constantly expose themselves to titillating erotica, sex-laced TV fantasy dramas, and all sorts of worldly garbage, unaware that their minds are slowly sliding downhill. I hear a whole gamut of justifications.

Excuses such as, "It's just entertainment." "It's not a big deal." "It won't affect me." "I'm strong enough." "I just ignore the bad parts." "I can't live in a bubble." Or the rationale that prompts an eyeball-roll and beats them all: "I need to be exposed to this so I can relate to my non-Christian friends." (Hmm. Wanna buy a bridge? I hear there's one for sale in Brooklyn.)

Our hearts can be desperately deceitful. Please don't think that I'm excluding myself from this pep talk. Sadly, I've used these justifications too.

Paul counseled his friends, "I want you to be wise as to what is good and innocent as to what is evil" (Romans 16:19). To be innocent is to be untainted, unspoiled, unravaged, unharmed. The Greek word used here means pure; without any defiling material added into the mix.[10]

So the question is, does that image, movie, TV show, magazine, website, book, song, article, idea, or thought subtly add defiling material into my mind? Does it taint my thinking? Does it ravage my imagination? Does it visit me in my dreams? Does it harm my purity? Does it sidetrack my attention? Does it work its way into my negative mental chatter?

To be untainted does not mean to be unaware. Paul was not suggesting for a moment that Christians stick their heads in the sand and remain unaware of culture's ideas and the ways the Devil seeks to deceive people. But he did suggest that a childlike inexperience and lack of exposure to evil is a good thing—a tremendously good thing!

There is great wisdom in remaining uninitiated and naive. "Do not be children in your thinking. Be infants in evil, but in your thinking be mature" (1 Corinthians 14:20). On the one hand, Paul urged believers to be mature and adultlike in their thinking. On the other hand, he urged them to be immature and childlike when it comes to evil.

The two ideas are not incompatible. Stated another way, Paul was saying that people who willingly expose themselves to evil are extremely immature. Spiritually strong women don't do that. They guard their minds, preserve their innocence, and make a habit of protecting themselves from being exposed to sinful garbage.

5. TAKE EVERY THOUGHT CAPTIVE TO OBEY CHRIST.

I opened this chapter describing Stockholm syndrome, a psychological condition in which a hostage gets captivated by a controlling, abusive creep. The weak-willed Christian women in Ephesus suffered from a spiritual type of Stockholm syndrome. They were taken captive by false ideas. If these women had been spiritually strong, they would have been in control of their minds. Rather than being taken captive by the false ideas, they would have taken the false ideas captive.

A weak woman is taken captive by lies, but a strong woman takes lies captive to truth.

Thankfully, God has equipped us for this battle. "The weapons of our warfare are not of the flesh but have divine power to destroy strongholds. We destroy arguments and every lofty opinion raised against the knowledge of God, and take every thought captive to obey Christ" (2 Corinthians 10:4–5).

These verses use military imagery to describe the clash between God's way of thinking and worldly ways of thinking. The two are on opposite sides. They fiercely war against each other. This verse informs us that the spiritual battle is ideological in nature. Worldly philosophies, arguments, ideas, and opinions stand in opposition and aggressively fight against the knowledge of God.

The battlefield of ideas is where the victory for hearts and minds is won or lost. Bad ideas captivate minds and keep people in bondage. Therefore, these ideas must be tracked down and brought into captivity. Every thought that is in rebellion to God must be made a prisoner of war and led to submit to the authority of God and the lordship of Jesus Christ.

This passage primarily refers to the external battle in which we counter the false ideas of others. But it's undeniable that we also combat these ideas internally. We are constantly engaged in a battle for our minds. If we do not fight to take lies captive, we will be in danger of being taken captive by them. We can passively let lies take us hostage, or we can actively fight to take lies hostage.

Taking thoughts captive simply means gaining control over what you think. When you notice a renegade thought, you don't let it run wild. You do something about it. You imprison that thought and shackle it to truth. If you find your mind running wild with worry, for example, you can meditate on a verse that talks about the faithfulness of God. You can pray. Or you can turn on some worship music. Instead of passively letting the thought control you, you actively battle to control it.

The battle for your mind will probably be the most challenging battle of your life. And not because taking a thought captive to Christ is hard. It's not that tough to counter one false thought with truth. But when you consider the sheer number of thoughts that pass through our minds, the task becomes more daunting.

On any given day you may need to take hundreds of wayward thoughts captive to Christ. If you want to close the gate to those ugly paths across your mind, you will need to make a lot of small correctives to your thinking.

You'll have to take thoughts captive all day.

Day. After day. After day.

The thing that makes this battle so challenging is the fact that it never ends. But, just as many footprints create a new path in a field, these small steps, taken consistently over time, will make a radical difference in your life. What's more, God's divine power gives you everything you need to stay on track.

You *will* become stronger bit by bit as you make a habit of mastering your mind.

HABIT 3

Pitch the Baggage

Unresolved sins and issues will
weigh you down and impair your
ability to navigate through life.

Overloading a vessel with excess cargo is one of the
most dangerous things a shipping company can do. That's why the sides
of ships are marked with a load line, which disappears below the water if
the ship is overloaded. Inspection authorities won't let a ship leave port
if its load line indicates it's carrying too much cargo. But companies still
find ways to break the rules and dangerously overload ships.

The load line on the hull of the South Korean ferry *Sewol* showed
that the ferry was safely loaded when it left port carrying 476 people,
the majority of whom were secondary school students.

Unbeknownst to those on board, the company had overloaded the
vessel with more than three times the maximum of cargo permitted.

To mask the weight of all the illegal cargo and bring the ship's load line up to the right level, the crew emptied all but 580 of the recommended 2,040 tons of the ferry's ballast water from the bottom compartment. The ballast water functions as a critical counterbalance to the weight of the cargo, vehicles, and passengers above.

On April 16, 2014, the ill-fated ferry departed for its holiday-island destination, top heavy and severely overloaded.

Things went smoothly until they reached the most challenging part of the journey, a narrow waterway with treacherous currents. The crew had to exercise extreme caution and manually steer the ship through this dangerous channel. Unfortunately, when the helmsman turned the wheel sharply to adjust course, stacks of heavy cargo containers suddenly shifted, throwing the ship's weight to one side. Water flowed in through the side door of the cargo loading bay.

It wasn't long before the ferry capsized. More than 300 of the 476 people on board died. Most of the victims were students.

The captain and three crew members were charged with murder. Dozens of ferry company officials, safety inspectors, and coast guard officials were jailed or convicted on various criminal charges related to the sinking. The disaster led to a manhunt and the death of the billionaire who owned the ferry company. It sparked anti-government protests and violent clashes with police that left dozens injured. The tragedy contributed to the impeachment of the country's president. It was one of the most traumatic episodes in South Korea's recent history.[1]

All those tragic consequences could have been avoided if the crew hadn't overloaded that boat.

UNAUTHORIZED BAGGAGE

Like the *Sewol*, the weak women in Ephesus were overloaded with unauthorized baggage. They were burdened with sins. The Greek word for *burdened* means to be loaded with a heap or pile of something. The verb was used in Hebrew literature to describe loading a wagon sky-high by piling more and more things on top. It suggests an accumulation that is heavy, cumbersome, and difficult to manage.

The image that comes to my mind is all the overloaded vehicles I saw on a visit to Thailand. Never have I seen bikes, motorbikes, and trucks with loads piled so treacherously high. Do an Internet search for "Thailand overloaded vehicle" images to see what I'm talking about. You'll be astonished. There's one photo of a small pickup truck that was so overloaded it broke in half! Seeing the overloaded vehicles on the roads of Chiang Mai and Bangkok was fascinating, but it was frightening, too, because it was obvious that these vehicles were unstable and could crash at any moment.

In much the same way, the weak women in Ephesus were overloaded with piles of sin that made them spiritually unstable and susceptible to crash.

There are burdens we are meant to carry and burdens we are not meant to carry. The Lord gives us strength to face the difficulties, hardships, and heartaches of life. We are meant to withstand these types of burdens. He promises that such burdens will never weigh us down beyond what we are able to bear. They will not sink us below a safe load line.

But we are *not* meant to carry the burdens of unconfessed sin, guilt, and shame. These unauthorized types of burdens will oppress us and make it difficult for us to navigate the waters of life safely. Loaded down with sin, we are far more likely to capsize and sink.

That's why a strong woman makes a habit of ridding herself of sin, guilt, and shame.

MISSING THE MARK

During the 2017 CMA Awards, country music singer Carrie Underwood sang an old hymn with the refrain, "Earnestly, tenderly

Jesus is calling—Calling, O sinner, come home!"[2] She sang it in memoriam of colleagues in the country music industry and the victims of the Las Vegas Harvest Festival mass shooting. Though the tribute was beautiful and touching, many took to social media afterward to criticize Underwood for referring to the deceased as "sinners."

The concept of sin isn't popular these days.

Most people believe they should be free to live how they want without anyone telling them what to do. They believe that as long as they do no harm, they have the right to decide for themselves what is acceptable based on their own opinions. They think that modern social missteps, such as hurting people's feelings by labeling their behavior "sinful," is the only real sin there is.

This mind-set is evident in the top definition of *sin* from the Urban Dictionary, which defines sin this way: "Sin means harm. Sinful means harmful. Sinless means harmless. Is a particular thought, word, or action sin? If it is harmful it is sinful. If it is harmless it is sinless."[3] In other words, if you feel hurt or offended—harmed—by what I say or do, then I have sinned against you.

Though "harm" may reflect the popular definition of sin, and though sin is undoubtedly harmful, this isn't in line with what the Bible says about sin.

What exactly is sin?

Scripture teaches that sin is failing to reach God's perfect standard. It's not about my failing to reach your standard or your failing to reach mine.

Billy Graham explained that sin is "any thought or action that falls short of God's will. God is perfect, and anything we do that falls short of His perfection is sin."[4] Sin means we've done something wrong. We've either done something that God says we shouldn't do, or we've failed to do something he says we should do (John 14:23; James 4:17).

We sin whenever we fail to love God—whenever we fail to esteem him, trust him, seek him, and obey him with our whole hearts.[5] Sin encompasses more than rules such as "Thou shalt not kill," "Thou shalt not steal," and "Thou shalt not commit adultery." Most people would agree that these actions qualify as sin. But Jesus taught that hidden attitudes, such as contempt, lust, and hardness of heart, are also sin, even if these attitudes don't result in sinful actions.

Anything that is not a faith-filled response to circumstances is sin. Therefore, anxiety, worry, and fear are sins too. And then there are the sins of neglect: leaving good works undone, failing to use our talents, or ignoring the injured.

The New Testament lists a lot of sins, such as:

jealousy	fornication
strife	sexual immorality
rivalries	sexual impurity
disputes	sensuality
resentment	homosexual acts
bitterness	adultery
unforgiveness	idolatry
malice	magical arts
cynicism	occult
envy	abuse
greed	slander
coveting	defamation
ungratefulness	angry outbursts
backstabbing	gossip
drunkenness	clamor
carousing	filthiness
swindling	coarse jokes
deceit	irreverence
lying	profanity
hypocrisy	willfulness
lust	impulsivity

bragging	lack of discipline
arrogance	self-indulgence
insolence	self-importance
self-centeredness	conceit
materialism	gluttony
self-promotion	cowardice
contempt	unholiness

This isn't a politically correct list. It's definitely not the list that most people would come up with if asked to catalog which attitudes and behaviors qualify as sin. But, like it or not, the Bible calls these attitudes and behaviors *sin*. And God is the one who defines what sin is. Not me, not you, not Hollywood, not the media, and not the Urban Dictionary.

Looking at the sins mentioned above, I think you'll agree that sin is something we *all* do every day.

Romans 3:23 says, "All have sinned and fall short of the glory of God." We all miss the mark. *But* (and this is the amazing part), we "are justified by his grace as a gift, through the redemption that is in Christ Jesus" (v. 24). Christ atones for our failure to hit the mark. Because of his sacrifice, God freely and generously pardons our sin.

The lyrics of the hymn Underwood sang, "Softly and Tenderly," point this out:

Oh, for the wonderful love he has promised,
Promised for you and for me!
Though we have sinned, he has mercy and pardon,
Pardon for you and for me.

Come home, come home,
You who are weary, come home;
Earnestly, tenderly, Jesus is calling,
Calling, O sinner, come home![6]

Sin wearies us. It weighs us down. It overloads us with heavy emotional and spiritual baggage. But the Lord invites us to ditch the baggage and come home. Just as the father in the parable of the prodigal son joyfully forgave and welcomed his boy home, so our heavenly Father forgives and welcomes all who turn to him in faith and repentance.

Sin, guilt, and shame are burdens we do not need to bear. He wants us to be free of the heavy load. When we receive Christ's forgiveness, he gives us the power to deal with sin on an ongoing basis. We can continually rid ourselves of this oppressive baggage.

We don't know what kinds of sin were weighing down the women in the church in Ephesus. Maybe they were caught up in sins of comparison and envy, or gossip and spreading hearsay. Maybe they were critical and cold toward their husbands. Perhaps they were entertaining lustful fantasies about good-looking theater stars, muscular gladiators, or the handsome traveling merchants who flirted with them down at the market. They could have been shopaholics, caught in the grip of materialism. Or they might have been resentful and unforgiving toward people who had hurt them—sinning in response to sins committed against them. Perhaps bitterness was the sin weighing them down.

Regardless of the specifics, we do know this: the phrase "burdened with sins" indicates that these women were encumbered with sins that had piled up and accumulated over time. Though they were churchgoers and professed faith in Jesus, they weren't getting rid of their baggage. They weren't laying "aside every weight, and sin which clings so closely" (Hebrews 12:1). Sin was burdening them, tripping them up, and making them weak.

So how do we keep that from happening to us? How do we get rid of our baggage?

The Bible teaches that we get rid of the unauthorized cargo by earnestly and habitually confessing our sins.

TIME TO FESS UP

Confession is an important habit. As 1 John reminds us, "If we say we have no sin, we deceive ourselves, and the truth is not in us. If we confess our sins, he is faithful and just to forgive us our sins and to cleanse us from all unrighteousness" (1:8–9). We all have sins to confess—every one of us. The apostle John didn't exclude himself; he said "we." And he wasn't just talking about past sins but present and ongoing sins too.

His words literally mean "if we keep on confessing our sins," or "if we make a practice of confessing our sins." John writes the word *sins* in the plural to indicate that they are many. He presented authentic Christian living as involving an honest, open, and ongoing acknowledgment of the ways we fail to live up to God's standard.[7]

The word *confess* is a translation of the Greek word *homologeo*, from *homos*, "same," and *lego*, "to speak." To confess means to say the same thing as another or to agree with another.[8] Confession of sin means that we agree with God; we say the same thing about our sin that God says about it and view it the same way he does.

Our confession of sin is first and foremost to God. But the word *confess* also contains an element of *open* acknowledgment or *open* witness. There's a public, social dimension to it. The acknowledgment of sin is not just a private matter between God and me. It's also a matter of being honest and transparent with other people, especially those in the faith community.

Scripture indicates that open confession is a highly effective way to deal with sin. "Confess your sins to one another and pray for one another, so that you may be healed. The urgent request of a righteous person is very powerful in its effect" (James 5:16 HCSB). What this verse is advocating for is a culture of authenticity. God's people ought to be honest and transparent, and eager to help and support each other in our battle against sin.

The verse doesn't say we need to confess to a pastor or priest. It doesn't say we need to confess publicly in front of the whole church. Nor does it say we need to tell everyone about every sin we commit. It simply teaches that confessing our sins to trusted, godly mentors or friends and asking them to pray for us is a highly effective way for us to gain victory.

In a healthy Christian environment, it's okay to be imperfect. We can tell people about our sin. We don't need to cover it up or hide it or pretend there's no issue. We can be real about our struggles. Though it can feel scary, it's important to do this. "Whoever conceals his transgressions will not prosper, but he who confesses and forsakes them will obtain mercy" (Proverbs 28:13). If you want to get rid of the sin, guilt, and shame that's weighing you down, openly confessing can really help.

I met twenty-seven-year-old Mindy at a conference on the East Coast. Mindy was on staff with a parachurch organization in full-time campus ministry. Nine years earlier in her freshman year at college, Mindy had gone to a bar with Ethan, a guy who was a regular at the coffee shop where she worked. She knew that her dad, a pastor in a small-town church, wouldn't approve. Neither would her mom for that matter. Her parents were constantly extolling the dangers of young women going out alone with young men and frequenting bars. Mindy brushed off their paranoid warnings. She was a strong woman; firm in her faith, spunky, and smart. Nothing bad would ever happen to her.

Ethan was polite and charming. His rugged good looks and deep brown eyes set Mindy's heart aflutter. She turned him down the first few times he asked her out, but his playful persistence won her over. *What's the harm?* she reasoned. Maybe she'd get a chance to witness to him.

Ethan was well-mannered and respectful at the bar that night. A perfect gentleman. So, after a few hours, Mindy dropped her guard. She didn't notice when he slipped a club drug into her drink.

The next morning Mindy woke up naked in a bed, feeling terribly nauseous, disoriented, and sore all over. That, and blood on the sheets, pointed to the horror that might have happened. Or was the blood from the scrape on her leg? She wasn't sure. Her head was pounding. Confused, traumatized, and ashamed, she numbly stumbled through the following days with a sick feeling in the pit of her stomach.

What happened? Why couldn't she remember? Did she drink too much? Was she raped? Was it her fault? How could she tell anyone? How could she face her parents? It didn't help that Ethan dropped by the coffee shop a few times afterward, flashing his dazzling smile and acting as though nothing had happened.

Mindy's predicament worsened a few weeks later when she discovered she was pregnant. Pregnant! She sat there stunned. She couldn't breathe. The test confirmed her worst nightmare. She couldn't even remember sleeping with Ethan that fateful night. She had planned on remaining a virgin until she married.

How could this happen? How could she tell her parents? How could she face the stares and the whispers at church? How could she explain this to the girls she mentored in her small Bible study group? How could she quit college and have a baby? It would ruin her life!

The doctor at the on-campus medical center calmly presented options. Panicked and desperate, Mindy grasped at the hope of keeping everything under wraps and winding the clock back a few months to the way things were before she met Ethan.

She quietly had an abortion.

Mindy hung her head in shame as she finished telling me her story. She explained that she had eventually disclosed the rape to her parents and a few close friends and had gone for counseling to work through the trauma. She felt that she had dealt with the emotional baggage caused by the assault—the self-blame, anger, resentment, and bitterness. But she still hadn't told a soul about the abortion. No one knew. I was the first person to whom she had disclosed this dark secret.

"I took a life!" she sobbed. "I had no control over the sin that Ethan committed against me . . . but it was my choice to abort my baby. *My* choice!" In agony she divulged that she had asked God for forgiveness every single day for the nine years since the abortion but wasn't sure that he had forgiven her sin, or that she could ever forgive herself. My heart broke. I could see that the enormous guilt and shame tortured her.

"Why don't you confess your sin to the Lord again right now, out loud, so I can be your witness?" I suggested. Sobbing and hardly able to get the words out, she did. I quietly interceded as she poured her heart out to the Lord. When she was finished, I gently lifted her chin to look her directly in the eyes and proclaimed, "Mindy, you are forgiven!"

I could hear something crack in the spiritual realm. Mindy gasped.

I laid hands on her and began to do battle for her mind. I prayed the truth of God's Word into her spirit. Truth about the sufficiency of Christ's sacrifice. The abundance of his forgiveness. His free gift of righteousness. The canceled debt.

I prayed scriptures like Ephesians 1:7: "In him we have redemption through his blood, the forgiveness of our trespasses, according to the riches of his grace."

Isaiah 1:18: "Though your sins are like scarlet, they shall be as white as snow; though they are red like crimson, they shall become like wool."

Psalm 103:12: "As far as the east is from the west, so far does he remove our transgressions from us."

I affirmed her standing in Christ Jesus, that she was chosen of God, holy and dearly loved (Colossians 3:12), a beloved daughter of God (2 Corinthians 6:18), a new creation (5:17), a righteous and holy one (Ephesians 4:24). Forgiven, without blame (Romans 8:1; Ephesians 1:4), a recipient of God's lavish grace (1:6–8). Established, anointed, sealed by God (2 Corinthians 1:21–22). A partaker of the divine nature (2 Peter 1:4). Firmly rooted in Christ (Colossians 2:7).

We prayed until the wee hours of the morning.

The next day a beaming young woman grabbed me outside of the conference room. "I can't begin to tell you what God did in my heart last night," she started. It took a moment for me to realize I was talking to Mindy. She looked so different! There was a radiance about her that dramatically changed her features.

"I feel so light and free and happy!" she confirmed. "I know beyond a doubt that God has forgiven me. Thank you for praying! This morning was the first time in nine years that I bounced out of bed with a smile on my face. God is *so* good!"

Indeed. My eyes welled up with tears. But Mindy's didn't. She laughed, gave me a big hug, and started to do a jig down the hallway.

Mindy confessed the sin of aborting her baby more than a thousand times before we met. Every night for nearly nine years she privately begged God for forgiveness. I believe that he forgave her the very first time she asked and arguably even *before* she asked. But to experience the full force of his forgiveness and be unburdened from the sin, guilt, and shame of the abortion, she needed to confess *openly*. She needed to bring her sin out into the light. To experience true freedom she had to tell someone, be prayed over, and audibly hear the declaration, "You are forgiven!" from a believer functioning as an "ambassador" (representative) of Christ, who alone has the power to forgive sins.

"If we confess our sins, he is faithful and just to forgive us our sins and to cleanse us from all unrighteousness" (1 John 1:9). What an amazing promise. And what an amazing privilege.

Notice that this verse contains a conditional statement. It says *if* we confess (keep confessing) our sins, he will forgive and cleanse us. Does that mean that if we don't confess every single sin that we commit every single day, God won't forgive us? Will he hold those unconfessed sins against us? Does my being cleansed from unrighteousness depend on me noticing every instance of sin in my life?

If it meant that, then we'd all be in big trouble. We often aren't even aware of all the ways we sin, much less taking care to confess them all.

Can you even recall the number of times in the past week that you said something that wasn't beneficial? Or the number of times you had a critical thought? Or the number of moments you failed to love God more than other things? If this verse meant that we are guilty and legally obligated to pay for each sin until we confess it, then we'd have no hope, because we'd never be able to confess everything we do wrong.

The Bible tells us that Jesus "erased the certificate of debt, with its obligations, that was against us and opposed to us, and has taken it out of the way by nailing it to the cross" (Colossians 2:14 HCSB). So when we confess our sins as believers, we can be confident that Christ has already dealt with our sin. It is finished! At the cross the guilt of each offense was transferred to him. This means that each debt has truly and fully been paid. His sacrifice covers every sin—past, present, and future.

Why, then, do we need to confess our sins on an ongoing basis? There's a very good reason.

It's because confession makes the forgiveness of the cross real to us. When we confess our sins, we recognize and declare the force of what Christ accomplished on our behalf. We claim the amazing mercy and forgiveness that became ours the moment of our salvation. The habit of ongoing, open confession of sin is simply about walking in the light. We openly and honestly admit the ways we've failed to live up to God's standard so that we might gain victory over sin and grow in godliness.

Confession is about *applying* the gospel. It's not something we have to do as much as it's something we get to do. We get to unburden ourselves. Feel the load lift. Experience the cleansing. We get to feel the force of God's love and forgiveness and make things right with him. We get to claim his power and victory. It's a privilege and joy inaccessible to those who don't know Jesus.

Each time we confess, we claim and reaffirm the truth of what our Savior did for us on the cross. The grace and forgiveness we receive makes the joy of our salvation more precious every time we receive it. We are reminded again and again about the reality and wonder of it all.

REAL AND COUNTERFEIT CONFESSIONS

Have you ever had someone hurt you and tell you he was sorry, but you suspected he really wasn't? Maybe he regretted getting caught. Or maybe he regretted the consequences he'd have to face. Or maybe he regretted that you felt the way you did. But you had a nagging suspicion that deep down he wasn't truly sorry. You sensed that he didn't really believe that what he did was wrong or all that harmful. His confession wasn't backed up with a resolve to do things differently. He said he was sorry, but he didn't demonstrate a change of heart.

Scripture teaches that there is a right way and a wrong way to relate to God after we've sinned. True confession is more than verbally acknowledging we did something wrong. As I mentioned earlier, confession means that we agree with God; we say the same thing about our sin that God says about it and view it the same way he does. Therefore, confession that isn't accompanied by godly sorrow and repentance isn't true confession.

It's counterfeit.

The Bible provides examples of people whose confessions were counterfeit and people whose confessions were true. There's a huge difference between someone who merely says he's sorry and someone who truly is. We're going to look at the way three different people in the Bible confessed their sins. Only one confessed in the right way.

SAUL, FIRST KING OF ISRAEL

King Saul, the first king of Israel, was tall, handsome, and capable, but he was spiritually weak. The reason for this was that he never truly confessed and repented of his sins. His confessions were counterfeit. Let me briefly highlight three scenes from his life.

First is the Pretend-I'm-a-Priest scene from 1 Samuel 13:8–12. The prophet Samuel gave Saul explicit instructions not to begin the battle against the Philistines at Gilgal until Samuel arrived to offer a sacrifice. Saul knew that only priests could offer sacrifices (this was a strict rule), but Saul was in a hurry to get the battle going. He chose not to wait for Samuel and took it upon himself to present the burnt offering. After all, he was the king. Later, instead of expressing genuine sorrow, Saul made excuses for his actions. He confessed,

- "I'm sorry, but I couldn't wait any longer. The soldiers were getting restless."
- "I'm sorry, but I was losing the window of opportunity for a successful defense."
- "I'm sorry, but you were late and didn't leave me with any other option."

We can see another example of Saul giving a counterfeit confession in the scene when Saul was hunting David. Saul was jealous of David, so he took an army of soldiers into the hills where David was hiding to seek him out and kill him. One night David stumbled onto Saul's hideout. David's men urged him to kill Saul and claim the throne, but instead, he took Saul's spear and water jug to prove that he had spared him.

The next day, when confronted with the evidence, Saul confessed, "I have sinned. Return, my son David, for I will no more do you harm, because my life was precious in your eyes this day. Behold, I have acted foolishly, and have made a great mistake" (1 Samuel 26:21). Saul felt remorse. He felt sorry and apologized. He said all the right things, but he didn't change. It wasn't long before he started hunting David again.

On a third occasion, the We-Deserve-a-Parade scene from 1 Samuel 15, Saul disobeyed God's instructions about how he should deal with the Amalekites, the archenemies of the Israelites. He was supposed to destroy everything and not take any spoil—no cattle, no sheep, no treasure, nothing. Saul only partially obeyed. Though he destroyed all the undesirable and worthless animals and goods, he let his men take the best plunder. Plus, he didn't kill the Amalekite king (vv. 1–9).

He and his officers likely planned to put on a big show for the people back home. They intended to parade out the bounty, make a spectacle of the foreign king, and grandstand their illustrious victory. When Samuel confronted Saul about his failure to follow through, Saul maintained that he had, in fact, obeyed the Lord and that his motives were honorable. Saul presumed that God wouldn't mind the slight deviation from plan. After all, his men were going to offer the plundered animals as burnt offerings to the Lord (vv. 12–21). He thought the Lord would be pleased. "I'm doing it for God—so what's the big deal, Samuel?"

Saul didn't acknowledge that he had done anything wrong. Therefore, Samuel uttered these distressing words: "Because you have rejected the word of the LORD, he has also rejected you from being king" (v. 23).

Saul decided he needed to make things right, and fast! He confessed, "I have sinned, for I have transgressed the commandment of the LORD and your words. . . . Now therefore, please pardon my sin and return with me that I may bow before the LORD" (vv. 24–25).

Samuel saw right through the counterfeit confession. He reiterated that God was going to depose Saul as king. Panicked, Saul again begged for forgiveness. "I have sinned; yet honor me now before the elders of my people and before Israel, and return with me, that I may bow before the LORD" (vv. 26–30).

Do you see the problem with his confession? Saul was more concerned about his reputation—about being honored in front of the elders—than he was about his sin. In all three scenes there was something terribly wrong with Saul's seemingly heartfelt confession.

JUDAS, DISCIPLE OF CHRIST

Let's consider another well-known and tragic personality in the Bible, Judas. After betraying Jesus, Judas realized the awful consequences of his actions. "When Judas, his betrayer, saw that Jesus was condemned, he changed his mind and brought back the thirty pieces of silver to the chief priests and the elders, saying, 'I have sinned by betraying innocent blood.' . . . And throwing down the pieces of silver into the temple, he departed, and he went and hanged himself (Matthew 27:3–5).

Again, notice carefully the words of Judas's confession: "I have sinned."

Judas fessed up, but he tragically did not make the changes God wanted him to make. He departed in shame. His guilt was so enormous that he hanged himself. He confessed his sin, but this acknowledgment of wrongdoing did not lead to the response God desired.

DAVID, THE HARP PLAYER

David's most glaring and infamous sins were his adultery with Bathsheba and the subsequent murder of her husband, Uriah, to cover up the pregnancy. These were terrible sins, and, from a human perspective, they appear even worse than Saul's sins. But there was an important difference between the ways the men responded.

Nathan the prophet told David a compelling story that led him to recognize his wrongdoing. David confessed to Nathan, "I have sinned against the LORD." And Nathan responded, "The LORD also has put away your sin; you shall not die" (2 Samuel 12:13).

"I have sinned." Those are the same words of confession both Saul and Judas used. Even though all three men expressed similar heartfelt sorrow, David's sins were *put away* and forgiven while Saul's and Judas's weren't. These stories demonstrate that although people may acknowledge their wrongdoing, feel sorry, intend to change, and pray, it doesn't necessarily mean that they have truly confessed and repented of their sin.

David confessed, "I have sinned," just as Saul and Judas did, but he said something else that's really significant. I don't know if you noticed. He said, "I have sinned against the LORD."

The expression "against the LORD" is highly important. David recognized that by sinning he had broken his Creator's eternal and righteous law and displeased him. In an emotional plea he cried out to God and asked for forgiveness. We see this pattern of repentance more than once in David's life. Notice how, in the words of this confession from Psalm 51, he also acknowledged that his sin was against God: "I know my transgressions, and my sin is ever before me. Against you [Lord], you only, have I sinned and done what is evil in your sight" (vv. 3–4).

David recognized the most important truth about sin: it is primarily rebellion against a holy God. While recognizing the person-to-person, horizontal nature of sin, the Bible consistently presents sin as mainly a person-to-God, vertical offense. Though David had undoubtedly sinned against Bathsheba, Uriah, their families, David's own family, his officers, and a bunch of other people, that's not what he focused on when he confessed his sin.

That's not to say David didn't also apologize to the people he had hurt. But he obviously understood that the thing that makes sin so incredibly heinous is the fact that it's a crime against the God of the Universe.

"Against you, you only, have I sinned and done what is evil in your sight."

WRONGING GOD

Whenever we do something wrong, we sin against God. This is the case even if we're not consciously trying to offend him, and even if, in the moment of our sin, God is the very last one on our minds.

When the wife of Potiphar tried to seduce Joseph, he refused and said, "How then can I do this great wickedness and sin against God?" (Genesis 39:9). Joseph knew that sleeping with his master's wife would be sinning against God. He was far more worried about wronging God than wronging Potiphar or Potiphar's wife.

The fact that all sin is sin against the Lord is well-documented in the Bible. Jealousy is a sin against the Lord (Numbers 16:8–11). Slander is a sin against the Lord (21:7). Failing to keep one's word is a sin against the Lord (32:23). Greed is a sin against the Lord (Joshua 7:20–21). Grumbling is a sin against the Lord (Psalm 78:17–18). Oppressing the poor is a sin against the Lord (Proverbs 14:31). Failing to pray for someone is a sin against the Lord (1 Samuel 12:23).

The Lord told the Israelites, "When a man or woman commits any sin against another, that person acts unfaithfully toward the LORD and is guilty" (Numbers 5:6 HCSB). Paul told believers that when they sinned against other people, they were "sinning against Christ" (1 Corinthians 8:12 HCSB). A legitimate confession recognizes that the sin was ultimately an offense against the Lord. All sin is a wrong committed against him.

TRULY SORRY

Sharla was horrified when she discovered pornography on her fiancé's phone. She and Todd had already set a date for their wedding. "I am unwilling to marry a man who's addicted to porn," she sobbed. "What should I do?" Todd was deeply sorry and seemed repentant. But Sharla worried that he was only sorry that he got caught and that his vow to change was only motivated by the threat of losing her. She decided to stay engaged but to put their wedding on hold. That way she'd have time to evaluate whether Todd's repentance was real.

"But how will I know?" she pleaded.

I advised her that if Todd was truly sorry, she'd notice a change in his character and mind-set over time, not just in his behavior. He'd become godlier. That's not to say that he'd completely vanquish the temptation to look at porn or that he'd never slip up, but his attitude toward that sin would fundamentally change. She would witness unmistakable growth.

Todd gathered together a small group of godly friends. He confessed to them, confessed to God before them, and had them lay hands on him and pray for victory. He installed software on his computer and phone to prevent him from visiting porn sites and to send reports to an accountability partner. He stopped using certain forms of social media. He read Christian books about how to defeat lust. He identified triggers and came up with strategies for dealing with temptation. He fasted and prayed. He begged God to break the addiction. He sought to discern the faulty beliefs underlying his behavior. He became open and transparent about his struggles.

Half a year after putting the wedding on hold, Sharla was ready to move forward and marry Todd.

"He's a changed man," she reported. "I see a brokenness, humility, and vulnerability in him that wasn't there before. And the thing that reassures me most is that he knows he doesn't have what it takes to conquer this sin apart from the power of Christ. He is depending on Jesus."

Their wedding was a joyful celebration, not only of the marriage but also of the power of Christ to redeem. And I'm happy to report that seven years later Todd is still winning the battle against lust and porn.

There was a time when the apostle Paul confronted his friends about sin, and their response is another great example of true repentance. In 2 Corinthians Paul referred to a previous letter he had sent to the church in Corinth (2:3–9; 7:8–12), an emotional letter that has been lost: "I wrote to you out of much affliction and anguish of heart and with many tears" (2:4). Apparently, it was a difficult letter for Paul to write. In it, he took his friends to account for failing to deal with sin.

Paul knew that he was taking a risk, that the letter would cause them grief and might irritate or offend them. We're not sure what the sin was. It may have been sexual immorality in the church that wasn't being addressed, or maybe something else. Regardless, Paul was immensely relieved when Titus brought word that his friends had responded positively to his rebuke.

They were truly sorry, and their repentance had led to genuine change.

Thrilled that they had repented in the right way, Paul noted, "Godly grief produces a repentance that leads to salvation without regret, whereas worldly grief produces death" (7:10).

Grief is the heartache, sorrow, and remorse we feel when we do something wrong. It's feeling sorry. According to Paul our sorrow can fall into one of two categories: godly or worldly. So, what's the difference?

Godly grief is inherently God-centered. We are sorry that we have sinned against God and that we've broken his holy, just, and good law (Romans 7:12). We are sorry that we've damaged our relationship with him.

Worldly grief is self-centered. It is caused by the loss or denial of something we want for ourselves. We're not really sorry that we've violated God's laws. We mainly feel sorry over the fallout.

Worldly grief results in counterfeit confessions, such as:

- "I'm sorry I got caught."
- "I'm sorry for the embarrassment this will cause."
- "I'm sorry I'm going to lose my good reputation."
- "I'm sorry for the guilt and shame I feel."
- "I'm sorry that you feel hurt and offended."
- "I'm sorry you think this is such a big deal."

- "I'm sorry about the consequences I'm going to face."
- "I'm sorry this has caused so much conflict and turmoil."
- "I'm sorry this has diminished my peace and happiness."

Confession motivated by worldly grief depends on human effort for change. The attitude is: "I've got this! I'll do better. I'll try harder. I'll make it right." There's an element of self-sufficiency and pride in addressing the predicament.

What's more, if the offender only views the sin through the lens of how it impacts herself and what she desires, she'll fail to get to the root of it. She won't address the underlying problem. As a result, she won't make any significant progress in changing her attitudes and behaviors. Her spiritual growth will be stunted. And her confession won't get rid of the weight of the sin.

If you feel deflated, discouraged, and diminished after confessing your sin, then you may be wallowing in the dangerous waters of worldly grief.

A "sorry" that is motivated by godly grief, on the other hand, relies on God to take care of the problem. This kind of sorrow is a healthy emotion. It will bring you closer to God and produce positive change.

It's life-giving. Redemptive.

It positions you to experience significant growth, victory, freedom, and joy.

As Paul pointed out, worldly grief only produces death, but godly grief produces life (2 Corinthians 7:10).

SEVEN SIGNS YOU'RE TRULY SORRY

How do we know we're truly sorry (with godly grief) and not just feeling remorseful in a self-centered way? In 2 Corinthians 7:11 Paul identified seven signs he saw in the lives of his friends that indicated they had truly confessed and repented: "Consider how much diligence this very thing—this grieving as God wills—has produced in you: what a desire to clear yourselves, what indignation, what fear, what deep longing, what zeal, what justice! In every way you showed yourselves to be pure in this matter (HCSB).

We can check for these signs to identify whether we've truly grieved and repented of sin. If we have, we should see more of the following attitudes in our lives:

I. WE TAKE SIN MORE SERIOUSLY ("DILIGENCE").

Paul's friends had been tolerating sin. Maybe they hadn't been aware that the sin in question was an offense against the Lord. Or maybe they'd been apathetic, thinking the sin wasn't really a big deal. Paul's bold letter woke them up to the gravity of the matter.

Diligence is the opposite of apathy. When we are truly repentant for a sin, we will experience a change of attitude toward that sin. We will no longer see it as something justifiable or acceptable, but rather we will desire to get it out of our lives and stay as far away from it as possible. We will no longer have a casual attitude toward it.

We will take sin as seriously as God does.

2. WE ARE EAGER TO CONFESS SIN ("DESIRE TO CLEAR YOURSELVES").

The Greek word *apologia*, from which we derive the word *apology*, is translated "desire to clear yourselves."

When we are truly sorry, we are eager to apologize. We can't wait to run to the cross to confess to the Lord. We also desire to confess openly to the person we've sinned against, as well as to godly friends who can pray for us and help us conquer the sin. We want to bring it out in the open, into the light, so it can be dealt with and cleared away.

Whenever I see someone try to keep her sin hidden or cover up the parts that were exposed involuntarily, I suspect that she isn't sorry. Or at least not sorry in the way God desires.

3. OUR HATRED FOR SIN GROWS ("INDIGNATION").

Indignation is a strong feeling of opposition and displeasure against something we judge to be wrong. It's righteous anger. When we start to see our sin the way God sees it, our love for that sin will decrease and our indignation toward it will increase.

Instead of being attracted to the sin, we will be repulsed by it.

We will hate the way it dishonors God. We will hate the way it destroys lives. We will hate all the ugliness and evil it contains. If we are truly sorry for our sin, we will abhor it as evil and cling to what is good instead (Romans 12:9).

4. WE FEAR GOD MORE THAN WE FEAR CONSEQUENCES ("FEAR").

When we fear God, we regard him with reverential awe. We have a knee-knocking respect for his holiness and justice. We do not take his forgiveness and mercy for granted. We understand that the wrath of God toward sin must be satisfied, that the penalty is more horrible than we can imagine, and that the only way we have escaped certain punishment is by accepting the abundance of grace and the gift of righteousness God offers through faith in Jesus Christ.

If we are truly repentant, we will fear God more than we fear being exposed. We will fear him more than we fear what others might think or the consequences of confessing. Fear of the Lord is a positive emotion. It brings about wholeness and joy.

Just listen to this promise: "Fear the Lord, and turn away from evil. It will be healing to your flesh and refreshment to your bones" (Proverbs 3:7–8).

5. WE YEARN FOR CLOSE RELATIONSHIP ("DEEP LONGING").

If I've sinned against my husband, Brent—if I've said something unkind, been critical, or snapped at him—it creates a palpable distance in our relationship. It hinders our connection and intimacy. I know that Brent will forgive me. He's faithfully done so for more than three decades. But, nevertheless, the disconnect gnaws at me and unsettles me. I long to reconnect. I long for the relationship to return to a healthy state.

That's the kind of feeling Paul was talking about when he said "deep longing." It's a powerful, inward drive to be in perfect fellowship with God. If we are truly sorry for our sins, we will experience this longing in an ever-deepening way. We will yearn for all hinderances to be removed in our relationship with the Lord so we may experience intimacy with him.

6. OUR PASSION FOR CHRIST GROWS ("ZEAL").

Simon the Pharisee was contemptuous of a woman who crashed his dinner party and made a scene. "A woman in the town who was a sinner . . . brought an alabaster jar of fragrant oil and stood behind [Jesus] at His feet, weeping, and began to wash His feet with her tears. She wiped His feet with the hair of her head, kissing them and anointing them with the fragrant oil" (Luke 7:37–38 HCSB).

Simon scorned her fanatical display of affection. But Jesus contrasted her lavish welcome with Simon's stoic one and sarcastically noted, "He who is forgiven little, loves little" (v. 47).

Simon's problem was that he had no concept of how sinful his heart really was. He didn't think he had much to confess. The woman, on the other hand, was aware of her sins and knew how much she needed forgiveness. She loved much because *she knew* she had been forgiven much.

If we genuinely confess our sins on an ongoing basis, we will be aware that we have been forgiven much, and we will respond with zeal and enthusiasm. Our passion for the gospel will grow. Our hearts will overflow with joy, gratitude, and a fervent desire to know Christ and make him known.

7. WE DESIRE TO MAKE AMENDS ("JUSTICE").

The Greek word translated *justice* means giving justice to someone who has been wronged. It's a desire to make restitution.

Justice describes the response of the wealthy tax collector, Zacchaeus, who resolved to make amends for his greedy, cheating ways. He gave away half of his fortune to the poor, and he paid back people he had defrauded fourfold the amount he had swindled (Luke 19:8). Jesus never asked him to do this. This wasn't a penance to pay for his sins. But it was a proper response to the forgiveness he had received. He had cheated people out of money, so it was appropriate for him to give their money back.

Restitution isn't always possible, but if we are truly sorry, we will do what we can to give justice to those we have wronged.

These seven signs showed Paul that his friends were truly sorry. He said they were "pure in this matter." *Pure* means innocent. Not innocent in the sense that they hadn't committed the offense, but innocent in the sense that the sin had been cleared. It was no longer weighing them down.

It had been ditched.

It was gone forever.

CONQUER THE LIES WITH TRUTH

Confession leads to spiritual growth, freedom, and victory. So why do so many believers remain crippled by feelings of guilt and shame? Mindy carried around the heavy burden for almost a decade. I know women who've spent a lifetime encumbered by this type of baggage. They are never able to rid themselves of feelings of self-condemnation and self-reproach. Why?

I think there are five basic reasons. First, they may not be confessing their sins to God on an ongoing basis. Second, they may be confessing with worldly grief instead of godly grief. Third, they may not have openly confessed to and been prayed for by other believers. Fourth, their ongoing struggle with a particular sin may cause them to think they have not truly repented. (More on that in a moment.) Fifth, and the most common reason by far, is that God has an archenemy who does his utmost to stop us from believing and walking in truth.

Satan is a liar. And he's a dirty fighter. If he can't deceive you one way, he'll deceive you another. On the one hand, he'll try to get you to believe that you aren't guilty of sin and don't need forgiveness. On the other hand, he'll try to get you to believe that you are hopelessly guilty and beyond forgiveness. Self-righteousness or self-reproach . . . either way, he wins.

As I mentioned earlier, Satan relentlessly accuses believers day and night (Revelation 12:10). He wants us to believe that our sin is bigger and uglier than everyone else's. He wants us to doubt that Christ's work on the cross has paid our debt. That liar wants us to disbelieve that God could or would completely pardon our sin. He wants us to be convinced that we still need to carry the weight of it all. The Devil wants to destroy our joy and cripple our usefulness for the kingdom. And he can do this by falsely accusing us and wrapping us up in guilt and shame.

The way to combat guilt and shame is with the truth of Scripture.

The Bible says, "God made [us] alive together with him, having forgiven us all our trespasses, by canceling the record of debt that stood against us with its legal demands. This he set aside, nailing it to the cross" (Colossians 2:13–14). If you are a believer, God has forgiven your sin.

Your debt is canceled. It is nailed to the cross. Your guilt is gone.

God pronounces you innocent. "There is therefore now no condemnation for those who are in Christ Jesus" (Romans 8:1).

That is truth.

If you insist that you are guilty when God says you are innocent, or if you insist on hanging on to feelings of guilt, then you are not believing and walking in truth.

Guilt is usually tied to an event: "I *did* something bad." Shame is usually tied to an identity: "I *am* bad." Guilt is the wound. Shame is the scar. Shame is internalized disgrace, humiliation, and degradation. It's a sense that we are despicable and unworthy, coupled with an overwhelming urge to hide. And, as we discussed in the previous chapter, it starts with the lies we believe.

We first see shame in the Bible in Genesis 3:7, when Adam and Eve sinned and then tried to cover themselves up with leaves because they felt ashamed of their nakedness. This is in marked contrast to the way things were before they sinned, when they were naked and unashamed (2:25).

God dealt with their sin and shame in a way that powerfully foretold the work of Christ. "The LORD God made for Adam and for his wife garments of skins and clothed them" (3:21). The sacrifice dealt with their guilt, and the garments that covered them dealt with their shame.

This was a sign that pointed to the work of Christ. He is the Lamb of God whose sacrificial death atones for our guilt and whose skin clothes us in righteous garments. "As many of you as have been baptized into Christ have put on Christ like a garment" (Galatians 3:27 HCSB).

The cross provides the answer for the problem of our guilt as well as the problem of our shame. Scripture assures us, "Everyone who believes in him will not be put to shame" (Romans 10:11). "Those who look to him are radiant, and their faces shall never be ashamed" (Psalm 34:5).

To deal with sin, we need to confess it openly before the Lord with godly grief. But to deal with guilt and shame, it's important to practice another kind of confession: confess the truth.

What truth? The truth about the gospel and the truth about our identity in Christ.

When I prayed for Mindy, I prayed Scripture verses over her. It was the power of truth that broke her bonds of guilt and shame. We can counter the voice of guilt with the gospel truth that we "are justified freely by His grace through the redemption that is in Christ Jesus" (Romans 3:24 HCSB), and that "if we confess our sins, he is faithful and just to forgive us our sins and to cleanse us from all unrighteousness" (1 John 1:9).

We can counter the voice of shame with the gospel truth that we are new creations (2 Corinthians 5:17), friends of God (John 15:14), adopted by God (Ephesians 1:5), saints (1:1), God's delight (Zephaniah 3:17), God's dwelling place (1 Corinthians 3:16), righteous and holy (Ephesians 4:24), citizens of Christ's kingdom (Colossians 1:13), coheirs with Christ (Romans 8:17), blessed with every spiritual blessing (Ephesians 1:3), recipients of God's lavish grace (1:6–8), complete (Colossians 2:10), and lacking nothing we need for life and godliness (2 Peter 1:3).

When Satan tempted Jesus with lies, Jesus fought back by quoting Scripture. That's the way we can fight back against Satan's efforts to keep us loaded down with false guilt and shame. Remember, those who look to the Lord are radiant, and their faces will never be ashamed (Psalm 34:5).

GOOD FOR THE SOUL

Don't let yourself get burdened down with sin. I suggest that you learn to confess quickly and frequently. Make it a habit. Like picking up the mess in your house, it's far easier to keep things clean if you clean regularly instead of letting things pile up. I had to confess sins of envy and discontentment this morning. And the sin of criticism this afternoon. I try to confess whenever I notice sinful attitudes, thoughts, or actions crop up in my life.

It's best to be as specific as possible when confessing. Identify the sin. Was it selfishness? Malice? Willfulness? Pride? A lack of love?

Besides confessing regularly as you go throughout your day, it's also wise to set aside some time to examine your heart. It doesn't have to take long. Just a few minutes. Rid yourself of distractions before you start. Turn off your phone, TV, computer, and stereo. Then wait on the Lord in stillness. Ask the Holy Spirit to examine your heart and convict you of sin.

"Search me, O God . . . see if there be any grievous way in me, and lead me in the way everlasting!" (Psalm 139:23–24).

It's a good idea to have a Bible and journal in hand. You may want to read through a passage like Psalm 51 to help you focus. You may find confession difficult at first, but as you flex those spiritual muscles, they'll strengthen and it will get a lot easier.

I also encourage you to confess *openly*.

Don't try to fight the battle against sin alone.

Be honest and transparent about your struggles with others. Ask for prayer. The prayer of a righteous friend is powerful and effective and will help you gain victory (James 5:16). Make sure you're confessing with godly sorrow and not worldly sorrow. Recognize that your sin is against God and that you cannot deal with it apart from him.

Keep a watch on your heart. Godly sorrow produces healthy spiritual and emotional fruit that makes you strong in the Lord. Worldly sorrow produces apathy or deadness of heart, guilt and shame, or the desire to cover up, ignore, shrug off, excuse, and deny sin. It makes you weak and vulnerable. If your confession is genuine, you should see some positive signs. If you feel deflated, discouraged, and diminished after confessing your sin, then you may be wallowing in worldly grief.

Make sure to counsel your heart with truth. Remind yourself of Christ's finished work on the cross and of your identity and inheritance in him.

Finally, I want to encourage those of you who have been fighting a relentless, revolving-door battle with a particular sin. Maybe it's pornography, lust, an addiction, or an explosive temper. You confess the sin, but then you fall right back into it and need to confess it again. It seems you've been confessing the same sin for years. You beat yourself up and wallow in guilt and shame because you can't seem to make any progress.

I think that victory over sin sometimes tarries because God is interested in the fruit that the struggle produces. He wants to teach you how to fight the battle persistently and to depend on him.

Yes, sin in our lives is a problem, but so is a life where we haven't learned how to rely on God. Defeating sin is often a process. This is particularly true if you have been sinned against and need to deal with resentment, bitterness, and unforgiveness.

So keep at it. Be persistent.

Continue to confess your sin and to pursue true repentance.

An old Scottish proverb says, "Confession is good for the soul." If you haven't been confessing your sins on a regular basis, it's time to lighten your load. It's high time to ditch the sin, the guilt, and the shame. Unburdening them is a privilege and joy. Each time you confess you'll claim and reaffirm the truth of what Jesus did for you on the cross. You'll be reminded again about the wonder of his amazing grace. Your walk with the Lord will grow closer, and you'll see positive spiritual growth and change.

As you unload the baggage, you'll become stronger.

So fess up! Make a habit of doing so. Because it's true: confession really is good for your soul!

HABIT 4

Engage Your Emotions

When aligned with your mind and will,
emotions can be used as a tool to help
you move in the right direction.

Are you a chocaholic? Does the thought of eating a decadent piece of Godiva make your mouth water?

I have a weakness for chocolate, so I don't normally keep any in my house. But I make an exception to that rule in the month of December. Every Christmas season Brent brings home a generous selection of chocolates he's received from patients and colleagues at his sports medicine clinic.

One doctor always gives him Belgian chocolates from the world-renowned chocolatier Bernard Callebaut. In this selection I'll find Hazelnut Praline. Sea Salt Carmel. Almond Ganache. Truffles. All sorts of dainty melt-in-your-mouth morsels nestled in a large shell of milk chocolate shaped like a Yule log. *Mmm, delish!* I get a chocolate craving just thinking about it.

Brent doesn't even like chocolate (his guilty pleasure is potato chips), so he rarely samples a bite of the Christmas haul. And that's the problem. I'm the one who eats them. All of them. I simply can't resist. I tell myself I'll just eat one . . . but then I eat three, or six. (Please don't tell.) I vow that I've had enough for the day, but inevitably a few hours later the delectable treats start calling my name again. They weaken my resolve, and I give in to the powerful urge to indulge.

By the time January rolls around, I'm frustrated with my inability to resist temptation, and I deal with the problem in one fell swoop by tossing any remaining chocolate into the garbage.

I'm guessing you know how it goes too. You're sitting at your desk or on the couch, and you suddenly get a hankering for chocolate—or maybe it's potato chips, soda, ice cream, pretzels, salsa, or popcorn. You know that if you don't satisfy the urge, you won't be able to think about anything else until you get what you want. And food isn't the only thing we yearn for. Other cravings can be even more powerful and difficult to resist.

Like a longing for affection or for sexual gratification, for instance.

Or a longing for power and prestige.

Or revenge.

The weak women in Ephesus had all sorts of cravings. Paul said they had been "led astray by various passions" (2 Timothy 3:6). Other translations say "impulses" or "desires." A passion is a powerful and compelling emotion. It's the feeling that accompanies an unsatisfied state. It's a strong desire, yearning, or craving that moves us toward a course of action. It has an unmistakable effect on behavior.

A passion impacts what we do, what we think about, and what we put our efforts and energies toward.

You're not really passionate about exercise, for example, if you don't ever bother to lace up your running shoes and break into a sweat.

Your behavior of watching TV every evening for hours on end indicates that you are far more passionate about being comfortable and entertained.

The Greek word for passion or desire, *epithymia*, can be used in either a positive or negative sense. For example, Paul's passion to be with Christ was a positive desire (Philippians 1:23), as was his yearning to see his friends (Romans 1:11; Philippians 1:8; 2 Timothy 1:4) and his encouragement for them to stand firm in their faith (Philippians 4:1).

But the context of our passage makes it clear that when Paul spoke about these weak women, he was using the word with its more typical negative sense of worldly passions, which are illicit in nature and lead people into sin.

The women's emotions were leading them in the wrong direction.

Used in a negative context, the word *passion* carries sexual overtones, implying lustful and forbidden sexual desires. But its meaning is also much broader than that. A sinful passion is any desire for what God says is off-limits.[1] It's any craving that displaces our love and longing for him and disrupts our obedience.

Paul included the adjective *various* in 2 Timothy 3:6 to make sure his readers understood that he was using the word *passion* in its broadest sense possible. Though some of the women in Ephesus may have been led astray by sexual desires, most were probably led astray by impulses that weren't sexual in nature. Many different types of longings were responsible for their weakened condition.

DEATH BY DESIRE

I suspect that the desires of the women in Ephesus were very much like our own. They likely longed for affection, attention, and affirmation; significance, security, and success; enjoyment, amusement, and ease.

These yearnings aren't necessarily bad. Given the right framework, they can be legitimate desires. But even a good desire can lead to sin if we try to satisfy it the wrong way.

For example, a legitimate desire for security can easily slip into a destructive ambition to get rich. Instead of relying on God to meet our needs, we can become discontented, envious, and crave more and more money. This certainly was a temptation for the women in Timothy's church.

As you know, Ephesus was a wealthy city. Opulent split-level homes on the terraced mountainside rose up over the metro area, in full view of women living in less-affluent neighborhoods. The grand marble-columned market in the downtown core carried an endless variety of merchandise—all the latest Roman fashions, jewelry, accessories, and beauty products. Shopping and consumerism were rampant. Opportunities to be pampered and entertained were numerous. Women undoubtedly felt the pressure to keep up with the Joneses.

No wonder Paul felt he had to warn them, "Those who want to be rich fall into temptation, a trap, and many foolish and harmful desires, which plunge people into ruin and destruction. For the love of money is a root of all kinds of evil, and by craving it, some have wandered away from the faith and pierced themselves with many pains" (1 Timothy 6:9–10 HCSB).

The desire to live extravagantly was a strong temptation in Ephesus. Some women probably gave in to that urge and were trapped in materialism. As a result, they were plagued with many foolish and harmful desires.

Nowadays a materialistic woman might have the impulse to buy those Jimmy Choo shoes or that Louis Vuitton purse, even though they are way over budget. Or she might struggle with the desire to lie to her husband about how much money she actually spent. Or the urge to criticize his spending habits and his meager earnings. Or the compulsion to max out credit cards, cheat on taxes, withhold charitable giving, and take on more and more debt.

Materialism leads to all sorts of foolish decisions and trouble—"Ruin and destruction," "all kinds of evil," and "many pains."

If a woman experiences trouble in her life, that trouble can usually be traced back to a desire that insidiously led her astray.

I think of Dora, a woman in her late fifties who had divorced multiple times (five and counting at the time we met) and sobbed on my shoulder, "Please pray that God will send me another husband. I just need someone to love me!"

And Amy, the boy-crazy sixteen-year-old who yearned for affirmation but ultimately ended up with an STI, pregnant, and alone.

I think of Justine, the girl whose longing for acceptance led to anorexia and cutting.

Jenna, whose yearning for fun led to a drug addiction.

And Abby, whose drive for success compelled her to seduce and sleep her way up the corporate ladder.

In each case the outcome of pursuing the desire was not what the woman had envisioned. Instead of bringing satisfaction, pursuing the passion only led to an increased sense of dissatisfaction.

The apostle James argued that every human passion is accompanied by a temptation to fulfill that desire in the wrong way. He explained, "Each person is tempted when he is lured and enticed by his own desire. Then desire when it has conceived gives birth to sin, and sin when it is fully grown brings forth death" (1:14–15).

James used two metaphors here. The first comes from fishing. The bait on the fisherman's hook attracts and entices the fish. Once hooked, the fish is dragged away and pays with its life.

In the second metaphor James pictured desire as conceiving—getting pregnant—and giving birth to sin. James implied that temptation is not sinful in and of itself. Only when desire *conceives*—that is, when we let it produce offspring—does sin come to life. It is when we give in to sinful desires that we sin.

The point is an important one. Strong emotional yearnings are not sin.

These longings are simply part of what it means to be human. Everyone has them. Even the Lord experienced powerful yearnings and temptations. He sympathizes with our weaknesses because he was tempted just as we are, yet he didn't sin (Hebrews 4:15).

It's also important to understand that our longings do not occur in the absence of other emotions. Desires are connected to the rest of our feelings.

When I anticipate that my longing will be met, I feel happy, excited, or hopeful. When I anticipate that my longing won't be met, I feel disappointed, disheartened, or dejected. If something or someone sidetracks or interferes with the fulfillment of what I want, I feel perturbed, annoyed, angry, or resentful. If I suspect that my wishes will never be fulfilled, I feel wistful, anxious, despairing, or depressed.

My desire is like an achy void that I feel compelled to fill. It's like an itch that I need to scratch. Having a desire fulfilled feels gratifying. Living with an unfulfilled desire feels painful. Wrestling against a compulsion to satisfy a powerful desire can feel like absolute agony. The deeper the desire, the deeper the emotions that accompany it.

Jesus was not unfamiliar with all these emotions. He felt joy when his desires were fulfilled (Luke 10:21), and he felt pain and distress when he had to resist temptation. The writer of Hebrews found this to be a great source of encouragement. "Because [Jesus] himself has suffered when tempted, he is able to help those who are being tempted" (2:18).

Thankfully, we are not left on our own to manage emotions. The Lord wants to help us navigate these powerful feelings and understand how to use them for his righteous purposes.

BEAUTIFUL EMOTIONAL COLORS

The women in Ephesus were spiritually weak because they had let their desires get the better of them. Their emotions had led them astray. That's not to say that emotions are bad. On the contrary, emotions are a good and precious gift, given to us by the God who *feels* deeply. They exist for God's glory and for our good.

Sadly, I think some Christian communities view emotions as a problem to be managed rather than a gift to be celebrated. Some teach that intellect is better than emotion because it's far more reliable. The subtle suggestion is that we should view our feelings with suspicion and do our best to stifle them. The message is, "Your emotions are always getting you into trouble. So deny them. Contain them. Wrestle them into submission!"

Unfortunately, this can leave us with the impression that one of the greatest mistakes we can make in the Christian life is to be *overly emotional*. Or to conclude that godliness requires us to lock up our emotions like animals at the zoo. But the Bible encourages us to feel deeply about things that are right and true. As Randy Alcorn pointed out, "Emotions are part of our God-created humanity, not sinful baggage to be destroyed."[2]

Our souls are comprised of our mind, emotions, and will. These three parts are meant to work in harmony with one another. Each part brings something unique to the table:

- Our minds are tasked with thinking.
- Our emotions are tasked with feeling.
- Our wills are tasked with doing.

The task of our emotions is different from that of our minds and wills, but it certainly isn't any less vital. Do you think that God wants you to think loving thoughts and do loving things but not feel loving emotions? Of course not! He wants you to be *all in*, to love with every part of your being.

Christ died to redeem every part of you, including your emotions. You will be unbalanced if you try to make your intellect and your will run your life and leave your emotions out of the picture. It's equally damaging to let your emotions run the show and leave your mind and will out of the picture. Or to use your mind and emotions but fail to engage your will.

The gospel brings our souls back into perfect balance so that we may be perfectly complete and whole. As Martyn Lloyd-Jones pointed out,

> The Christian position is threefold [mind, will, emotions]; it is the three together, and the three at the same time, and the three always. A great gospel like this takes up the whole man. . . . What a gospel! What a glorious message! It can satisfy man's mind completely, it can move his heart [emotions] entirely, and it can lead to whole-hearted obedience in the realm of the will. That is the gospel. Christ has died that we might be complete men, not merely that parts of us may be saved; not that we might be lop-sided Christians, but that there may be a balanced finality about us.[3]

Jesus experienced deep human emotions. Because he was without sin, his feelings were rich, vivid, and pure. As we touched on earlier, he felt all sorts of feelings. He often felt sympathy, tenderness, and pity. Sometimes, he was annoyed, exasperated, or indignant. Jesus sighed and cried. At times, he felt pained. Troubled. Distressed. Or deeply moved. He moaned in agony. He was surprised and astonished. He enjoyed greatly. He loved intensely. He desired passionately.[4]

No one experienced the depth of pure emotion as Jesus did.

God doesn't want you to suppress your emotions. No. He wants you to feel the depth and breadth of pure, holy emotion and experience a kaleidoscope of rich, vivid, brilliant emotional colors, as Jesus did. Christ died for your whole person. He didn't just die for your mind and will. He died for your emotions too. He wants to redeem your emotions along with the rest of your body, soul, and spirit.

Everyone who truly encountered Jesus had their emotions awakened. Their lives went from darkness to light, from monochrome to vivid technicolor. They didn't remain emotionless. How could they?

When Jesus healed their sicknesses and rid them of demons and forgave their sins, they exploded with joyful exuberance. They worshiped with abandon. They served enthusiastically. They loved deeply. They were overcome with awe and wonder. They felt passionately and intensely. They experienced what it felt like to be truly alive.

Jesus came that you might experience an abundant life. Your emotions are an integral part of that.

Matthew Elliott, an expert on the biblical view of emotions, put it this way: "We can no sooner . . . turn [our emotions] off than an eagle can clip its own wings. And emotions *are* our wings. They are what carry us to a soaring Christian life—to the abundant life we were created to live. . . . God wants you to soar. He wants a 'you' more full of vitality and spirit than you've ever imagined."[5]

EMOTIONALLY DAMAGED

The sad reality for many of us is that our emotions aren't carrying us to a soaring Christian life. They're dragging us down and tripping us up. We need the Lord to set our emotions right because sin has made them go so terribly wrong.

Just imagine the vibrant emotions the first woman must have felt before the fall, in a world untainted by sin. She felt no negative emotions—nothing troublesome, nothing hurtful, nothing discouraging, no ungodly passions. All her feelings were pure, wholesome, and life-giving. She experienced sheer happiness, merriment, delight, contentment, excitement, inspiration, anticipation, trust, wonder, and love. Eve had the type of feelings we all yearn for but can never perfectly attain this side of paradise.

But then along came Satan with his persuasive sales pitch, underhandedly toying with her emotions.

Satan suggested that God was holding out on her and that she ought to focus on her own interests. He implied that she'd experience amazing benefits from eating the forbidden fruit. As she listened she began to experience some puzzling new emotions, such as confusion, doubt, and a twinge of indignation. These strange, new feelings were accompanied by a growing desire to indulge in what was forbidden. It wasn't long until she gave in to the powerful urge.

What a powerful flood of negative emotions must have come rushing in when innocence was lost. It must have been mind-boggling.

The shame. The fear. The guilt. The overwhelming sense of grief and loss. The cold chill of evil wrapping its black, ugly tentacles around her heart.[6]

For the first time ever, Eve felt embarrassed. Damaged. Unsafe. Exposed. Betrayed. Hurt.

Sin unleashed a torrent of negative and destructive feelings into her heart. What's more, it put her soul into a perpetual state of conflict. It shattered the harmony between her emotions, mind, and will.

What we need to remember in the wake of Eve's brokenness is that God created our emotions to work in conjunction with our minds and wills.

Emotions provide our minds with valuable information and insight. A sense of indignation informs us that an injustice may have occurred. A sense of sadness informs us of some kind of loss. A sense of fear informs us of possible danger. A sense of empathy tells us a compassionate response is called for. A sense of hesitation tells us to exercise caution. The mind needs emotional input. Otherwise our thinking descends into cold, unfeeling rationalism. Without emotional input, we might miss critical information, draw the wrong conclusions, and make poor decisions.

The way we feel also impacts our resolve and willpower. Os Guinness observed that feelings "are highly influential. Once persuaded, they become the powerful persuaders."[7] The stronger we feel about something, the more motivated we are to act. Empathy moves us to embrace and serve the one who is suffering. Righteous anger arouses us to defend the one who is mistreated. Sorrow prompts us to seek comfort. Fear propels us to seek protection. Despair disposes us to look for solutions. Emotions are a catalyst that help put us in motion. You know how difficult it is to do something when you don't feel like doing it. It's much easier when your emotions are engaged and aligned with your will.

Before the fall, there was a harmony and a unity to our souls. Mind, will, and emotions all worked together for the common good. But sin changed all that. Now our passions fight against our well-being. Instead of working in harmony with our minds and wills, our emotions battle against them.

Peter said that the passions of the flesh "wage war" against our souls (1 Peter 2:11). Likewise James asked, "What causes quarrels and what causes fights among you? Is it not this, that your passions are at war within you?" (4:1). Instead of agreeing with our reason, our feelings are now at odds with our minds. Our emotions battle against us.

Have you ever battled your emotions? Have you ever felt like they were at war with what you knew you should do? Or with what you wanted to do? I think we've all experienced this battle.

Sin has broken us. There's a disconnect in our souls. That's why it's tough to get our minds, wills, and emotions to move in the same direction.

We tend to deal with this problem by managing our emotions in one of two equally destructive ways: we either *deny* them, or we *rely* on them.

Both approaches are unhealthy. Neither response puts our emotions back into proper balance.

After being molested as a young girl, Bonnie spent the next four decades trying to stifle her emotions. She kept them locked up in a dark box in her heart, refusing to acknowledge or look at them. Though she pushed them down, the feelings of pain, shame, and self-reproach never completely disappeared. They festered in the dark recesses of her heart, robbing her of vitality and crippling her ability to interpret and interact with her world appropriately.

On the surface Bonnie pretended to be happy and went through all the right motions. No one would have guessed that fear, anxiety, and depression constantly threatened to burst out of her heart.

The suppressed emotions distorted Bonnie's self-awareness and self-perception and waged war against her soul. Over the years she struggled with a hidden eating disorder and with a tendency toward substance abuse. She became locked into the habit of trying to make everyone else happy while denying her own true feelings.

When she hit a marital crisis in her midfifties, all the unresolved emotions came to a head and simply became too much to handle. She couldn't keep the lid closed anymore. A lifetime of pain and frustration surged out like a hurricane. It totally undid her. Her journey of healing will likely be longer and more difficult than it would have been had she acknowledged and dealt with her emotions much earlier in life.

Denying your emotions is not the right way to handle them.

Emotional suppression is essentially an avoidance of emotion—a coping strategy. But it's important to understand that unacknowledged feelings don't just disappear. They fester inside and impact you negatively in ways you don't even realize. There is a heavy price to be paid when feelings are denied or suppressed. Apathy, boredom, and a sense of deadness toward life may be the sad consequence. People who feel emotionally numb may turn to bigger and stronger forms of stimulation to feel happy and alive.

Denying your feelings interferes with the way you interpret the world and impairs your capacity to make wise, rational choices. You might turn to food, TV, alcohol, drugs, unhealthy relationships, or compulsive work patterns to help keep your feelings suppressed. Unresolved emotions can impact your physical health too. They can weaken your whole immune system and be a precursor to chronic pain and crippling disease. Sadly, many women try to squelch their emotions and end up with their bodies and souls out of balance.

When we do this, we lose a part of ourselves. We hinder our minds from coming to a full and complete understanding of the situation. And we make it much more difficult for our wills to move us in the right direction. As Carolyn Mahaney and Nicole Whitacre wrote, "Emotions are not to be stifled or stamped out, but rather they are to propel us to God and godliness."[8]

Some of us hide our unhappy emotions, keep a tight lid on them, stuff them deep down into a dark box. Others of us let our emotions take over. We explode and vent, or compromise and indulge. We put an undue emphasis on following our hearts. We put our brains in *park* and let our emotions drive us around.

I suspect the women in Ephesus were doing things they knew were wrong. They probably used their feelings to rationalize and justify their behavior. They had succumbed to what I call the "I know, but" syndrome. I'm sure you're familiar with it. It's a common sickness. I've definitely been afflicted from time to time. With this syndrome, a woman knows the right thing to do, but she lets the powerful tug of her emotions take her in the opposite direction. For instance, she might say:

- "I know I shouldn't date a non-Christian, but he's nicer than church guys."
- "I know I shouldn't have screamed at him, but he pushes my buttons."
- "I know I shouldn't retaliate, but he disrespected me."
- "I know it's wrong to sleep with my boss, but he makes me feel so special."
- "I know it's wrong to give her the cold shoulder, but I resent what she did."
- "I know it's wrong to drink so much, but I just needed to relax."
- "I know it's wrong, but it feels so right."

Have you ever been stricken with the "I know, but" syndrome? Is it making you spiritually sick even now?

Emotions are powerful. Reason seems to stand little chance against the forces of fear, anger, hatred, jealousy, or whatever emotion is moving us. It's so much easier to let emotions take the lead rather than do the hard and necessary work of bringing our emotions in alignment with what we know we ought to do.

Whether you tend to deny your feelings or rely on them, both these approaches fail to respect the rightful place and function of your emotions. They do not bring your emotions back into alignment with the rest of your soul. Martyn Lloyd-Jones said that the lack of balance between mind, will, and emotions "is one of the great causes not only of unhappiness, but of failure and of stumbling in the Christian life."[9]

Unless we learn how to bring our minds, will, and emotions back into balance under the lordship of Jesus Christ, it's virtually inevitable that we will be "led astray by various passions."

Satan wants to exploit your emotions for evil. But you can put emotions to work for good. Whether your emotions are positive or negative, you can use them as a tool to help propel you in the right direction. You can engage them to be used for God's purposes.

WEAPONS FOR RIGHTEOUSNESS

So where do we start? How can we grow stronger in this area?

When it comes to our emotions, we tend to start with how we feel, how we want to feel, or how others expect us to feel. But if we want our emotions to be set right, we need to start with God as our reference point.

True emotions start with God. His emotions are our true north.

When we know how God feels about things and what he desires, we'll know how we ought to feel about things and what we ought to desire.

We need his help to learn which emotions and desires are holy because our emotions can be twisted and manipulated. We can feel good about something God feels bad about. We can long for something he says is off-limits. Our emotions were created to reflect *his* emotions and put *his* feelings and *his* desires on display.

We bring God glory by having our feelings and desires line up with his feelings and desires—and by running to him for help whenever they don't. Our fallen nature tempts us to think that our emotions are all about us, but ultimately our emotions do not exist for our sake. They exist for the glory of God. Most people fail to understand this crucial point.

> Because sin permeates our emotions, we're inclined to seek emotions for our sakes, rather than for God's sake. Sin ruins God's good gift by turning our emotions in the wrong direction. Instead of directing our affections toward God, sin turns our emotions toward us. . . . We become, as Martin Luther put it, "curved in" on ourselves. "Sin," he wrote, "bends the best gifts of God toward itself." We take this great gift of emotions and twist it around toward ourselves. We seek emotions for our selfish satisfaction.[10]

Sin turns our emotions in the wrong direction. It makes us "slaves to various passions and pleasures" (Titus 3:3).

Many of us are living as slaves to powerful and destructive desires. We battle with self-indulgence, cravings, lusts, and all sorts of obsessions and addictions, whether it's alcohol, drugs, caffeine, smoking, food, purging, cutting, money, shopping, gambling, gaming, social media, pornography, sex, romance, work, or even exercise.

In an attempt to fulfill our longings, we damage our personal well-being, our relationships, and our spiritual lives.

But we can't seem to resist the powerful urge that's driving us to fill the void.

Sin arouses our desires in such a way so as to corrupt us (Ephesians 4:22). It twists our emotions and uses them as weapons for unrighteousness (Romans 6:12–13). It ruins God's good gift of emotions by turning them in the wrong direction.

Thankfully, God provides the remedy. The apostle Paul explained, "We ourselves were once foolish, disobedient, led astray, slaves to various passions and pleasures. . . . But when the goodness and loving kindness of God our Savior appeared, he saved us, not because of works done by us in righteousness, but according to his own mercy, by the washing of regeneration and renewal of the Holy Spirit, whom he poured out on us richly through Jesus Christ our Savior" (Titus 3:3–6).

It's true. We were once foolish, disobedient, led astray, and slaves to various passions and pleasures, but when the goodness and loving-kindness of God our Savior appeared, *he saved us.*

Do you see the significance of this?

When Christ saves our souls, he saves us from being slaves to various passions and pleasures. He doesn't just save our minds and our wills; he also saves our emotions. He puts the parts back into alignment so that our emotions can function the way they were supposed to.

The amazing news of the gospel is that Christ sets us free from the grip of ungodly desires (Romans 7:5–6). We are no longer at the mercy of our emotions. That doesn't mean we won't ever feel strong impulses or unpleasant emotions. It simply means that the Holy Spirit gives us the power we need to respond in the right way. We are no longer doomed to obey human passions and desires.

Paul told his friends, "Do not let sin reign in your mortal body, so that you obey its desires. And do not offer any parts of it to sin as weapons for unrighteousness. But as those who are alive from the dead, offer yourselves to God, and all the parts of yourselves to God as weapons for righteousness" (6:12–13 HCSB).

"All the parts" of you includes your emotions.

According to the Bible, your emotions are like weapons. You can passively let Satan use them against you, or you can offer them up to God as weapons for righteousness. You can allow your emotions to be used for evil, or you can use them for good.

GET A GRIP ON YOUR EMOTIONS

A strong woman manages her emotions; a weak woman is managed by them.

The Bible doesn't encourage us to get rid of all unpleasant feelings; rather, it shows us that God has a purpose for those feelings. Good or bad, our feelings can be a valuable source of information and motivation. They play a good and useful role when they work together with our minds and wills to move us toward godliness. Emotions present an opportunity to alert the mind and engage the will. They are essential to the process of making wise decisions and taking the right kind of action.

You will never be a strong woman if you don't get a grip on your emotions.

So how do we engage our emotions for good and not let them be exploited by our sinful nature?

Paul said that this takes some practice. "The grace of God has appeared . . . training us to renounce ungodliness and worldly passions, and to live self-controlled, upright, and godly lives in the present age" (Titus 2:11–12).

We need training in order to deal with our emotions and desires in a godly manner. It doesn't just happen. If you want this ability, you'll need to sign on as a student in God's Emotions 101 course. It's a lifelong practicum. But as someone who's been in the program for decades, I can assure you that the Holy Spirit is a faithful mentor. He will help you learn how to manage your emotions for God's glory.

Here are some tips that can help you get started:

1. UNPACK YOUR EMOTIONS.

One of the top trends in the business world in the past two decades is training leaders how to deal with emotions—both their own and other people's. In 1990 two Yale psychologists coined the term *emotional intelligence* to describe a person's skill in perceiving, understanding, and managing emotions and feelings. They defined it as the "ability to monitor one's own and other people's emotions, to discriminate between different emotions and label them appropriately, and to use emotional information to guide thinking and behaviour."[11]

In many ways this insight from the business industry taps into key biblical truths. God is interested in helping you perceive and manage your emotions and feelings—far more than you probably realize. Emotional information can help you understand what's going on and make the right choices. That's why it's important for you to be emotionally intelligent.

Unfortunately, many of us are not even emotionally aware. We aren't in touch with our true feelings. Apart from the three broad categories of *happy*, *sad*, and *mad*, we haven't developed the necessary self-awareness or language to identify them. What are you feeling? Anger? Annoyance? Aggravation? Agitation? Frustration? Contempt? Disgust? Irritation? Scorn? Are you paying attention? Can you tell the difference? Do you even know?

Wise King Solomon said, "The purpose in a man's heart is like deep water, but a man of understanding will draw it out" (Proverbs 20:5).

In other words, it's important to examine and unpack the deep emotions, motivations, and desires of our hearts. Those who are wise will draw this information out like a bucket of water from a deep well. It's not always easy to evaluate clearly and accurately our own emotions and motivations. We can easily get the wrong read. But the Lord knows our true feelings. He probes and tests the hearts and minds of the righteous (Jeremiah 20:12). You will get the best insight into your emotions when you engage his help in the process.

As you seek to understand your emotions better, pay attention to the complex interaction between your emotions and your body. Emotions often show up physically:

- Sadness rolls down your cheeks.
- Surprise takes your breath away.
- Anger makes your face flush and heart pound.
- Fear puts a squeeze on your chest.
- Nervousness flutters around in the pit of your stomach.
- Worry ties up your muscles in knots.

Don't forget to consider that exercise, eating habits, and overall health all influence how we feel. And then there are our hormones (oh, those hormones!), which can make managing our emotions more difficult during that time of the month, or during the big hormonal changes that occur with puberty, childbirth, or menopause.

When emotions talk, we need to listen. We should pay careful attention to what they are saying.

That doesn't mean we *obey* our emotions. We don't put our brains in park and let emotions drive us around. No. Hearts are out of balance when emotions take the lead.

We listen to our emotions in order to gain valuable information.

We listen to understand. We listen because our feelings are not trivial or useless. They tell us a lot. They are often a better indicator of what's going on in our hearts than anything else. That's why the first step in getting a grip on your emotions is figuring out what those emotions actually are.

2. USE EMOTIONS AS A GAUGE RATHER THAN A GUIDE.

One way we can engage our emotions for good once we've learned to identify them is to determine what they reveal about how closely our hearts are aligned with the Lord's. The problem with the weak-willed women in Ephesus was that they were being *led astray* by their passions. They had a bad habit of letting their emotions drive their behavior. But emotions were created to function as a gauge, not a guide. They are like a car's dashboard indicators—not its steering wheel.

The dashboard gives us information about how the vehicle is functioning: what's going on under the hood, fluid levels, whether doors are open or seat belts are on, tire pressure, engine temperature, and service needs. In the same way, our emotions provide valuable information about our spiritual condition. They are often more truthful than our minds in telling us what we value, what we believe, and how much we value and believe these things.

Here's an example to show you what I mean. Say you were to drop an everyday cup on the floor and it smashed. You'd probably feel annoyed. But if you were to drop and break an irreplaceable cup from the set your grandmother gave you, your feelings would be a lot stronger. You'd feel the loss more keenly because you value the object more highly. Or say a stranger in a crowd calls you an ugly name. You'd probably feel irritated and slightly offended. But if your father called you an ugly name, your emotions would be much more intense. You'd feel deeply hurt. Your emotions would be stronger because you place a higher value on the relationship with your father than with the stranger.

Can you see how the emotion is connected to the value you place on the object of the emotion?

Matthew 6:21 says, "Where your treasure is, there your heart will be also." Virtually everyone recognizes that there is something wrong when wives love their dogs more than they love their husbands. Or when dads are more excited about their golf games than spending time with their children. Or when a boyfriend is more concerned about his damaged car than his injured girlfriend. In relationships, our emotions speak louder than our words.

And emotions are a good gauge of a person's spiritual state too.

If I say I love the Bible but don't ever feel excited to read it, that indicates that I don't actually love it as much as I say I do. If I feel stirred up by the championship game but never feel moved in worship, my emotions indicate which champion holds a greater place in my heart.

And not only do our emotions tell us what we value, they also tell us what we believe. Our feelings say a lot about what we hold to be true. Say your colleague rushes past you without acknowledging you or saying hello. If you believe she's snubbing you, you will feel offended, but if you believe she's stressed because of a pressing deadline, you will feel empathy. Or say you've been invited to a party. If you think the party will be fun, you'll feel excitement and anticipation. But if you think you're going to have to endure boring small talk and be endlessly interrogated by relatives on your marital status, you may feel reluctant to attend. In both these scenarios, your feelings stem from your underlying beliefs.

Your emotions and desires tell you what you truly cherish and believe. As Matthew Elliott wrote, "Emotion is not an illogical reflex, unreliable and fickle. Emotions cut through all our talk, all our spin, and take us right to the truth of the matter."[12]

For example, Vicky knows that the Bible teaches that sexual immorality and impurity are "improper for God's holy people" (Ephesians

5:3 NIV). But the sex scene from last week's HBO show has been looping a tantalizing replay in her mind. She's longing to watch the next episode. Not only that, she's lusting over the sexy guy at church and daydreams about playing out the scene in bed with him. Her emotional fantasies intrigue and arouse her.

What do Vicky's emotions and desires reveal about her true values and beliefs?

They indicate that her passion for sexual gratification is greater than her passion for God. She gets more pleasure from her imaginings than she does from loving the Lord. Her desire for God is several notches lower on the scale. What's more, she doesn't believe that filling her mind with illicit sexual images and daydreams and lusting after guys is quite as bad as God says it is. Vicky claims she loves God and believes the Bible, but her emotions tell the truth about what she really values and believes.

Vicky's problem is that she's allowing her emotions to drive her behavior. Remember, *emotions are meant to function as gauges, not guides.* If Vicky understood this and took the time to evaluate her emotions, she could get some valuable information about the condition of her heart. Rather than letting her emotions steer her in the wrong direction, she could use the information to help her make corrective choices and move in the right direction.

As author Jon Bloom pointed out, "God designed your emotions to be gauges, not guides. They're meant to report to you, not dictate you. The pattern of your emotions (not every caffeine-induced or sleep-deprived one!) will give you a reading on where your hope is because they are wired into what you believe and value—and how much. That's why emotions such as delight (Psalm 37:4), affection (Romans 12:10), fear (Luke 12:5), anger (Psalm 37:8), joy (Psalm 5:11), etc., are so important in the Bible. They reveal what your heart loves, trusts, and fears."[13]

Emotions present an opportunity to evaluate and understand what's going on in my heart. What's causing the emotion? Am I feeling what God wants me to feel? Do I value what God values? Do I believe what he says is true? Do I feel the same way about things that he does? Do I desire the things he says are valuable?

Not only should I have the right kinds of feelings, but I should also feel them with the right intensity. I want to feel the feelings God says I should feel with the intensity that he says I should feel them. Therefore, I shouldn't merely dislike sin, I should hate it. If I find that I don't, I can use that as an opportunity to run to God for help in getting my values, beliefs, and emotions right.

3. GIVE YOURSELF SOME GODLY ADVICE.

When we understand that emotions reveal our beliefs and values, we can go after our wrongly oriented emotions at their source. We can target the beliefs and values that underlie ungodly feelings. While it's true that we can't change our emotions directly, we can begin to address any faulty beliefs and values that negatively fuel our emotions.

Yes, we need to listen to our emotions carefully. But the problem is that most of us stop there. We let our emotions do all the talking. We listen, but we don't talk back. We don't counsel our hearts with truth. Martyn Lloyd-Jones asked, "Have you realized that most of your unhappiness in life is due to the fact that you are listening to yourself instead of talking to yourself?"[14]

Remember when we discussed how thoughts can cripple us? That can happen with our feelings too. One of the best ways to train our emotions is to speak truth to them, just like we do with our thoughts. King David made a habit of doing this too. The Psalms provide dozens of examples of him telling himself how he ought to feel and why he ought to feel that way:

"My soul, find rest in God; my hope comes from him" (62:5 NIV).
"Return, O my soul, to your rest; for the LORD has dealt bountifully with you" (116:7).

"Why are you cast down, O my soul, and why are you in
turmoil within me? Hope in God; for I shall again praise him,
my salvation" (42:5).
"Bless the LORD, O my soul, and forget not all his benefits"
(103:2).

David made a habit of giving himself godly advice, especially at
night when he lay awake mulling things over and his emotions were on
the verge of overwhelming him. "In the night also my heart instructs
me" (16:7). Whenever his emotions were out of sorts David gave himself a truth pep talk to remind himself of God: who God is, what God
is like, what God has done, and what God has pledged himself to do.

His emotions were running amok. He felt overwhelmed by dis-
couragement and defeat. But instead of letting his emotions talk to
him, he chided them. "Why, my soul, are you downcast? Why so
disturbed within me?" (43:5 NIV).

David called time-out and said, "Wait a minute, self, you need
some perspective here. I need to remind you of what's true."

He took himself in hand, addressed himself, questioned himself,
preached to himself, and exhorted himself. Instead of passively listening
to his emotions and letting them drag him down, he fought back against
what his emotions were telling him and counseled them with truth.

Jude suggested a similar strategy. After noting that many people
are given to negative emotions and the urge to follow ungodly desires,
he told his friends how to avoid being sidetracked like this. "You,
beloved, building yourselves up in your most holy faith and praying in
the Holy Spirit, keep yourselves in the love of God" (Jude vv. 20–21).

In other words, the way to manage negative, destructive, ungodly
emotions, is to build yourself up in your faith, ask the Lord for help, and
keep yourself in his love. The Lord gives you his power, his truth, his
precious and very great promises—everything you need to manage your
emotions and escape the powerful pull of sinful desires (2 Peter 1:3–4).

So when your emotions talk, listen.

But don't give them the final word.

4. RESOLVE TO DO WHAT'S RIGHT, EVEN WHEN YOU DON'T FEEL LIKE IT.

God frees us from being a slave to our emotions. He gives us the power to think and choose so that we can bring all the parts of our soul back into alignment with what he wants for us.

I am fascinated by the fact that the Lord calls us to account not only for actions and attitudes that miss the mark but also for emotions that are not what they ought to be. We tend to think emotions are beyond our control. We think we can't help that we've *fallen* in or out of love, that we're happy or sad, that we're overwhelmed by powerful longings, or that we do or don't have a certain emotion.

But that's not the message of the Bible.

Scripture teaches that we *can* change our emotions by engaging our minds and wills. When we *think* and *choose* the right way, our emotions usually start to *feel* the right way.

This is exactly how the Bible instructs us to deal with wayward emotions.

We see this in Christ's corrective letter to the church in Ephesus (Revelation 2:1–7). The women in Ephesus obviously weren't as passionate about Jesus as they were about other things. And apparently they weren't the only ones in the church who had lost their enthusiasm. In this letter Christ accused the whole congregation of waning love.

At that time the congregants were doing a lot of things right. They had rejected evil. They were patiently enduring hardship. They had corrected false doctrine. They were working hard for the sake of the gospel. But their emotions weren't what they should have been. Christ said to them, "I know you are enduring patiently and bearing up for my name's sake, and you have not grown weary. But I have this against you, that you have abandoned the love you had at first. Remember therefore from where you have fallen; repent, and do the works you did at first" (vv. 3–5).

Note that Jesus corrected them for not having the right emotion. He took them to account for not having the right feelings. Their lack of passion was a sin.

But he also told them how to fix that.

They were supposed to think back to the way things were when they were first in love and again do the things that a head-over-heels-in-love person does. To correct their emotions, they had to engage their minds ("remember") and their wills ("do the works you did at first"). They had to make a choice to behave as though they loved God. As they obediently engaged their minds and wills, their feelings would follow. Honeymoon-like behavior would lead to honeymoon-like affection. Even though they weren't feeling it, Jesus wanted the believers in Ephesus to behave in a way that inspired the emotion they wanted to cultivate. (By the way, this is also great advice for any wife who has "fallen out of love" with her husband.)

The Bible instructs us to engage our minds and wills when dealing with wayward impulses and passions. We need to *think* the right way about our emotions and then *do* the right thing with them. This doesn't mean we pretend to have an emotion we don't have. It simply means we ought to do something to bring our emotions in line with what God wants them to be.

Scripture uses all sorts of action words on this topic (emphasis added). We are to:

"*abstain* from the passions of the flesh" (1 Peter 2:11)

"*put off* [our old selves]," which are "corrupt through deceitful desires" (Ephesians 4:22)

"*put to death* . . . sexual immorality, impurity, lust, evil desire, and greed" (Colossians 3:5 HCSB)

"*flee* youthful passions" (2 Timothy 2:22)
"*walk* by the Spirit" (Galatians 5:16)

You can't always choose your feelings, but you can always choose how to respond to them. And when you consistently respond the way the Lord wants you to, your feelings will usually come around.

THE PURSUIT OF HAPPINESS

All of our passions stem from a deep-rooted desire to be happy. That was what motivated the behavior of the women in Ephesus, and it's the motivation of all our actions too. "All men seek happiness," explained the great French philosopher Blaise Pascal. "This is without exception. . . . This is the motive of every action of every man, even of those who hang themselves."[15]

The women in Ephesus thought they'd be happy when they indulged their desires. Yet ironically, this pursuit led them away from the very thing that would bring them true and lasting joy. Has that ever happened to you? Have you ever pursued what you thought would bring you happiness, only to find, when you got it, that it didn't make you any happier and perhaps even made you less so?

God promises to satisfy the desire of those who honor him (Psalm 145:19). He boldly invites us to seek happiness in him. "Delight yourself in the LORD, and he will give you the desires of your heart" (37:4). David said to God, "In your presence there is fullness of joy; at your right hand are pleasures forevermore" (16:11).

Scripture promises incredible blessings to those who desire God above all else. Ultimately, the only way to be truly happy is to say a resounding yes to God and a resounding no to the temporary pleasures of sin. We attain supreme joy when we sacrifice lesser pleasures for greater ones. I love this quote by C. S. Lewis: "It would seem that Our Lord finds our desires not too strong, but too weak. We are half-hearted creatures, fooling about with drink and sex and ambition when infinite joy is offered us, like an ignorant child who wants to go on making mud pies in a slum because he cannot imagine what is meant by the offer of a holiday at the sea. We are far too easily pleased."[16]

The best way to get a grip on your emotions is to cultivate a greater desire. And by that I mean a desire for greater things. You will have much more success in resisting the pull of the world's melody if you are listening to a sweeter song.

Homer's *Odyssey* tells the story of an island inhabited by beautiful sirens, which were dangerous creatures that made sailors shipwreck on jagged rocks by luring them with enchanting music.

When Odysseus sailed past the island, he had his sailors plug their ears with wax so they couldn't hear the beguiling but deadly song. Odysseus was curious and wanted to listen, though he knew it would render him incapable of rational thought. So he had his crew bind him to the mast. When his boat sailed past the sirens, the bewitching music drove him temporarily insane. He struggled with all his might to break free from the ropes so he could respond to the powerful pull. The desire—and the agony—were unbearable.

When Jason knew he had to sail past the island, he came up with a different strategy. He asked the renowned musician Orpheus to ride along. The song of Orpheus was sweeter and more beautiful than the song of the sirens. Jason and his crew didn't need to plug their ears with wax or be tied up and tormented by unfulfilled desire. They just had to listen to the melody coming from Orpheus's lyre. It kept them from hearing the sirens' song. They joyfully rowed past the island, barely even noticing that the sirens were there.

Like Odysseus binding himself to the mast, many Christians deal with the pull of worldly desires by binding themselves to following rules. They know that sin is deceptive and that if they give in they'll end up shipwrecking their lives. But they still hear sin's song. They still feel the pull. Though they know they can't, they still have the urge to *go there*—and are miserable as a result. The Bible proposes a different strategy. It encourages us to be captivated by something far more beautiful.

As our affection for Jesus grows, our attraction to the world will fade. And our emotions will increasingly be put in order.

Our emotions are the most beautiful, tender, and vibrant parts of our souls but also the most vulnerable and difficult to manage. Satan will try to exploit our emotions to get us to make bad choices and lead us astray. We can be sure of that.

We can also be sure, however, that Jesus will give us the power to use our emotions in the right way. We don't need to be slaves to our emotions. We can offer our desires and emotions to God to be used as weapons for righteousness. Instead of our emotions working against us, we can make them work for us—for our good and for God's glory.

A strong woman makes a habit of engaging her emotions to work together with her mind and will to keep her on track. Instead of serving her emotions, she makes her emotions serve her.

HABIT 5

Walk the Talk

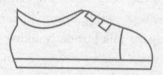

You haven't really learned until you've
put your knowledge into practice.

Just do it. You've probably heard this Nike slogan. It's
one of the most famous in advertising history.

The first time the world heard the phrase was in a 1988 television
commercial featuring an eighty-year-old marathon icon, Walt Stack.
In the ad the shirtless octogenarian lumbered across the Golden Gate
Bridge. "I run seventeen miles every morning," he told the audience
without breaking his stride. "People ask me how I keep my teeth from
chattering in the wintertime," he continued. A few moments later he
wryly retorted, "I leave them in my locker."

The scene then cuts out to the white-on-black message: Just do it.

The commercial was quirky, endearing, and motivating. It left view-
ers thinking that if a wrinkled eighty-year-old could do it, they could too.

This, along with many subsequent Nike ads, presented a vignette of a hero who worked hard to overcome adversity and ultimately emerged victorious against a daunting foe. But the foe wasn't always a literal enemy; it was usually the hero himself. He needed to overcome his own procrastination, inactivity, fears, and excuses in order to succeed.

The idea deeply resonated with people. The words *just do it* are simple and true. Whatever it is you should be doing, you should do it right now with no excuses. When there is something to be done, be proactive and just do it.

The problem with the weak women in Ephesus is that they were not just doing it. They were taking information in but not working it out. They were talking the talk but not walking the walk. They were "always learning and never able to arrive" (2 Timothy 3:7).

Their knowledge wasn't changing their hearts. It wasn't propelling them to grow and make progress.

Their spiritual lives were stagnating.

They were essentially in the same place they had been the previous year—and the year before that, and the year before that. The same problems. The same issues. They were just spinning their wheels. Have you ever felt like that?

If you live in the southern States or near the equator, you may not be familiar with the expression "spinning your wheels." I live in a region in Canada that's covered in snow for several months each year. Here, cars commonly spin their wheels.

It happens when the snow on the street accumulates and your car gets stuck or snowed in, and the tires get encased in an icy rut. When you press on the gas, the wheels spin furiously, but your vehicle doesn't move. Your speedometer might indicate that you're traveling at fifty miles per hour, but you're actually just getting nowhere fast.

To remedy this situation, you need to dig the snow out from around the tires, throw down some sand or gravel to get some traction, and enlist some bystanders (preferably some burly, strong men) to help heave-ho your car out of the rut.

ALWAYS LEARNING BUT NEVER DOING

The women in Ephesus were stuck in a spiritual rut. They were hearers but not doers. They were spiritual learnaholics who consumed a lot of information but didn't bother to apply it. This was true even though these women would have had access to far fewer Christian resources than we do today.

Nowadays, with the accessibility of print and e-books and with the growth of the Internet, we have access to a staggering amount of teaching. Translators have published about nine hundred English translations and paraphrases of the Bible since Tyndale printed the first one in 1526.[1] Amazon currently carries more than eighty thousand Christian book titles, and iTunes publishes more than a thousand Christian podcasts. And then there's YouTube, GodTube, online magazines, social media, blogs, church websites, sermons, streaming video conferences, and webcasts. Not to mention radio and TV.

Never before have people had access to so much Christian teaching.

While the abundance of Christian resources is undoubtedly a good thing, there's a downside. This availability has led to the same problem of Christian consumerism that was so prevalent among the women in Timothy's church.

Unfortunately, our churches are filled with people who have heard what the Bible has to say but haven't applied that information to their own lives.

I don't think I'm overstating the case.

Surveys show that there is little difference between the average churchgoer and the average nonchurchgoer when it comes to most moral beliefs and behaviors.[2]

Many years ago I sat at a table with a French-Canadian pastor who bemoaned what he had observed with some young men and women returning to their local churches after spending four years at Bible school. Speaking with a thick Quebecois accent and demonstrative hand gestures and facial expressions, he lamented, "We send them with 'earts like this [arms spread full width] and 'eads like this [fingers pinched together], and they come back with 'eads like this [arms spread full width] and 'earts like this [fingers pinched together]."

It's not that he disliked Bible schools. He was a great proponent of Christian education. I'm sure he'd agree that there is enormous value in pursuing a theological education. The problem was not that these students studied the Bible; the problem was that they didn't let it change them. They were taking in lots of information but experiencing very little transformation.

Their heads were growing bigger as their hearts were growing smaller.

Not much has changed.

A friend recently told me about a young woman who was extremely excited to go to Bible school. When she got there, she was shocked and disappointed to discover that the majority of students slept around, told dirty jokes, watched R-rated movies, gossiped, backstabbed, and embraced culture's view on gender fluidity and same-sex marriage.

Those students studied the Word of God and theology. They knew the lingo. They knew the difference between Arminianism and Calvinism. They could tell you if someone was a three-, four-, or five-pointer. They could debate complementarianism versus egalitarianism. They were well-versed in christology, soteriology, ecclesiology, eschatology, hermeneutics, and exegesis. Of course, they attended all the biggest and best Christian conferences, and they were attracted to high-profile Christian bloggers like ants to a picnic.

Like the women in Ephesus they were "always learning." Yet somehow all that learning hadn't transformed their hearts or changed their attitudes and behavior. They were hearers of the Word but not doers of the Word. They were becoming more and more religious, but they weren't becoming any more righteous.

If we are to be strong women, we need to make a habit of putting what we learn into practice.

Jesus said, "Blessed rather are those who hear the word of God and keep it!" (Luke 11:28). True obedience requires hearing *and* doing. Jesus soundly condemned the Pharisees of his day who were putting themselves forth as religious know-it-alls while keeping their hearts far from him.

Pharisees were Jewish scholars and educators. They weren't Levitical priests. They were more like a religious theological society of lay professors and teachers. Their primary focus was teaching common people how to apply the Torah, the Prophets, and Jewish oral traditions to everyday life.

Pharisees were highly regarded for their religious knowledge. They were committed to studying, learning, and teaching the Scriptures and engaging in scholarly debate. But many of them were so puffed up with information and so obsessed with arguing the finer points of the law that they ended up going against the very things that God wanted them to do. This problem was so widespread that some gospel writers used the word *Pharisee* almost interchangeably with *hypocrite*—two-faced religious fakes. The Pharisees' great knowledge didn't always translate into the right attitude or action.

How can we avoid the always-learning-but-never-doing problem of the Pharisees, the weak women in Ephesus, and so many people in the church today? How do we stop spinning our wheels and break out of our spiritual ruts? A good place to start is to examine our lives for signs that we, too, may be a religious fake.

SIGNS YOU ARE A RELIGIOUS FAKE

Jesus said, "Not everyone who says to Me, 'Lord, Lord!' will enter the kingdom of heaven, but only the one who does the will of My Father in heaven. On that day many will say to Me, 'Lord, Lord, didn't we prophesy in Your name, drive out demons in Your name, and do many miracles in Your name?' Then I will announce to them, 'I never knew you!'" (Matthew 7:21–23 HCSB).

It's sobering to think that we can be involved in all sorts of religious activities, listen to all sorts of religious teachers, and gain all sorts of religious knowledge but not actually have a genuine relationship with Jesus.

Are you fooling yourself? Are you in danger of becoming a hypocrite like the Pharisees and those weak women in Ephesus? Here are seven signs that you might be:

I. YOUR PUBLIC FACE IS DIFFERENT FROM YOUR PRIVATE ONE.

The word *hypocrite* comes from the Greek word for an actor in a stage play. In ancient Greek comedies and tragedies, the actors wore masks to represent the character they were playing. Hiding their true selves behind a mask is what hypocrites do.

A hypocrite playacts. She pretends to be very good or religious when she is aware she is not. There's a contradiction between who she is on the inside and who she outwardly presents herself to be. She knows there's sin in her heart, but she doesn't do anything about it. To cover it up, she feigns being righteous. She is two-faced, just like the scribes and Pharisees of Jesus' time. "Woe to you, scribes and Pharisees, hypocrites! For you are like whitewashed tombs, which outwardly appear beautiful, but within are full of dead people's bones and all uncleanness. So you also outwardly appear righteous to others, but within you are full of hypocrisy and lawlessness" (Matthew 23:27–28).

A woman once wrote to me about an emotional affair she was having with her pastor. It had been going on for two years. Every week she went to church and pretended to be good, but during the sermon she fantasized about being with him. After the service she and the pastor would exchange glances and subtly flirt. Their hands would linger as they shook hands.

They hadn't followed through on their escalating sexual attraction . . . not yet. But they'd started exchanging increasingly personal and suggestive text messages. It was clear that if she didn't do something to stop it, the emotional affair would soon give way to a physical one.

To her church friends this woman appeared very righteous. But at home she was withholding love from her husband and becoming increasingly critical, judgmental, argumentative, mean-spirited, and defiant. There was a contradiction between who she pretended to be and who she really was.

Though a two-faced woman is usually an excellent pretender, at some point her duplicity will be exposed. She will not be able to pretend forever. Jesus warned, "Beware of the leaven of the Pharisees, which is hypocrisy. Nothing is covered up that will not be revealed, or hidden that will not be known. Therefore whatever you have said in the dark shall be heard in the light, and what you have whispered in private rooms shall be proclaimed on the housetops" (Luke 12:1–3).

If you are a hypocrite, you will:

- try to keep your sins hidden,
- put on a mask so other people will not see your struggles,
- be scared that people will discover that you aren't who you pretend to be,
- be afraid to be authentic and let people see the real you, and
- feel anxious and stressed about maintaining the charade.

Are you wearing a mask? Are you covering up who you really are? Are you afraid of being found out? How would you feel if what you have done in the dark were brought out into the light? If what you have whispered in private were made public, and your secret thoughts brought out into the open?

A weak woman wears masks. A strong woman is authentic about her struggles and does not try to hide. She is truthful about her spiritual condition and genuinely seeks and pursues growth.

Sadly, there's an unproductive type of authenticity in many Christian blogs and social media posts nowadays. It's displayed by people who are bold—proud, even—to speak openly of their sins and failures. They wear their shortcomings on their sleeves like a badge of honor. They constantly share their struggles but make no progress in winning the battle. They do not hold themselves or their readers accountable to God's standard of holiness. Their authenticity is misleading, because they have no desire and no intention to change. Their openness is only a front to convince followers that they are superspiritual. A woman who is open about her sin for the purpose of appearing spiritual is just as two-faced as the one who hides her sin for the purpose of appearing spiritual. Both wear masks and pretend to be what they are not.

2. YOU HAVE A VENDING-MACHINE VIEW OF GOD.

A second sign that you may be a religious fake is if you are self-indulgent. A hypocrite loves pleasing herself more than she loves pleasing God (2 Timothy 3:4–5). She wants God to do things for her, but she doesn't want to do things for him. She doesn't want to change her sinful behavior and desires.

So she treats God like a vending machine.

She puts her coins of prayer and religious service into the slot and expects him to dispense the goods that she wants, how she wants, and when she wants.

According to Scripture this self-indulgent vending-machine type of perspective is common among double-minded people. Jesus called out the scribes and Pharisees for acting religious while having hearts "full of greed and self-indulgence" (Matthew 23:25). These hypocrites pretended to be interested in what they could give but were actually far more interested in what they could get.

A woman with a vending-machine view of God expects him to do what she desires, but she doesn't have any intention of doing what *he* desires. She constantly asks the Lord for things, but they are the wrong things. She merely wants him to indulge her sinful passions. According to James 1:7 a woman like this "must not suppose that [she] will receive anything from the Lord." This isn't because God doesn't want to give. It's because she doesn't want to receive what he wants to give.

I told the woman who wrote me that she should confess the emotional affair to her husband and to a trusted friend. She should repent, cut off all contact with the pastor, and seek out a different church. From the tone of her e-mail, I don't think she will. She does not seem sorry for her sin. She is merely sorry that God is keeping her from being with the man she wants to be with. She's praying for the situation to be resolved, but she doesn't want it resolved God's way.

She wants things her way.

And she wants God to support and bless her as she hurtles head-long toward an affair.

Do you treat God like a vending machine? Ask him for things to indulge your own sinful passions? Get upset with him when he doesn't give you what you want? Do you ask him to do your will while you are unwilling to do his?

A weak woman is preoccupied with what she wants God to do for her. A strong woman focuses on what God wants her to do for him.

3. YOU ARE HIGHLY CONCERNED ABOUT WHAT OTHERS THINK.

A third sign of hypocrisy is a focus on externals. A hypocrite is very concerned about outward appearances, how she looks to others and what people think about her. She desperately wants to blend in. So she acts like a chameleon. She changes color depending on the environment she is in.

When she's around spiritual people, she acts superspiritual. She does her Bible study homework, volunteers, does good things for the Lord, and is glad when people notice and praise her knowledge and virtuous behavior. But she isn't nearly as eager or careful about pleasing the Lord in quiet, unnoticeable ways. She won't serve or do good things if her religious friends don't notice, appreciate, and affirm her efforts. What's more, she quickly drops the religious façade when she's with other groups of friends.

The scribes and Pharisees did all their deeds "to be seen by others" (Matthew 23:5–7). These religious leaders wanted to draw people's attention to their "goodness" so that they would be praised (6:2). But they were like chameleons, different people when they were out in public than when they were at home (Luke 13:15). They operated by a different set of rules. Their conduct changed depending on the environment they were in and the people they were with.

My son's friend Nate said of a girl we know, "The Krista you get at a party is different from the Krista you get at church. She's only as spiritual as the people she's with."

A hypocritical woman is guilty of chameleonlike conduct. Like Krista, she is only as spiritual as the situation demands. When she's at church she acts like a church girl. But when she's at a party she acts like a party girl. She behaves differently depending on where she is and who she is with.

How about you? Are you focused on externals? Are you worried about what people will think? Do you change colors to blend in? Do you behave differently with your church friends than you do with your non-church friends?

A weak woman is concerned about what people think of her. A strong woman is far more concerned about what God thinks of her.

4. YOU ARE SELECTIVE ABOUT WHICH PARTS OF THE BIBLE TO OBEY.

In Matthew 23 we see that the Pharisees did some things right, such as tithing mint and dill and cumin, but they "neglected the weightier matters of the law: justice and mercy and faithfulness" (v. 23).

Hypocrites are guilty of partial obedience. They pick and choose which parts of the Bible they're willing to put into practice. They will be doers of the Word when it suits them but won't obey when it doesn't suit them. They are seldom willing to do anything hard, uncomfortable, or culturally unpopular.

My husband and I once went out of town for the weekend and left our teenage sons home alone. I assigned each son one chore to complete while we were gone. My youngest son had to empty the dishwasher. My middle son had to cut the back lawn. I asked my oldest son, Clark, to fold the load of laundry that I had just pulled out of the dryer and piled up on the coffee table. "I don't want the clothes sitting there for days with the wrinkles setting in," I explained, "so please get to it as quickly as possible."

When we got home my oldest son, Clark, greeted us. Beaming, he told me that he had vacuumed the carpet, dusted the furniture, and washed the kitchen floor. (I wondered what he'd spilled.) I was surprised and pleased that he had done all these things. But then I saw the crumpled pile of laundry still stacked up on the coffee table. I could see that he had vacuumed the carpet all around the coffee table while the laundry on top was untouched. And the wrinkles had definitely set in. *Arghhh!*

Clark had done all sorts of things I hadn't requested, but he hadn't done the one thing I had requested. I was annoyed to say the least. All those extras felt meaningless in light of his fundamental failure to follow through on the one job I had assigned.

Clark was crestfallen when I pointed it out. "But I vacuumed and dusted and cleaned. I did way more than you asked me to do! I did way more than my brothers did."

"Yes. But they obeyed, and you didn't. Had you added these other chores to your obedience, I would have received them as a great gift. But you did these other chores to *avoid* doing the chore you don't like. You thought you could skirt doing what I asked you to do by doing all these other things."

Afterward I was struck with the spiritual lesson illustrated by my son's behavior. I wondered if God felt the same way toward my lack of obedience as I did toward Clark's. I was doing a lot of good things for God. But I was procrastinating and putting off the one hard thing that the Lord had asked me to do. I knew that he wanted me to reach out and forgive someone who had wounded me and try to patch up the difficult relationship. That was the pile of laundry I didn't want to fold. Studying and writing and traveling and speaking and serving were easy acts of obedience by comparison. I was busying myself doing all these good things, but there was one thing God wanted me to do that I didn't want to do.

As I mentioned earlier, Jesus said, "On that day many will say to Me, 'Lord, Lord, didn't we prophesy in Your name, drive out demons in Your name, and do many miracles in Your name?' Then I will announce to them, 'I never knew you!'" (7:21–23 HCSB). Those Pharisees were busy doing good things for God. But partial obedience isn't really obedience. If we don't wholeheartedly obey in the little things—in the hard things—then all our religious busyness is for naught.

What's your pile of laundry you don't want to fold? What's the thing the Lord is asking you to do that you are avoiding? Are you being selective in the ways you are willing to obey?

A weak woman picks and chooses the ways she is willing to follow the Lord. A strong woman follows Christ wholeheartedly and is ready to do the hard things.

5. YOU RATIONALIZE YOUR DISOBEDIENCE.

The scribes and Pharisees were masters at rationalizing their sin and excusing their lack of follow-through. They came up with all sorts of elaborate loopholes and arguments to justify disobeying God. For instance, they argued that their commitment to charitable giving justified their failure to support their parents financially. "God understands how much I've given. He wouldn't expect me to support my parents too."

Jesus accused them of voiding the Word of God with their clever rationalizations (Matthew 15:3–6). Two-faced people come up with all sorts of rationalizations as to why their selective obedience is justified. I've heard many from women over the years:

"Everyone's doing it."

"It's really not that bad."

"That was a sin in that culture, but not in ours."

"If the Bible were written today, God would have something different to say."

"God made us with sexual desires that need to be fulfilled."

"I prayed about it."

"That other sin is far worse than mine."

"It isn't wrong if we don't go all the way."

"God wants me to be happy."

"I can't help that I feel this way. It's the way God made me."

"How can it be wrong when it feels so right?"

Have you ever used any of these excuses?

The woman who e-mailed me justified her emotional affair

because both she and the pastor had emotionally abusive spouses and loveless marriages. In her mind this made their behavior okay. Their spouses had driven them to seek solace elsewhere. Solomon said, "This is the way of an adulteress: she eats and wipes her mouth and says, 'I have done no wrong'" (Proverbs 30:20).

Hypocrites rationalize sin. And I'm not just talking about the sin of emotional or physical infidelity.

Maybe you justify speaking unkindly to your husband.

Or giving your relative the cold shoulder.

Maybe you justify gossiping about a coworker behind her back.

Or not reporting income on your tax return.

We are hypocritical whenever we rationalize our sin—whenever we make excuses or blame our sinful attitudes and behaviors on circumstances or other people.

Coming up with excuses to justify our disobedience is one of the most glaring signs that we are religious fakes. Hypocrites always find a way to justify their failure to obey. They have plenty of excuses to let themselves off the hook.

Weak women come up with excuses for why they can't or don't have to obey. Strong women don't make excuses. They take God at his word and get it done.

6. YOU ARE HIGHLY CRITICAL OF OTHERS.

Not only does a hypocrite justify her lack of obedience, she is also judgmental and contemptuous of others.

- She looks down on others with a holier-than-thou attitude (Luke 18:11–12).
- She sees the speck in other people's eyes but fails to notice the log in her own. She doesn't think that her own sin is a big deal and considers the sin of everybody else to be much worse (Matthew 7:5).

- She has very high expectations of what other people should do but isn't willing to apply that same standard to herself (23:4).
- She is highly critical when other people fail or let her down. She self-righteously thinks that she is beyond such weakness (vv. 29–30).
- She feels malice toward anyone who tries to teach or correct her (22:15–18).
- She easily takes offense (15:10–12).

A religious hypocrite shines the spotlight on other people's short-comings. She gossips about their failures and maligns them behind their backs. She is critical, disrespectful, and contemptuous. Everyone is a hypocrite except for her.

A weak woman looks for signs of hypocrisy in other people's lives. A strong woman looks for signs of hypocrisy in her own life.

7. YOU NEVER MAKE ANY PROGRESS.

The final and overriding sign that you may be a religious fake is that you fail to make any significant spiritual progress. Like the weak women of Ephesus, a religious fake constantly learns but does not progress from one level of maturity to the next. She is not transformed "from one degree of glory to another" (2 Corinthians 3:18).

Her character does not improve. She does not make progress or gain any victory over her anger, impatience, anxiety, doubt, grumbling, negativity, criticism, resentment, or lack of self-control.

She doesn't grow stronger.

Jesus warned that those who hear the Word but fail to act on it won't be strong. They'll be weak and shallow and have trouble withstanding the storms of life:

Why do you call Me "Lord, Lord," and don't do the things I say? I will show you what someone is like who comes to Me, hears My words, and acts on them: He is like a man building a house, who dug deep and laid the foundation on the rock. When the flood came, the river crashed against that house and couldn't shake it, because it was well built. But the one who hears and does not act is like a man who built a house on the ground without a foundation. The river crashed against it, and immediately it collapsed. And the destruction of that house was great! (Luke 6:46–49 HCSB)

There were no diggers and bulldozers in Bible times. If you wanted to dig a hole for a foundation you had to use a shovel. You had to put in some sustained effort, especially if you were digging all the way down to the bedrock. It took days to dig the hole because the work only progressed one shovelful at a time.

The point of the analogy is that it takes a series of small, consistent steps of obedience to build a solid spiritual foundation. You won't become a strong woman overnight. It's the consistency of applying God's Word on a daily basis over the long haul that will strengthen your core.

The woman who doesn't put in a consistent daily effort will remain spiritually weak. Her foundation will be as shallow as the Leaning Tower of Pisa's, history's most famous architectural mishap. This white marble bell tower, which workers began constructing in 1173, had such a shallow foundation that it was doomed from the start. Builders didn't bother to dig down deep.

At first, this careless omission didn't seem to matter. But when they began work on the second floor, the tower began to lean. In an effort to compensate for the tilt, they built the upper floors with one side taller than the other. The lean plus the uneven weight created even more problems. Several builders tried but failed to complete the increasingly bungled project.

The tower was finally completed in 1399, more than two hundred years after construction began. But because of all the architectural fudging, it was embarrassingly crooked. What's more, the foundation kept right on sinking. The lean just kept getting worse. Over the centuries there were a number of attempts to correct the tower, or at least to keep it from falling over. Most of these efforts failed, and some even worsened the tilt.

In the late 1990s Italy finally undertook a massive modern engineering operation to fix the foundation. The project cost more than $40 million and spanned more than a decade. It was only these efforts that kept the Leaning Tower of Pisa from catastrophic collapse.[3]

A woman who is not a doer of the Word will have a shallow foundation. She will not be strong; she will be spiritually weak. So many Christian women have not done what is necessary to build a strong foundation. They are learning but not applying Scripture. As a result, they experience significant struggles. And no matter how they try to fix things up, their lives just keep tipping over. Unless they put in some major repair work, they'll be in danger of catastrophic collapse.

Are you seeing significant progress in your spiritual life? When you look back, can you see how you've grown? Are you becoming kinder, more patient, less critical, less stressed, more disciplined, more joyful, and more loving? Or is your character increasingly leaning away from those upright attitudes? Is the tilt so bad that you're on the verge of a spiritual collapse?

A weak woman learns a lot but doesn't make a lot of progress. A strong woman digs down deep, applies what she learns, and experiences significant spiritual growth.

HYPOCRISY AND SELF-DECEPTION

Are you a religious fake? If you are honest, I think you'll be able to identify some, if not all, of these seven signs in yourself. At least I hope you do. I've certainly seen them in myself at various times.

I studied the marks of hypocrisy a few years ago when I was writing *Girls Gone Wise in a World Gone Wild*, a book that contrasts the prototypical wild woman and wise woman from the book of Proverbs.[4] But as I revisited the topic, I was convicted all over again.

It's *me* who is the hypocrite.

It's *me* who needs to check that I'm putting what I learn into practice.

It's *me* who needs to be careful not to teach anything that I am not first applying.

If I want to fight against the ever-encroaching sin of hypocrisy, my attitude needs to echo the words of that old traditional spiritual song, "It's me, it's me, O Lord, standin' in the need of prayer. . . . Not my brother, not my sister, but it's me, O Lord, standin' in the need of prayer."[5]

The most dangerous aspect of hypocrisy is the self-deception that accompanies it. The problem is not when we notice the hypocrisy in our lives; the problem is when we don't.

Paul warned his audience in Ephesus that "impostors will go on from bad to worse, deceiving and being deceived" (2 Timothy 3:13). James taught believers, "Do not merely listen to the word, and so deceive yourselves. Do what it says" (1:22 NIV).

It's easy to convince ourselves that we're applying the Word and getting it done, when, in fact, we're not. Especially if we're fortunate enough to be exposed to a lot of good information and teaching. It's easy to self-righteously point our fingers at the weak women in Ephesus for failing to put what they learned into practice. But we must keep the teaching of 1 John 1:8 in mind: "If we claim to be without sin, we deceive ourselves" (NIV).

Acting on truth is a lifelong quest.

So is the fight against hypocrisy and self-deception.

It takes a strong woman to avoid self-deception and keep pursuing godliness over the long haul.

PROOF IN THE PUDDING

James learned how to be a doer by watching the behavior of his big brother, Jesus. It's one thing to wear a mask and pretend to be good in front of your friends. It's a lot harder to maintain the charade at home, in front of your family. The people closest to you normally have the best perspective on whether your character is as good as you make it out to be.

As the half brother of Jesus, James had the unique opportunity to observe Jesus up close over many years. He saw how Jesus conducted himself at home and at work, how he acted when he was tired or asked to do things. He saw how he responded when things didn't go right or when his parents were grouchy or unfair. He witnessed Jesus' reaction when his siblings were mean and when their dad, Joseph, died.

James concluded that Jesus was authentic. He didn't just talk the talk; he walked the walk. He was the real deal.

It's interesting that it was James who wrote the book of the Bible that puts the most emphasis on practicing what we preach. Jesus' little brother probably finally came to faith because he saw Jesus doing just that.

James stressed that there had to be proof in the pudding. Faith can't just be an intellectual exercise. If it's real, it inevitably works its way into our hearts, changes our character, and impacts the way we live. If faith doesn't change us, then it likely isn't authentic. James indicated that it was possible to tell the difference between someone who applies truth and someone who doesn't.

Ridding yourselves of all moral filth and evil, humbly receive the implanted word, which is able to save you. But be doers of the word and not hearers only, deceiving yourselves. Because if anyone is a hearer of the word and not a doer, he is like a man looking at his own face in a mirror. For he looks at himself, goes away, and immediately forgets what kind of man he was. But the one who looks intently into the perfect law of freedom and perseveres in it, and is not a forgetful hearer but one who does good works—this person will be blessed in what he does. (James 1:21–25 HCSB)

Some of you are gardeners. You love to plant seeds and watch them grow into beautiful flowers or delicious herbs, fruits, and vegetables. You are fascinated by the miracle of transformation and growth you get to witness. I am so excited to see my herb garden flourishing with fragrant rosemary, basil, oregano, and thyme this summer, and my wooden tub of strawberry plants spilling over with blooms, buds, and ripening fruit. The growth delights me.

Or maybe the closest you've ever come to gardening was during a school project, when your science teacher made you plant a bean seed in some soil in a disposable cup. I remember racing to the window of my grade-school classroom to water the cup with my name on it. I always glanced down the row of Styrofoam cups to compare the growth of my bean seed with the others.

Some grew faster and taller, but they all sprouted and grew. Each seed turned into a green bean plant that would (if the science project lasted long enough) keep growing and produce more beans.

Because that's what bean seeds do.

James indicates that God is a gardener and the Word of God is a seed. God *implants* the seed in our hearts. Once implanted, it will grow and bear fruit.

If it doesn't, something's wrong.

James was probably thinking back to the parable Jesus told about the sower and seed and various types of soil (Matthew 13:1–23; Mark

4:1–20; Luke 8:4–15). Jesus underscored that genuine faith always produces results.

How do we tell if we're actually applying the Word? Jesus said that "every healthy tree bears good fruit" (Matthew 7:17), and the same can be said about the faithful. If we are truly following Jesus, we'll grow in "love, joy, peace, patience, kindness, goodness, faithfulness, gentleness, self-control" (Galatians 5:22–23), and all sorts of other ways that are "good and right and true" (Ephesians 5:9).

SIGNS THAT YOU'RE GETTING IT DONE

So far in this chapter we've covered the signs of a religious fake that Jesus identified in the Pharisees. Jesus' brother James indicated that there are also some clear signs that a person isn't a fake but is, in fact, authentic.

God encourages us to make an accurate assessment of our own spiritual condition (Romans 12:3). It's easy to get discouraged by the hypocrisy we see in our lives and forget about all the growth we've experienced.

If Satan can't get you on the left, he'll try to get you on the right.

In other words, sin generally creates two ditches along the path of truth. When we move away from the ditch on one side, we must be careful not to fall into the ditch on the other. On the one side, Satan would like to trap us in the sins of pride and hypocrisy. But he's just as happy to trap us in the opposite ditch of defeat and self-condemnation.

It is important to watch for signs of hypocrisy in our lives. That's undeniable. But it's just as important to celebrate signs of growth.

Here are some signs gleaned from the book of James (aka Just-Do-It James) that indicate you're growing and your faith is for real.

1. YOUR CHARACTER IS IMPROVING.

James uses the analogy of a mirror to illustrate the difference between a person who merely hears the Word and a person who hears and applies it. The Word of God is like a mirror. When we peer into it, we can see things about our spiritual condition that need to be corrected.

The *hearer* looks at her image in the mirror, then turns away and forgets what she saw. She doesn't do anything about it.

The *doer* carefully studies her image and then does something about what she sees.

Imagine that a woman was getting ready to meet a friend for dinner at a nice restaurant after a day of painting and renovating. The woman looks in a mirror and sees that she has a big streak of Benjamin Moore color-of-the-year paint smeared on her cheek; a glob of dried mustard at the corner of her mouth; ghoulish, smudged, black mascara under her eyes; and a snarl of tangled hair sticking straight out at a right angle from her head.

Do you think that she would take a quick glance at her reflection and walk away without doing anything about it? Do you think that she would just forget about her appearance and drive to the restaurant?

Of course not. The whole point of a mirror is to check if things look right.

If the woman saw that things were amiss, she'd get out a washcloth and a brush. She'd clean her face and untangle her hair. She'd fix her appearance. And she'd keep looking in the mirror to check on her progress until she was satisfied that she had gotten things right.

When a *doer* looks into the Word of God and sees that there's something about her spiritual appearance that needs fixing, she sets about to fix it with the help of the Holy Spirit, and she "perseveres" in this (1:25).

James said that doers work to rid themselves of "all moral filth and evil" (v. 21 HCSB). Throughout his book he identified several ways applying the Word impacts a person's character.

A woman who applies the Word will gain greater control over her tongue and her temper and become a better listener (v. 19). She'll complain less (5:9), criticize less (3:9), and be less envious and less selfish (1:14; Titus 3:3; 1 Corinthians 13:4). She'll be more patient (James 5:8), open to reason, honest, peaceable, forgiving, gentle (3:17), and steadfast in her faith (1:4).

Over time she will grow into a nicer, more self-controlled, stronger, godlier woman. The change will be obvious to her and those around her. I think of Karin, whose husband came to faith six months after she did, telling her, "I want to know this Jesus who is making you into a better you!"

Are you becoming a better you? When you examine your character, can you tell that there's been an improvement over time? Maybe the paint is washing off your cheek or your eyes don't look quite as ghoulish as they once looked. When you look at your spiritual reflection, can you see the ways you've changed? Can those closest to you tell that you are changing for the better?

Almost every fall, I ask the Lord for clarity on one or two things he'd like me to work on in my life. (Fall seems to be a much better season for reflection and goal-setting for me than the New Year.) My areas of focus in years past have been having more gratitude, being a better encourager, being a better steward of my body, learning to rest, working on spiritual habits, practicing more hospitality, reading more, and complaining less. This year I sense that the Lord wants me to focus on deepening some relationships.

Ridding ourselves of sin and growing in godliness is obviously a lifelong habit. When we look into the mirror of Scripture, we will always see something that requires attention. We will never fully arrive, not this side of heaven. But we should be able to look back and see a series of small *arrivals*, significant steps of progress and transformation "from one degree of glory to another" (2 Corinthians 3:18).

The direction and constancy of the change is just as meaningful as the size of the change. You may not have completely vanquished your volatile temper, for example, but you can be encouraged if you've made some slow, steady progress in getting it under control, and if you can see yourself becoming a more patient person.

Seeing change like this is one of the best ways to be assured that we are doers of the Word, not hearers only, and that we are growing in spiritual strength.

2. YOU'RE BECOMING MORE OTHERS-FOCUSED.

A second sign that you're a doer of the Word is that you are becoming more others-focused and less *me*-focused.

James wrote, "Religion that is pure and undefiled before God the Father is this: to visit orphans and widows in their affliction" (1:27). He asked, "What good is it, my brothers, if someone says he has faith but does not have works? . . . If a brother or sister is poorly clothed and lacking in daily food, and one of you says to them, 'Go in peace, be warmed and filled,' without giving them the things needed for the body, what good is that?" (2:14–16).

According to James, doers aren't just concerned about loving God. They are also concerned about fulfilling the second part of "the royal law according to the Scripture: 'You shall love your neighbor as yourself'" (v. 8).

Ephesus was an affluent city. The always-learning-but-never-able-to-arrive women were probably rich or at least financially comfortable. They obviously devoted significant time and resources to satisfy their own intellectual curiosity and desire to learn. But sadly it appears they weren't nearly as interested in using their time and resources to serve others, including the people they should have been the most devoted to—their own families.

Paul commanded them, "If any believing woman has relatives who are widows, let her care for them" (1 Timothy 5:16). He chided, "If anyone does not provide for his relatives, and especially for members of his household, he has denied the faith and is worse than an unbeliever" (v. 8).

Worse than an unbeliever? Wow. That's strong language. Apparently Paul was as passionate as James was about the need to put our faith into practical action.

In recent years there has been a renewed emphasis on social justice among Christians. We are encouraged to care for the weak and broken, for those who are poor, homeless, hungry, trafficked, orphaned, abused, or afflicted. These are worthy and highly critical causes and reflect God's care for the oppressed. But, interestingly, Scripture indicates that our concern and service should begin with those closest to us and then spread out from there.

Many Christians are concerned about the atrocities and needs in other parts of the world while they neglect the glaring needs that exist in their own biological and church families. Paul argued that our selfless service ought to start with the people who are closest to us. He insisted that women "first learn to show godliness to their own household" (v. 4). "If anyone does not provide for his relatives, and especially for members of his household, he has denied the faith" (v. 8).

Next, our concern and sacrificial service should extend to our Christian brothers and sisters. Finally, it should extend to people out in the community and around the world. Paul said, "As we have opportunity, let us do good to everyone, and especially to those who are of the household of faith" (Galatians 6:10).

The wealthy women in Ephesus may have been giving plenty of money to disaster relief efforts for the folks in Galatia. But they likely weren't putting the right kind of emphasis on loving and serving the needy women in their own circles.

We can learn from their omission.

The women around us have so many needs. Like the sister who has a colicky baby and would benefit from an evening out. Or the mother who has bad arthritic knees and could use some help weeding her garden. How about the grandma with Alzheimer's who sits lonely and forgotten in the nursing home? Don't forget the aunt whose son is in the hospital and whose family would love some home-cooked meals. Or the single mom from church who is hauling her kids around on the bus and wishes she had a car. The neighbor who threw out her back and needs someone to shovel her walks. The employee who is having a hard time making ends meet and could really use a bonus.

As you become a doer of the Word, you will see the needs of those around you far more clearly, and the Holy Spirit will stir your heart to address these needs in practical ways. You will become less selfish and more selfless in your service of others. This is another clear sign that you are putting your faith into action.

3. YOU'RE BECOMING HUMBLER.

James said that we need to receive the implanted Word with meekness in order to become a doer (1:21). Meekness means having a humble attitude. It's the opposite of the arrogant, conceited, know-it-all attitude that was prevalent among believers in Ephesus. They had a lot of knowledge, but it was the type that swells the head and shrinks the heart. They "wandered away into vain discussion, desiring to be teachers of the law," without fully understanding what they were confidently asserting (1 Timothy 1:6–7).

Paul said that the knowledge of these people had puffed them up. What's more, it had given them "an unhealthy craving for controversy and for quarrels about words, which produce envy, dissension, slander, evil suspicions, and constant friction" (6:4–5). These were the type of religious know-it-alls you might find nowadays on social media, posting vehement, ugly, condescending theological rants.

In Paul's assessment, the people in Ephesus who thought they knew so much actually knew nothing at all (vv. 3–5). "'Knowledge' puffs up," Paul told his friends in Corinth. "If anyone imagines that he knows something, he does not yet know as he ought to know"

(1 Corinthians 8:1–2). In other words, if you're puffed up with knowledge, then your knowledge is deficient. True wisdom is always clothed in humility. As the Sage said, "The fear of the LORD is what wisdom teaches, and humility comes before honor" (Proverbs 15:33 HCSB).

If you are a doer of the Word, you will grow humbler over time. The more truth you absorb, the more you'll become aware of how much you have yet to learn, how desperately you need to learn it, and how utterly dependent you are on the Holy Spirit to instruct you.

I flinch a bit when I look back at my twenty-five-year-old self. That young woman thought she knew a lot. She had far more swagger and was far more brash and dogmatic than the woman I am today. I can look back and see how my attitude has matured. My younger self was reliant on her own smarts; my older self is far more reliant on the Holy Spirit. Every day I am increasingly aware of my own fallibility and of my need for the Lord.

How can you tell if you are becoming humbler?

Generally speaking, you'll be more convinced of your need for God's guidance. You'll be less argumentative, less intent on being proved right, less condemning, less condescending, more willing to be corrected, and more careful to listen and consider what others are saying.

None of us can ever claim to have arrived when it comes to humility. But if we are doers of the Word, we will see this trait steadily increase.

4. YOU'RE BECOMING MORE SPIRITUALLY ATTENTIVE.

A fourth sign that you're a doer is that you pay close attention to what God asks and you don't forget about it. James said a doer "looks intently into the perfect law of freedom and perseveres in it, and is not a forgetful hearer" (1:25 HCSB). He contrasted this attentive, determined, sustained response to someone who is just a hearer.

A hearer *forgets*.

Forgetting to do something is not the same as willfully not doing it. Forgetfulness isn't an intentional neglect or omission. No one plans to be forgetful.

Nevertheless, forgetting is often an indication of how important something is to us. Our mindfulness and attentiveness usually match the value we place on an object. We tend to forget things that we regard as trivial.

Someone might forget to pick up the dry cleaning or forget to buy a new bottle of ketchup at the grocery store, for example. But chances are a bride won't forget her wedding. A mother won't forget to take her child to school or forget to pick him up afterward. An employee won't forget when payday is. When something is important to us, we generally don't forget.

A second reason we might forget is that our lives are bursting at the seams with other things that clamor for our attention. Often we focus our efforts on all sorts of activities that seem urgent and mistakenly think that they are also important. Most people spend large portions of time doing urgent, unimportant things but don't intentionally set aside time to do nonurgent, important things.

Spiritual growth usually falls into this latter category.

It's highly important. But because it doesn't constantly text, e-mail, call, ping, beep, buzz, or nag us, we often set it aside to attend to later and then inadvertently forget about it.

A doer is not indifferent, careless, or lackadaisical about applying what she learns. She places a high value on obedience and spiritual growth. Therefore, she makes a habit of putting what she learns into practice.

She doesn't put it off.

She doesn't forget.

It's a good thing that the Holy Spirit helps us with this, as Jesus explained, "The Helper, the Holy Spirit, whom the Father will send in my name, he will teach you all things and bring to your remembrance all that I have said to you" (John 14:26). We tend to forget, but the

Holy Spirit helps us remember. He is our counselor and teacher, our mentor and coach. He trains us to be more attentive. He reminds and helps us *just do it.*

You can be assured that you are a doer if you are becoming more sensitive to the promptings of God's Holy Spirit and more attentive to spiritual things.

5. YOU'RE BECOMING MORE COUNTERCULTURAL.

James said that authentic followers of Jesus keep themselves set apart, "unstained from the world" (1:27). People who follow Jesus will be out of step with popular culture. They will think and live differently than most of the people around them.

As Christians, our beliefs, values, and morals are not the same as the world's. Our priorities, motivations, and aspirations are different. We march to the beat of a different drum. Or at least we ought to.

James reprimanded his readers for being worldly. "You adulterous people! Do you not know that friendship with the world is enmity with God? Therefore whoever wishes to be a friend of the world makes himself an enemy of God" (4:4).

The Bible frequently compares the covenant relationship between God and his people to a marriage relationship (Isaiah 54:1–6; Jeremiah 2:2). The Old Testament prophets repeatedly accused Israel of being unfaithful to her husband (Isaiah 54:1–6; Jeremiah 3:7–10; Ezekiel 16:23–26; Hosea 3:1). New Testament writers extend the bridegroom-bride imagery to the covenant relationship between Jesus Christ and the church (2 Corinthians 11:1–2; Ephesians 5:22–23; Revelation 19:7; 21:9). James undoubtedly had this important imagery in mind when he scornfully branded his hearers, "You adulterous people!"

James was disgusted that his Christian readers were cheating on their husband (Jesus) and messing around with an illicit lover (the world). They were more in love with the world than they were with their bridegroom, Jesus. He expected their attraction to the world to taper off as they grew in their love for Christ. He anticipated that they would progressively turn away from worldly ways of thinking and acting as they grew in Christian obedience and maturity.

How about you? Can you identify ways you might be becoming less in step with culture?

- You've refused to read the latest best-selling shade of erotica that all your girlfriends are tittering about.
- You've unsubscribed from the raunchy TV channel that packages and sells deviant sex under the guise of historical fiction.
- You've decided you can't violate your conscience by participating in your colleague's bachelorette party.
- You've stopped going to the bar.
- You told the truth when your friend pressed you to tell a little white lie.
- You won't listen to gossip or an off-color joke.
- You've stopped cussing like a sailor, as all the other girls on your rugby team do.

If you are seeking to obey Christ, you will increasingly find yourself to be the odd man out. Like a salmon swimming upstream, you will find yourself surrounded by fewer and fewer swimmers who have the strength to go against the flow.

If this is the case, take heart. It's a clear sign that you're a doer of the Word.

As Malcolm Muggeridge once said, "Never forget . . . that only dead fish swim with the stream."[6]

6. YOU'RE BECOMING MORE COMMITTED TO DOING THE HARD THING.

Remember the story I told you about my son failing to fold the laundry I had piled on the coffee table? I explained that one of the marks of a religious fake is selective obedience. It should come as no surprise, then, that one of the marks of a doer is prompt and complete obedience. A doer is willing to do the hard thing—and to do it promptly.

James cited the example of Abraham, who obeyed when God asked him to sacrifice his son, Isaac (2:21–23). Isaac was the miracle baby God had promised to Abraham and Sarah. They waited a long time for God to fulfill that promise—twenty-five years to be exact. Sarah was more than ninety years old and Abraham was more than one hundred years old when Isaac was finally born.

Imagine Abraham's shock, years later, when God commanded him to sacrifice his son. By then Isaac had grown into a young man.[7] Abraham promptly carried out what God asked him to do. He took Isaac up the mountain, laid him on an altar, and was poised to plunge a knife into Isaac's heart when God intervened and stopped him.

Abraham obediently followed through on what God asked of him, even when it was hard and he didn't understand why (Genesis 22). The writer of Hebrews explained that Abraham's confidence in God's goodness and power was so strong that he obeyed without question. "He considered that God was able even to raise [Isaac] from the dead, from which, figuratively speaking, he did receive him back" (Hebrews 11:19).

Wow. That's quite the story. It's mind-blowing to me that Abraham was willing to go to that extent to obey the Lord. In the end, his great obedience was rewarded with a massive blessing from God. "Because you have done this and have not withheld your son, your only son, I will surely bless you, and I will surely multiply your offspring as the stars of heaven and as the sand that is on the seashore. And your offspring shall possess the gate of his enemies, and in your offspring shall all the nations of the earth be blessed, because you have obeyed my voice" (Genesis 22:16–18).

Obedience always results in God's blessing. Doers know this.

That's not to say that doing the right thing is easy. It can be hard. And it can cost. Sometimes it can cost a lot.

But doers are willing to do the hard thing, because they are confident in the goodness and power of God and in the blessing that he will bestow on those who trust and obey.

Becoming increasingly willing to do the right thing—even when it isn't easy—is another sign that you are truly a doer of the Word.

7. YOU'RE BECOMING A HAPPIER PERSON.

James said, "The one who looks into the perfect law, the law of liberty, and perseveres, being no hearer who forgets but a doer who acts, he will be blessed in his doing" (1:25). Do you know what the word *blessed* means? Blessed means happy . . . happiness of a deep, joyful, unshakable kind.

Obedience produces happiness.

James undoubtedly heard this truth from his brother Jesus, who guaranteed that "those who hear the word of God and keep it" will be blessed (Luke 11:28).

Have you ever stopped to consider that God is infinitely happy? He is "the blessed God" (1 Timothy 1:11) who rejoices in doing good for his people (Jeremiah 32:41). Jesus invites us to spend eternity with a happy, joyful God (Matthew 25:23). He lived and died so that his own joy—God's joy—might be in us and that our joy might be full (John 15:11; 17:13).

Happy are "those who hear the word of God and obey it!" (Luke 11:28 GNT).

If obedience produces happiness, then doers of the Word will be happy people.

It's inevitable.

The more you obey, the happier you will be.

That's not to say you won't experience sorrow or hardship. Jesus was "a man of sorrows and acquainted with grief" (Isaiah 53:3). But even sad and difficult things, when endured with obedience, will produce joy. It was "for the joy that was set before him" that Jesus obediently endured the cross (Hebrews 12:2).

This kind of happiness is not the same as the shallow, fleeting, worldly kind of happiness, which depends on circumstances and disappears in a poof at the first sign of trouble. No. The happiness of a doer is far deeper, richer, and stronger and lasts longer than that.

How happy are you? Have you ever considered that you can increase your level of happiness by increasing your obedience? One of the signs that you're a doer of the Word is that you are turning into a happier person.

GET IT DONE

Unlike my youngest son, I'm not much of a fitness guru. I don't know how to put together my own workout, nor am I self-motivated enough to follow through on a set program. If I go to a gym, I get overwhelmed by all the different types of equipment. After wandering around and doing some feeble pushes on a variety of machines, I give up, pack up my stuff, and go home.

A few years ago, however, I started attending a fitness center that provides a trainer. In hour-long sessions the trainer guides a small group of us through an ever-changing series of cardio and strength exercises. She tells us what we need to do and how long we need to do it, then she sets targets for the heart rate zone she wants us to reach.

Our heart rates, effort, and achievements are tracked on big, colorful monitors that are visible from every part of the room. The trainer monitors our progress, gives us personal coaching and feedback, corrects any problems she sees with our form, and continually shouts out praise and encouragement.

Having a trainer keeps things simple.

It really works for me. All I need to do is show up, strap on my heart rate monitor, and put in the effort to follow my trainer's instructions.

Obeying God is like that. It's not complicated. He has given us the gift of his indwelling Holy Spirit to be our ever-present coach and trainer. All we need to do is show up, put our focus on God, and follow his lead.

As I've stressed throughout this book, little choices compound over time. Small things done consistently produce big results. It's the consistency of the habit over time rather than the magnitude of each individual action that makes the difference.

It's not the random big push on that impressive machine at the gym that will make me strong. No. What it takes is a lot of small, repetitive efforts over time.

Don't get me wrong. Sometimes obedience does require a big push and lots of effort. But most of the time, it just happens over the course of each day in the hundreds of small decisions I constantly make.

Am I going to lose my temper?
Am I going to say something cruel?
Will I repeat the gossip?
Will I resort to complaining?
Am I going to compromise?
Am I going to be kind?
Will I offer forgiveness?
Will I return good for evil?
Am I going to obey what my coach tells me to do today?
Am I even listening to his voice?

Most of us know what it is that God is asking us to do. We also know that when he asks us to do something, he gives us the strength to get it done. Often I think the reason we are weak—always learning but never able to arrive—is that our hearts are like Captain Naaman, the commander of the Aramean army who wanted God to cure him of leprosy.

This proud and capable captain we read about in 2 Kings 5 balked when Elisha instructed him to submerse himself in the Jordan seven times. The request was just too ordinary and too simple.

Captain Naaman had shown up at Elisha's door with an impressive glittering entourage. Elisha didn't even bother to come out and personally meet him. He merely conveyed his instruction through a servant. The great captain was insulted.

Submersing himself in that muddy little stream Israel called a river was beneath him. It was an affront to his great power and dignity. He was a mighty man of valor. Had Elisha asked him to do something challenging and monumental, he would have certainly done it. But something so small and trivial and common? *Pfft!*

The captain turned his horse around and stormed off in a rage. Thankfully, a servant talked some sense into him and convinced him to give it a try. The act of obedience was so simple, and he had traveled all that way. Really, what did he have to lose?

Can you imagine what it must have felt like for the great captain to get off his high horse, strip off his impressive armor, wade into that cold, muddy water in his skivvies in front of all his underlings and servants, and humbly dip down under the surface seven times?

In the end, it was that small, repetitive, and seemingly trivial action that healed him.

Had Paul challenged those highly knowledgeable Ephesian women to do something great and illustrious for Jesus, I suspect they would have done it. That's what we want. We want to do something big and impressive for God. We'd be happy to do that. But obeying in the little things? *Pfft!* Who's got time for that? What difference would it even make?

It's important for us to understand that growth doesn't generally come through big and illustrious acts of obedience. It comes through all those small, daily, repetitive, and seemingly trivial ones. Flexing our spiritual muscles to do all the little things God asks of us is what will make us strong.

Do you want God to transform your weakness into strength? Then it's time to show up, listen to your trainer, and just do it!

HABIT 6

Stand Your Ground

Without solid doctrinal convictions you will
be weak and will slide away from the truth.

The young Israeli soldiers stood at attention in the
darkness, awaiting the final part of the ceremony that would complete
their basic training. The commander walked up and down the lines
of their formation, presenting each trainee with two essentials: a new
rifle and a personal copy of the Jewish Scriptures, the Tanakh, which
contains the Torah and the writings of the Hebrew prophets.

When all of them were armed with Scripture on the right and a
weapon on the left, the commander gave the order to light the fire.

The night sky lit up with a massive series of blazing Hebrew letters
that spelled out an unmistakable message. Loudly, and with conviction, the commander shouted out the burning phrase, "Masada will
not fall!"

In response, the soldiers raised their Tanakh and rifles toward the fiery anthem and pledged, "I swear! I swear! I swear!"

The old Israeli ex-paratrooper who was our tour guide paused for a moment after sharing this vivid memory. We were standing on Masada, the remains of King Herod's ancient desert fortress, where the last Jewish standoff against Roman invasion took place, and on the very spot where, as a newly minted military soldier, our guide had taken his vow.

According to the historian Josephus, the Romans' lengthy siege of Masada ended in the mass suicide of nearly a thousand Jews. They had sworn that they would never be servants to the Roman emperor nor to any god other than the Lord God himself.[1] They were willing to die for their convictions, as was our guide, Moshe, who had spent the better part of his life in the military.

"Masada hasn't fallen," Moshe quietly declared, "and it won't—not on my watch."

He meant this figuratively, of course, alluding to protecting the nation that he served and loved.

As we walked around the crumbled ruins, I pondered whether I would be willing to die for my convictions. The question became even more poignant as I came across the sole occupant of Masada, a Jewish scribe who daily cloistered himself into one of the few remaining structures to painstakingly copy the Torah by hand—line by line, letter by letter. I watched as he carefully and respectfully moved the nib of his feather quill across the parchment, transcribing the book of Leviticus. It was obvious he was convinced that the scroll he was duplicating was the holy Word of God.

Over the centuries multitudes of believers have been persecuted and martyred "for the testimony of Jesus and for the word of God" (Revelation 20:4). Do I have that kind of commitment? Do I have that kind of conviction? Am I willing to stake my life on the fact that Scripture is God's Word? Am I willing to stand for truth unflinchingly and uncompromisingly? Are you?

THE PURSUIT OF KNOWLEDGE

The weak women of Ephesus had no convictions—none they were willing to die for, in any case. Our text says they were "always learning and never able to arrive at a knowledge [Greek: *epignosis*] of the truth" (2 Timothy 3:7).

The Hebrew word for "knowledge" is *yada*, and it means more than just intellectual understanding. It also carries a sense of experience, emotion, and personal relationship. This contrasts with the Greek word for knowledge, *gnosis*, which is limited to intellectual knowledge. The New Testament writers, however, tended to use the word *gnosis* in a way that was more in line with the Hebrew connotation.[2]

At times, they chose to use the compound word *epignosis* instead, adding the prefix *epi-* to *gnosis*, to indicate that this broader definition was the one they had in mind. The prefix *epi-* indicates that something is deeper, fuller, or more intensive. *Epignosis* means full knowledge—intellectual, experiential, emotional, and intimately personal. This full knowledge of truth is what the weak women in Ephesus were unable to attain.

According to Paul the entire aim of learning was to reach a level of certainty and conviction about what one believes.

God "desires all people to be saved and to come to the knowledge of the truth" (1 Timothy 2:4). Paul argued that for this very reason he "was appointed a preacher and an apostle, . . . a teacher of the Gentiles in faith and truth" (v. 7). His whole mission as an apostle was "to build up the faith of God's elect and their knowledge of the truth that leads to godliness" (Titus 1:1 HCSB).

The Bible says we can *know* truth.

With certainty.

What's the point of learning if we can't be sure that what we're learning is true and reliable? And what's the point if we don't personally embrace the truth and live it out?

The women in Timothy's church were wishy-washy in their beliefs. They were eager to learn but never arrived at any firm conclusion. They were like "little children, tossed by the waves and blown around by every wind of teaching" (Ephesians 4:14 HCSB). Why were they like this? If we look at their culture, we can see what may have contributed to their being so fickle.

Broadly speaking, Greek philosophy was the dominant philosophy of the era and served as the backdrop for all the books of the New Testament.[3] One well-known characteristic of Greek culture was a love of learning. The Greeks were thinkers. Their philosophers thought of themselves as scientists and prided themselves in being seekers and lovers of wisdom.[4] Paul noted that this was a well-known cultural trait. "Greeks seek wisdom," he wrote in 1 Corinthians 1:22.

Since Ephesus was a Greek city, it placed an extremely high value on learning, knowledge, and the presentation and deliberation of ideas. Its library, speakers corners, public square, halls, and theater were explicitly designed to host discourses, orations, lectures, and debates. And it wasn't just men who were interested in attending. As I noted previously, upper-class women often invited teachers to give private lectures to groups of women who gathered in the parlors of their terraced homes. Debating new ideas was a normal part of life in Ephesus for both men and women.

Four philosophical schools flourished during that period: the Skeptics, Cynics, Epicureans, and Stoics. They all addressed the popular question of what would bring people happiness. The women in Ephesus were probably familiar with these trendy new ideas. A metropolitan center like Ephesus certainly would have been abuzz with them. The book of Acts notes that when Paul was in Athens, he debated with Epicurean and Stoic philosophers (17:18).

Skepticism refers to a questioning and doubtful state of mind. The word comes from the Greek verb *skeptomai*, which means to look carefully, to reflect. Skeptics believed that knowing truth was impossible, that there was no such thing as certainty in human knowledge. It was the viewpoint that Pontius Pilate espoused when he rhetorically asked Jesus, "What is truth?" (John 18:38). Skepticism is the opposite of dogmatism, the idea that a set of established beliefs exist and that they are not to be disputed, doubted, or diverged from.

Skeptics said: "There is no way to know for sure what's true. Don't you dare tell me that your way is right and my way is wrong. You believe what you want to believe. I'll believe what I want to believe. That's what will make us happy."

Cynics believed that happiness was gained by satisfying one's natural urges for food, sex, and shelter in the simplest manner, free from social constraints. The word *cynical* means to show contempt for accepted standards, to be bitterly or sneeringly distrustful and contemptuous. This is exactly what Cynics were like. They rejected religion, marriage, wealth, power, and fame. And they tried to live a life free from all possessions and property.

Cynics believed that the world belonged equally to everyone and that suffering was caused by all the worthless customs, conventions, and power structures in society. Cynics were particularly critical of any show of capitalistic greed or excess, which they viewed as a major cause of suffering. This philosophy is similar in many ways to the hippie movement of the 1960s or to the Occupy movement of more recent decades.

Cynics said: "I don't trust you. I resent that you have power and are trying to dictate my behavior. I do what I feel is right and am happy when I do what comes naturally."

Epicureans claimed that happiness came from being content and finding pleasure in the here and now. The modern use of the term *Epicurean* is associated with the saying "Eat, drink, and be merry." Epicurus, the philosopher behind this school of thought, encouraged his followers to enjoy their current state. He also promoted self sufficiency and self-determination. He said, "It is folly for a man to pray to the gods for that which he has the power to obtain by himself."[5]

Epicurus believed in equality and welcomed women and slaves into his school along with men.[6] He taught that as long as they followed the guiding principle "neither to harm nor be harmed," people should be free to pursue happiness in whatever way they wished.[7]

Epicureans said: "This life is all there is, so I'm going to make the most of it. As long as I don't harm anyone, I'm free to do whatever makes me happy." When Paul was in Ephesus, he wrote a letter to the church in Corinth, citing what appears to be an Epicurean saying: "Let us eat and drink, for tomorrow we die" (1 Corinthians 15:32).

Stoics believed that the path to happiness was to accept each moment as it presented itself. They aimed to be self-controlled and unmoved by emotion regardless of what life brought their way.[8] Stoics believed that you should take responsibility for things that you have control over but remain emotionless and unmoved about things that you don't have control over.

Stoics put the onus on the individual to suppress their emotions and take calm, measured action in response to the things that happen in his or her life. It was famously practiced by Cato, Seneca, and Marcus Aurelius.[9]

Stoics said: "I can't control what happens to me, but I can control how I respond to it. Happiness means being calm and in control of my emotions."

Nowadays most people are familiar with what it means to be skeptical, cynical, epicurean, and stoic. These words stem from the philosophical teachings that were promoted during New Testament times. Back then, however, the ideas were brand-new and represented the cutting edge of progressive thought.

A woman living in Ephesus would have heard talk on the street about all these new notions. She would have been exposed to the idea that it was impossible for her to know anything for sure (Skepticism), that she ought to distrust people in positions of power who tell her what to do (Cynicism), that as long as she did no harm, she should do whatever makes her happy (Epicureanism), and that she should focus on what she can control and avoid intense emotion (Stoicism).

Everyone is impacted by the culture they live in, and the women in Timothy's church were no exception. While their secular friends were busy learning and discussing philosophical ideas, these churchgoing women were busy learning and discussing religious ones. I suspect that they had absorbed at least some of the philosophy that was in vogue in secular society. And not just the philosophy but also the attitude toward learning that accompanied it.

People in Ephesus loved learning for the sake of learning. Just like the residents of Athens, who "spent their time on nothing else but telling or hearing something new" (Acts 17:21 HCSB).

They were far more interested in the process than in the result. The philosophers had convinced them that "never knowing" was actually a virtue.[10] As a result, people cared about learning more than they cared about truth. It's kind of like the guy who is more interested in the thrill of the chase than in finding true love and settling down. New ideas were the better ones, not because they were truer but simply because they were newer.

This popular attitude toward truth presented a challenge for the New Testament church. Christianity was dogmatic that Jesus Christ was *the* truth and that all alternatives were counterfeit (John 14:6). Christ himself repeatedly stressed that he was revealing eternal, unchanging truths from God. His favorite phrase "I tell you the truth" occurs more than eighty times in the Gospels.

Christians believe that "all Scripture is breathed out by God" (2 Timothy 3:16), that Scripture is the "word of truth" (2:15), and that Scripture is "the full expression of knowledge and truth" (Romans 2:20 HCSB).[11]

A major reason why the women in Timothy's church were never able to arrive at a knowledge of the truth was that they were fond of listening to other ideas. They wanted to hear something new. They had become bored with Timothy's teaching. *Same old, same old.* They had heard it all. They wanted something current and exciting.

So they explored other content, just like we do.

Here are some modern-day equivalents:

- reading a blockbuster by a controversial religious author who is questioning and challenging all the norms
- listening to podcasts of trendy religious commentators known for their funny, biting critiques
- updating our social media accounts to follow that feisty, provocative, forward-thinking megachurch pastor (who looks so good in skinny jeans)
- reading a "discernment website" run by self-appointed heresy-hunters to get the latest dirt about a stodgy, old theologian who is so *yesterday* and needs some help out the door
- following blogs of up-and-coming religious gurus who question the status quo and present new ways of looking at things

Paul warned, "The time is coming when people will not endure sound teaching, but having itching ears they will accumulate for themselves teachers to suit their own passions, and will turn away from listening to the truth and wander off into myths" (2 Timothy 4:3–4).

It was already a problem in Timothy's day. I believe it has become an even greater problem in ours. If we are to become strong women, we need to be grounded in the truth and be careful not to embrace trendy new ideas blindly.

THE PROBLEM OF FAKE KNOWLEDGE

A theological storm had hit the congregation in Ephesus. Certain people in Timothy's church were promoting ideas that were "falsely called 'knowledge'" (1 Timothy 6:20). In other words, they were broadcasting things that weren't true. And to Paul's dismay the women were lapping it up.

The false teachers were flooding the church with ideas that were politically correct but theologically wrong. They likely wanted to make Christianity more palatable so that it would line up better with their culture and make for a better sell. They were undoubtedly great speakers, and oh-so-engaging, popular, and provocative. If they lived in our day, they'd have fantastic blogs and innumerable social media followers. But the so-called knowledge they were promoting was kicking up a storm of controversy, a storm so bad that it was impacting the whole Christian community.

Paul described the problem extensively in his first and second letters to Timothy. These false teachers liked to teach and make "confident assertions" but had no idea what they were talking about (1 Timothy 1:7). Their ideas were progressive, to be sure. They taught a new and "different" doctrine (v. 3) that swerved from historic truth (2 Timothy 2:18) and didn't line up with the sound words of Jesus (1 Timothy 6:3) or with sound doctrine (1:10).

They did not use Scripture in the right way (v. 8). Their theology was based on "speculations" and complicated arguments (v. 4). It introduced a lot of urban myths and politically correct ideas into the mix (v. 4), along with what one translation calls "worldly fables" (4:7 NASB). Though their arguments sounded persuasive, their reasoning was inconsistent and filled with contradictions (6:20).

The creeps promoting this false knowledge were combative and argumentative (2 Timothy 2:14). They liked to be controversial (v. 23), "quarrel about words" (v. 14), and get into pointless discussions (1 Timothy 1:4). They engaged in a lot of "irreverent babble" (2 Timothy 2:16).

This indicates that they were disrespectful and condescending. And that they talked a lot . . . an awful lot. They always had an opinion to share and were never at a lack for words. Nowadays they would tweet and post vociferously.

Paul indicated that the ideas these teachers pushed caught on quickly and had spread through the Christian community "like gangrene" (v. 17).

Gangrene.

False information can be dangerous.

In 1938 Orson Welles took to the airwaves of CBS radio to perform a dramatized adaption of the science-fiction classic *War of the Worlds.* The faux newscast about a Martian invasion of Earth was supposed to be for laughs, but Welles had little idea of the havoc the broadcast would cause. Listeners believed that a real Martian invasion was under way.

Panic broke out across the country. Terrified citizens jammed highways seeking to escape the aliens. The Associated Press reported that one man in Pittsburgh returned home in the middle of the broadcast to find his wife holding a bottle of poison. She told him, "I'd rather die this way than like that."[12] While the media's reports of the mass hysteria were likely exaggerated, there were accounts of stampedes, suicides, and—once it became clear that the broadcast was fake—angered listeners threatening to shoot Welles.[13]

In more recent news an alarming announcement appeared on April 23, 2013, in the hacked Twitter account of the Associated Press: "Breaking: Two Explosions in the White House and Barack Obama Injured." The panic was immediate. The Dow Jones dropped 120 points within two minutes.[14]

Last year, the U.S. Food and Drug Administration recalled a blood pressure medication due to a potentially life-threating label mix-up. The label falsely identified the drug inside the bottle as a different medication.

False information isn't benign; it can be extremely dangerous, especially when it relates to matters of life and death.

The false doctrine making its way through the congregation in Ephesus ruined its hearers (2 Timothy 2:14) and upset the faith of some (v. 18). The people who embraced it ended up on a slippery theological slope that progressed "from bad to worse" (3:13), led to "more and more ungodliness" (2:16), and eventually totally shipwrecked their faith (1 Timothy 1:20; 4:1).

No one knows for certain exactly what false doctrines were being promoted in Ephesus. Scholars have made some educated guesses. Most think that the teachings were an early form of Gnosticism, which in Greek means having knowledge. This group of heretical teachings appears to have blended together ideas from Christianity, Greek philosophy, and several other religious traditions.[15] Regardless of the specifics, Paul maintained that this special knowledge wasn't really knowledge at all. He told Timothy that it was "falsely called 'knowledge'" and to avoid it (6:20).

What is most apparent about what was going on in Timothy's church is that it involved a lot of speculations, controversies, and chatter. The imposters loved to discuss and debate religion and philosophy.

There is a wonderful line from T. H. White's novel of King Arthur, *The Book of Merlyn*, when Queen Guinevere in her old age became the abbess of a convent. White described her as extremely adept at religion but devoid of devotion: "Guinevere never cared for God. She was a good theologian, but that was all."[16]

We could justifiably say the same thing about the people in Ephesus who had embraced false doctrine.

They talked a lot about religion, but that was all.

FAKE KNOWLEDGE IN LATER TIMES

The problem of false knowledge isn't confined to New Testament times. Paul warned that it would be an ongoing problem. In his first letter to Timothy, he said God expressly told him that "deceitful spirits and teachings of demons" would infiltrate the church "in later times" (1 Timothy 4:1).

In his second letter, right before he launched into the nineteen qualities of a creep, Paul reminded Timothy of this ever-present danger. "There will be terrible times in the last days" (3:1 NIV).

The Greek word translated *terrible* refers to something that is difficult. Some Greeks used the word to describe fierce animals or a violent sea. It referred to a dangerous situation that was tough to control and not easy to get through safely.[17]

This terrible situation would happen in the last days, which refers to the final segment of history between the time Jesus left and the time he will return. This time period is not our future but our own present age.[18]

According to Paul, we are living in terrible times. And the thing that makes these times so terrible is not the hardship and persecution that Christians face. Although that's tough, it's not the problem Paul had in mind. What he was referring to was the terrible problem of fake knowledge, the type that is full of "deceitful spirits and teachings of demons" (1 Timothy 4:1).

This deceptive fake knowledge comes from inside—not outside—the Christian community and it leads many astray.

Even though the church was established by God to be "a pillar and buttress of the truth" (3:15), Paul warned that there would always be people in the church who would "oppose the truth" (2 Timothy 3:8). He foresaw that this era would be replete with falsehood. It would be tough to contain and control. And God's people would not go unscathed. Many would be hurt and destroyed.

There have always been people who have promoted false knowledge. But now, the time of Christ's return is much nearer. We are in the latter part of the last days. And it seems to me that the problem is getting worse.

Much worse.

As I am sure you have noticed, there is enormous pressure for Christians to modernize the church's historic teaching on morality, marriage, and gender; the meaning of sin and salvation; the judgment, wrath, and mercy of God; and the reality of hell. And this push isn't primarily coming from outside the church. It's coming from within.

In recent times we've witnessed the rise of numerous popular Christian teachers who have departed from truth, taking scores of loyal fans with them.

These teachers started out by questioning whether the things the church traditionally called wrong might actually be right. They appealed to new and alternate interpretations of the Bible to support their ideas. They claimed that they were the actual defenders of truth, while those who clung to old ways were steeped in falsehood.

This is nothing new.

When it comes to the truth of God, there have always been "those who call evil good and good evil, who put darkness for light and light for darkness, who put bitter for sweet and sweet for bitter!" (Isaiah 5:20). What is new, however, is the sheer volume of Christian teachings we need to sift through. There are so many voices, and so much controversy and discussion, that it's hard to figure out who is telling the truth and who is not. It can get really confusing.

We already talked about the fact that the women in Ephesus were learnaholics who consumed a lot of information but didn't bother to apply it. In this chapter we're looking at a closely related problem. Not only did those women fail to apply what they learned, they also failed to discern whether the knowledge they were taking in was real.

They weren't strong enough to put the knowledge into practice, nor were they strong enough to figure out whether they even should.

The challenge for us today is even greater. If we want to be strong women, we need to develop some solid convictions about truth and firmly resist being swayed by falsehood.

We need discernment.

TRUE AND HEALTHY KNOWLEDGE

Paul's overriding concern in his two letters to Timothy was that believers would firmly embrace what is true and reject what is false. He used the Greek word for doctrine/teachings/instruction eleven times and discussed *sound* doctrine five times (1 Timothy 1:10; 4:6; 6:3; 2 Timothy 1:13; 4:3). He urged his young protégé, "Watch your life and doctrine closely" (1 Timothy 4:16 NIV).

For some of you *doctrine* is a slightly intimidating church word. But it simply means teachings. The dictionary defines doctrine as "any set of beliefs that are held and taught."[19] Doctrine is what you believe about God, the world, yourself, how to live, and what's right and wrong.

Everybody has a doctrine.

LGBT groups have a doctrine.
White supremacist groups have a doctrine.
Greenpeace has a doctrine.
Feminists have a doctrine.
CNN has a doctrine.
Fox has a doctrine.
The Netflix series you are watching has a doctrine.
Your local school has a doctrine.
Everyone who posts opinions on Facebook or Twitter has a doctrine.

Paul argued that, for Christians, not just any doctrine will do. We need to adhere to a specific doctrine: the set of beliefs revealed by God through Scripture, through Christ Jesus and his apostles. According to Paul, that's the only doctrine that qualifies as sound.

Certain people in the Ephesian church were pushing a mishmash of beliefs, which included Christian beliefs and a bunch of secular beliefs. Paul told Timothy to charge them "not to teach any different doctrine" (1 Timothy 1:3). He told his friend, Titus, who worked in Crete, to deal sternly with the people in his congregation who pushed false knowledge. "Rebuke them sharply, that they may be sound in the faith!" (Titus 1:13).

That word *sound* is important.

The Greek word is *hygianio*. It's the root from which we get our English word *hygiene*. To be *hygianio* means to be healthy, correct, or accurate, free from contaminants, infirmity, or disease.

When we think of the English word *sound*, we usually think of something that's reliable, dependable, and trustworthy, as in "sound advice." Or we think of something that's in good shape and not damaged, as in "she came back safe and sound." But we don't often consider that *sound* can also mean healthy and free from contaminants, which is the major idea behind the Greek word *hygianio*.

It's like the difference between a glass of pure spring water that comes from a sterile bottle versus a glass of water scooped from a sewage outlet. The spring water is sound. It's pure and clear. It's wholesome and free from contaminants. I would gladly drink it, knowing it'd be safe and healthy for me to do so.

The water from the sewage outlet is *unsound*. It's impure. It contains all sorts of unhealthy microorganisms and bacteria. Drinking the contaminated water is not a good idea. If I did, I would get extremely sick and might even die. The clear water is *sound*, and the contaminated water is *unsound*.

You get the idea.

When Paul told Timothy to make sure that people in his church embraced sound doctrine, he was not primarily concerned about theological accuracy. His concern was that they consumed what would bring them health. False knowledge contains dangerous contaminants. It makes people spiritually sick.

It can make you and me spiritually sick.

Several years ago I traveled to Asia to equip and encourage Christian women throughout the region. My husband met up with me afterward in Bangkok, Thailand, to do some sightseeing. We decided to take a canal tour on an old teak boat, navigated by an elderly Thai man. After taking us through the colorful floating market and past the glittering temples and garden condos, he took us into the slums of central Bangkok.

I could tell from the very start of the tour that the water in Bangkok was polluted and filthy. It was murky brown and littered with debris and smelled bad. There was no way I was going to dangle my fingers over the side of the boat! But what I saw when we got to the slums stunned me.

There, the canal was lined with shacks and rundown shanties. In many areas the water was thick with household waste and smelled putrid. To my utter shock and disbelief, I saw children playing in the polluted water. A few of the children in the area had visible physical deformities. Several had large white skin lesions on various parts of their bodies.

And then I saw her . . . an adorable girl about five years old with tussled raven-black hair, wearing a bathing suit, and playing beside her mama at the side of the canal.

The girl turned to look at me and gave me a shy grin. My heart broke as I noticed the massive festering skin lesion that covered nearly half of her face and neck.

When she started clambering over the rocks to jump in the canal, it was all I could do to stop from screaming at her, "No! Stop! Don't go in the water! It's making you sick!" and yelling at her mama, "Stop her! Don't let her play in this contaminated water! Can't you see how bad it is? Don't you know that it's hurting her?"

But I remained silent—I didn't speak their language. They wouldn't have understood. As we glided by, tears streamed down my face.

The little girl was content to play in contaminated water. She had no idea how unhealthy and dangerous it was. If I could have, I would have taught her and her mom about the dangers of water contamination and provided them with a clean water source.

That's exactly what the Lord does for us in Scripture. He provides a clean, healthy, uncontaminated source for us to drink from.

But sadly, many women don't believe that what they read in the Bible is good and healthy. In our culture we are constantly exposed to the message that the teaching we find in the Bible is not good for women, and is, in fact, harmful. Some argue, for example, that it is toxic to exhort women to cherish purity, modesty, a gentle and quiet demeanor, a heart for the home, femininity, and especially (horror of horrors) a submissive spirit. Many voices tell us that we need to add a scoop of feminist ideology to our doctrinal buckets.

I disagree.

I believe that the Bible is the Word of Truth, and that it is what will truly heal our pain and brokenness and set us free. Scripture—and Scripture alone, without other ideological contaminants—is the most wholesome, life-giving, and life-sustaining teaching that women can embrace. Nothing else has the power to save or the power to change.

The pure teaching of sound doctrine is what we must offer disciples of Christ if we want to see them become increasingly healthy and whole. Do you believe this too?

The teaching found in God's Word is sound. It's nourishing and life-giving. Paul told Timothy, "In pointing out these things to the brethren, you will be a good servant of Christ Jesus, constantly nourished on the words of the faith and of the sound doctrine which you have been following" (1 Timothy 4:6 NASB).

Sound doctrine nourishes people. It makes them healthy and strong.

The women in Ephesus were listening to all sorts of interesting religious ideas, but they weren't embracing the sound teaching of

Scripture. And as a result, they were sickly and weak, not healthy and strong. Healthy doctrine leads to healthy faith, healthy speech, healthy thinking, healthy attitudes, and healthy choices. I'm convinced that all the failures and flaws in our lives flow out of some sort of doctrinal error or deficiency.

Sound doctrine is the critical foundation for living a godly life. That's why Paul was so adamant that we hold fast to sound doctrine. One of the most important qualities of an overseer (a pastor or elder) is that "he must hold firm to the trustworthy word as taught, so that he may be able to give instruction in sound doctrine and also to rebuke those who contradict it" (Titus 1:9).

Holding firm to Scripture isn't just for people who hold official teaching positions in the church. It's for everyone. Including you.

The Lord wants you to develop some solid convictions. He doesn't want you to remain immature, being tossed about by "every wind of doctrine" or taken in "by human cunning, by craftiness," and by deceitful ideas that are falsely called knowledge (Ephesians 4:14).

No. He wants you to "stand firm and hold to" the teachings of God (2 Thessalonians 2:15). He wants you to watch your life and your doctrine carefully. He wants you to stand strong "with the belt of truth buckled around your waist" (Ephesians 6:14 NIV).

HOW CAN I KNOW IF IT'S REAL OR FAKE?

"*Sssneaky* snake!" That was my three-year-old granddaughter's takeaway from the Bible story her mama had read to her the previous evening.

I was amused by the way she dramatized it. She squinted her eyes, furrowed her eyebrows, and shook her finger at the *sssneaky* snake as the condemning accusation rolled off her tongue.

There was no way that snake would've tricked her into eating the forbidden fruit. Uh-uh! Her little three-year-old mind was wise to his game. She knew he was *sssneaky*.

I had to smile. If only it were that simple. It's not easy to spot deception. Especially in the church.

That's because false knowledge always contains a good portion of truth. It usually twists the truth only slightly. It adds a little, subtracts a little, or casts things in just a bit of a different light. The distinction is subtle and not readily apparent.

What's more, the people who push deception are usually also deceived by it. They are deluded, sincerely believing that what they are proposing is true (2 Thessalonians 2:11). Not only that, the deceiving spirit that has sunk its claws into their minds makes them crafty, cunning, and manipulative in the way they pitch the falsehood (Ephesians 4:14).

They seem friendly, charming, well-spoken, spiritually knowledge-able, and well-informed. They look like true believers, and even more devout than most. They don't come across as *sssneaky* snakes. But no wonder . . . as I said earlier, "Satan himself masquerades as an angel of light" (2 Corinthians 11:14 NIV).

Like a knockoff designer purse, false teachers appear genuine. And it's not easy to spot the illusion. If the falsehood were easy to spot, people wouldn't fall for it. That's what makes the deception so beguiling and dangerous.

So, how can you tell if what you are learning is real or fake? It's important that you discern the difference. You don't want to get spiritually sick, do you?

Here are some questions you can ask to test whether those religious ideas you're hearing are true or false:

1. IS IT BASED ON THE TRUTH OF SCRIPTURE?

Paul reminded Timothy that the Scriptures are "sacred writings," saying, "All Scripture is breathed out by God" (2 Timothy 3:15–16).

Peter explained, "Prophecy never had its origin in the human will, but prophets, though human, spoke from God as they were carried along by the Holy Spirit" (2 Peter 1:21 NIV).

Scripture has some powerful things to say about itself. It teaches us that the Word of the Lord is "right and true" (Psalm 33:4 NIV), "perfect" (19:7), and "flawless" (18:30 NIV). It says that Scripture is "the embodiment of knowledge and truth" (Romans 2:20) and that the entirety of God's Word is truth (Psalm 119:160 HCSB). Those are incredible claims!

We can trust the Bible.

Jesus constantly appealed to the authority and truth of Scripture. He quoted from it often, saying, "It is written . . ." On the road to Emmaus, Jesus used the Scriptures to convince two travelers that the death and resurrection of the Christ was necessary. "Beginning with Moses and all the Prophets, He interpreted for them the things concerning Himself in all the Scriptures" (Luke 24:27 HCSB).

It's interesting to me that he built his argument from Scripture when he could have just shown them the wounds in his hands and appealed to the miracle of his resurrection. But obviously it was important to Jesus that they grasped that he wasn't pushing a new or different truth. He was fulfilling Scripture. Jesus said, "For this purpose I was born and for this purpose I have come into the world—to bear witness to the truth. Everyone who is of the truth listens to my voice" (John 18:37).

Shortly before Jesus was delivered to be crucified, he prayed, "Sanctify them in the truth; your word is truth" (17:17). This verse is highly significant because Jesus did not use an adjective here. He did not say, "Your word is true." Rather, he used a noun. He said, "Your word is truth." God's Word is not only true but also the measure of truth.

"The difference is significant," says one theologian, "for this statement encourages us to think of the Bible not simply as being 'true' in the sense that it conforms to some higher standard of truth, but rather to think of the Bible as being itself the final standard of truth."[20]

The Bible is God's sacred, holy Word. It defines for us what is true and what is not. Therefore, we are to regard it "as the ultimate standard of truth, the reference point by which every other claim to truthfulness is to be measured."[21]

What then is true?

Truth is what God says, and we can read that in the Bible. If any teaching does not line up with the Bible, then it is false. If it is contrary to Scripture (Romans 16:17; 1 Timothy 1:3), you should reject it. It's not true.

The challenge is that Satan is good at subtly twisting what the Bible says. During Christ's temptation in the desert, Satan quoted Scripture to try to get Jesus to sin. So it should come as no surprise that imposters constantly misuse the Bible. They distort it (Galatians 1:7), twist it (Acts 20:30), tamper with it (2 Corinthians 4:2), add to it (Proverbs 30:5–6), misrepresent it (1 Timothy 4:2), mishandle it (1 Timothy 1:7–8), and fail to use it in a legitimate way (1:8).

There is a right way and a wrong way to handle the Word of God. Paul urged Timothy, "Do your best to present yourself to God as one approved, a worker who has no need to be ashamed, rightly handling the word of truth" (2 Timothy 2:15).

Paul refused "to practice cunning or to tamper with God's word" (2 Corinthians 4:2). There's a fascinating phrase he used in 1 Timothy 1:4 that summarizes how his approach toward Scripture differed from that of false teachers. He explained that false teachers were interested in "speculations rather than . . . stewardship."

What exactly does that mean? What's the difference between stewardship and speculation?

A *steward* is a person who manages another person's property. A *speculator* is someone who indulges in conjecture, who guesses at something or formulates an opinion or theory without sufficient evidence.

A person who views himself as a steward will approach the Bible with seriousness, deep respect, and great care. The Bible doesn't belong to him. It belongs to God. So he'll aim to be responsible and extremely conscientious with the way he handles it. Paul urged Timothy, "Guard the deposit entrusted to you" (1 Timothy 6:20). He wanted Timothy to be a faithful steward of God's Word.

A false teacher isn't worried about being a good steward. He's just interested in speculation, that is, in his own ideas. He wants to use the Bible in a way that supports and furthers his cause and his preconceived notions of what he thinks God should say. He may pretend that he believes that all Scripture is breathed out by God, but his cavalier attitude demonstrates that he really believes it belongs to him, to do with as he pleases.

The way people use the Bible (or fail to use it) is a strong indication as to whether they are pushing real or fake knowledge. If you pay careful attention, you can usually spot the difference.

2. DOES IT UPHOLD THE PERSON AND WORK OF JESUS CHRIST?

The second test that will help you determine whether something is true is what the teacher or his teaching says about the person and work of Jesus Christ.

Satan likes to throw people into confusion and "pervert the gospel of Christ" (Galatians 1:7 NIV). He wants to twist the truth about Jesus.

He doesn't mind if people believe in Jesus, as long as they don't believe everything the Bible says about Jesus. A benign, watered-down version is okay. If people want to believe that Jesus is merely a righteous teacher sent by God who loved people enough to die for them, that's all right. That suits Satan's purposes just fine.

As long as they don't believe that Jesus is the incarnate Son of God who was sent by God the Father to die a substitutionary death, atone for sin, and appease God's wrath. That Christ lived a sinless life and died for our sins according to the Scriptures, that he was buried, that he was raised on the third day according to the Scriptures. That Jesus is the way, the truth, and the life and that no one comes to the Father except through him. That Jesus is the *only* way to be forgiven of sin and reconciled to God. That he will one day return, leading the armies of heaven, and in righteousness will judge and make war. That people who believe in Christ will live eternally with him in heaven, while those who do not believe will incur judgment and face the eternal fires of hell.

These truths can sound grating to modern ears. But this is what the Bible teaches about Jesus.

The way you can tell if a teacher is false is if he or she proclaims *another Jesus* than the one portrayed in Scripture. Paul wrote,

> I am afraid that as the serpent deceived Eve by his cunning, your thoughts will be led astray from a sincere and pure devotion to Christ. For if someone comes and proclaims *another Jesus* than the one we proclaimed, or if you receive a *different spirit* from the one you received, or if you accept a *different gospel* from the one you accepted, you put up with it readily enough. (2 Corinthians 11:3–4, emphasis added)

Jude said this about false teachers: "Certain people have crept in unnoticed, . . . ungodly people, who pervert the grace of our God into sensuality and deny our only Master and Lord, Jesus Christ" (Jude v. 4).

A feeble view of Jesus leads to a feeble commitment.

False teachers often uphold Jesus as a great example to love and emulate, but most of the time they do not uphold him as the *only* Master and Lord who is to be honored and obeyed in everything (1 Corinthians 12:3; 1 John 2:20–23; 2 John vv. 7–11).

3. DOES IT HAVE A PROVEN TRACK RECORD?

Truth has a proven track record. That's why Jesus was so careful to establish that his teachings were in line with what God's prophets said. He was not going against the history of truth. "Do not think that I have come to abolish the Law or the Prophets," Jesus stressed. "I have not come to abolish them but to fulfill them" (Matthew 5:17).

The apostles assured the fledgling believers that Jesus' teachings aligned with the truth that the Jewish prophets had so carefully guarded and passed down through the centuries. The apostles had tested Christ's ideas. They'd compared them with Scripture and with the beliefs of earlier generations and concluded that they were true.

How can you know if a belief is true? Examine its track record. That will help you decide.

Remember, Paul warned that false teachers would "go on from bad to worse" (2 Timothy 3:13). The word translated as "go on" means to advance, progress, or proceed. "But as for you," he encouraged Timothy, "continue in what you have learned and have firmly believed, knowing from whom you learned it and how from childhood you have been acquainted with the sacred writings" (vv. 14–15).

Did you notice the difference? False teachers *go on*. Truth-teachers *continue in*.

Timothy had a strong spiritual heritage. The beliefs he held had been passed down to him from his Jewish grandmother, Lois, and his mother, Eunice (2 Timothy 1:5). He had been acquainted with the sacred writings since he was a child. What's more, Paul had mentored Timothy and reminded him, "You, however, have followed my teaching, my conduct, my aim in life, my faith, my patience, my love, my steadfastness" (3:10).

The point Paul was making is that Timothy's beliefs were not new or untested. He could be confident and continue in those beliefs because other trustworthy people had tested them and found them to be true.

Scripture warns, "Everyone who goes on ahead and does not abide in the teaching of Christ, does not have God. Whoever abides in the teaching has both the Father and the Son. If anyone comes to you and does not bring this teaching, do not receive him into your house or give him any greeting" (2 John vv. 9–10).

People who embrace false doctrine do not *continue in* the truth. They *go on* or *proceed beyond* what the church has upheld as true. Paul told Timothy to avoid this error.

"Continue in truth, Timothy. Don't move on to other beliefs. Hold firmly to the beliefs that have a proven track record. You learned these things from your grandmother and mother and me. You know that we are trustworthy. Don't get enamored with new ideas and be led astray by them."

This test for truth is not infallible. In the Reformation, for example, a major corrective to the church's doctrine was necessary, and Martin Luther led the way by pointing back to the unchanging source of truth that is even older than the Catholic church: Scripture. It's important to hold up every teaching to Scripture. But as we just discussed, it is also a good general rule to pay attention to what has been historically tried and tested. If you hear any new interpretation of Scripture that has not been historically tried and tested, you ought to be highly suspicious of it. Especially if that teaching mirrors a cultural trend, and especially if people you know to be trustworthy are holding firm to time-tested beliefs and not buying in.

4. ARE THE PEOPLE WHO EMBRACE IT INCREASING IN GODLINESS?

Another test that can help you determine if a belief is true is observing the character of the people who embrace it. "You will recognize them by their fruits" (Matthew 7:16).

Sound doctrine "promotes godliness" (1 Timothy 6:3 HCSB). It is "profitable for teaching, for reproof, for correction, and for training in righteousness" (2 Timothy 3:16–17). It doesn't just tickle our ears, as fake knowledge does (4:3). It challenges and changes us.

True knowledge produces righteousness, faith, steadfastness, love, gentleness, godliness, patience, and kindness (Galatians 5:22; 1 Timothy 6:11). The character growth it produces is undeniable. The progress can be seen by all (4:15). Don't expect to see perfection. But you definitely should notice some positive change.

A person who embraces true knowledge becomes godlier. But false knowledge leads people "into more and more ungodliness" (2 Timothy 2:16).

False knowledge produces arrogance, envy, greed, dissension, slander, evil suspicions, constant friction, and disrespect (1 Timothy 6:3–6, 20; 2 Peter 2:3). It has the appearance of godliness but doesn't have its power (2 Timothy 3:5). It's of no value in helping people curb self-indulgence (Colossians 2:20–23). On the contrary, it gives people permission to sin. Those who embrace it become increasingly sensual and compromise their moral standards (2 Peter 2:2, 18–19). False knowledge gives people liberty to do things the Bible says they shouldn't do.

False teachers "disguise themselves as servants of righteousness" (2 Corinthians 11:15). They pretend to have godly character so they can fool you. But as you grow in maturity and discernment, you'll get better at sensing the difference between someone who merely seems godly and someone who actually is.

5. IS IT PRODUCING MORE OR LESS CERTAINTY?

A truth-teacher encourages you to ask questions about your faith; a pretender encourages you to question your faith. The former leads you into deeper certainty while the latter leads you into deeper uncertainty.

It's not always easy to spot the difference. Not at first, anyhow. After all, both involve inquiry. The truth-teacher wants you to know that asking questions will lead to greater understanding; the pretender wants you to wonder whether understanding is even possible. Pretenders would have you believe that reaching certainty is narrow-minded and legalistic and that uncertainty equals genuine belief. The only thing they are sure of is that you can't be sure of anything.

But that's not the message of the Bible.

Paul assured Timothy that God's foundation was firm (2 Timothy 2:19). Pretenders don't have faith in this firm foundation. They don't trust it. They don't abide in it (2 John vv. 9–10). "As for you," Paul told Timothy, "continue in what you have learned and have firmly believed" (2 Timothy 3:14).

Faith involves firm belief. It involves certainty and confidence. "To have faith is to be sure of the things we hope for, to be certain of the things we cannot see" (Hebrews 11:1 GNT). Truth gives us "an anchor for the soul, firm and secure" (6:19 NIV).

A woman who embraces truth grows more certain about her convictions, while she who doubts "is like a wave of the sea that is driven and tossed by the wind" (James 1:6).

Paul wanted the women in Ephesus to grow up and reach a firm faith and knowledge of truth. When they attained that level of maturity, they'd "no longer be children, tossed to and fro by the waves and carried about by every wind of doctrine, by human cunning, by craftiness in deceitful schemes" (Ephesians 4:14). They would have firm convictions and be confident in what they believed.

Do you have firm convictions?

Are you confident in what you believe?

Confidence in what we believe is not cockiness about our own intellectual capacity. It doesn't mean that we never have questions or doubts. Confidence is accompanied by a deep humility that recognizes how prone we are to deception and how desperately we need the Holy Spirit to continue to teach, reprove, correct, and train us in the truth of Scripture. Our confidence is based on a deep certainty that God is faithful to teach us what is true. If we seek we will find. God wants us to know with certainty. He wants us to have convictions so strong that we are willing to die for them.

I often joke that I regret getting older because I knew so much more when I was young. It's a playful poke at the arrogance that often accompanies youth. As I have learned more about God's Word, I have become more aware of how much I have yet to learn. On the one hand, I have so many more questions. On the other hand, I have so much more certainty.

I *know* that I *know*.

I know that I know Jesus. I know that I know truth. The Spirit of truth guides me "into all the truth" (John 16:13). I know that the sacred, holy Bible is the Word of Truth. Of this I am certain. And in my better moments, this is a conviction that I am willing to die for.

Truth produces unshakable certainty in the gospel and in the trustworthiness of God's Word. "We have come to share in Christ, if indeed we hold our original confidence firm to the end" (Hebrews 3:14).

Firm. To the end.

6. DOES IT DEMONSTRATE THE RIGHT APPROACH?

The sixth test you can use to figure out whether someone is a truth-teller or promoting false knowledge is analyzing their approach. A truth-teller will have a genuine love for God's church and will patiently, kindly, and clearly explain their position from Scripture.

Paul expected truth-tellers to behave a certain way. "The Lord's servant must not be quarrelsome but kind to everyone, able to teach, patiently enduring evil, correcting his opponents with gentleness" (2 Timothy 2:24–25). He instructed them to "preach the word; be ready in season and out of season; reprove, rebuke, and exhort, with complete patience and teaching" (4:2).

He held himself to the same standard. "We have renounced disgraceful, underhanded ways. We refuse to practice cunning or to tamper with God's word, but by the open statement of the truth we would commend ourselves to everyone's conscience in the sight of God" (2 Corinthians 4:2).

Jesus warned that people who promote falsehood would come to us as wolves in sheep's clothing (Matthew 7:15). They're extremely difficult to identify and expose. Especially because they have a habit of using smooth and slippery speech (Romans 16:18). "From among your own selves will arise men speaking twisted things, to draw away the disciples after them" (Acts 20:30).

It's exceedingly difficult to engage in a logical, reasoned discussion with people like this. They twist words, twist what you are saying, and twist Scripture (2 Peter 3:16). They are quarrelsome and thrive on controversy (1 Timothy 6:4). The more they talk, the more twisted and convoluted and confusing their argument becomes. On the surface, their words sound plausible and persuasive (Colossians 2:4), but "they deceive the hearts of the naive" (Romans 16:18).

These wolves in sheep's clothing are highly adept at "human cunning with cleverness in the techniques of deceit" (Ephesians 4:14 HCSB). They come across as sweet-as-pie while stabbing daggers in the backs of the faithful. They delight in the downfall of others.

Paul chided believers in Corinth for putting up with people like this. "You even put up with anyone who enslaves you or exploits you or takes advantage of you or puts on airs or slaps you in the face" (2 Corinthians 11:20 NIV).

Obviously his friends didn't think they were being enslaved, exploited, or pushed around. Paul's point was that they were blind to what was really going on. The celebrity teachers were pulling the wool over their eyes.

Here are some clues that may indicate that someone is pushing false knowledge:

- She rarely reasons from Scripture, and when she does, she selectively twists the verse out of context.
- She misrepresents the ideas of the people she criticizes.
- She slanders her opponents. She attacks the person instead of engaging with the idea. She uses straw men, syllogism, and all kinds of other logical fallacies in her reasoning.

- She sets herself up as the persecuted one. She accuses those who tell the truth of being harsh, unkind, and mean-spirited (and narrow-minded and dogmatic too, of course).
- She claims to love the church but demonstrates a negative and critical attitude toward it.
- She has an insubordinate, disrespectful, and snarky attitude toward spiritual authority.
- She exhibits a false humility and love. There is an undercurrent of nastiness and malevolence in her spirit toward those who disagree with her. She sees the speck in other people's eyes but doesn't notice the log in her own.
- She is more concerned about growing her own kingdom than growing God's.

James warned, "Not many of you should become teachers, my brothers, for you know that we who teach will be judged with greater strictness" (James 3:1).

That's sobering.

I tremble to think of the times I have been nasty or quarrelsome or tried to win arguments through human cunning instead of simply presenting an "open statement of the truth" (2 Corinthians 4:2) and trusting the Holy Spirit to confirm it in the hearts of those who love God. I don't think any truth-teller can claim to be above reproach. We all fail to meet the standard perfectly.

Nevertheless, a person's overall approach is one of the tests that indicates whether that person is the Lord's servant or simply pushing her own agenda.

7. DOES IT HAVE STAYING POWER?

Have you ever heard the saying, "It will all come out in the wash"? It means that things will become known or apparent in the course of time. False teachers may be highly popular for a season, but over time they will inevitably depart from the faith. Paul reminded Timothy that this was the case with two well-known fraudsters. Though they fooled a lot of people, their true nature was eventually exposed.

Timothy could be sure that the people pushing false knowledge in his congregation would also one day be exposed as imposters. Their falsehood would become plain and apparent to all. Paul told him, "Just as Jannes and Jambres opposed Moses, so these men also oppose the truth, men corrupted in mind and disqualified regarding the faith. But they will not get very far, for their folly will be plain to all, as was that of those two men" (2 Timothy 3:8–9).

Scripture warns that people who embrace false teaching will eventually "depart from the faith" (1 Timothy 4:1). They will not hold their original confidence in Jesus "firm to the end" (Hebrews 3:14). Instead of *continuing on* in the truth of the Word of God, they will *move on* to other beliefs.

Falsehood is progressive in nature. It doesn't have staying power. It leads a person farther and farther away from the beliefs they once held. Sometimes that happens slowly and sometimes that happens quickly. This was the case with Paul's friends in Galatia. "I am astonished that you are so quickly deserting him who called you in the grace of Christ and are turning to a different gospel" (Galatians 1:6). Regardless of whether it happens quickly or slowly, sooner or later, people who embrace false doctrine will turn to a different gospel. And it will be apparent to those who hold firm to the Word of God that they have abandoned ship.

It all comes out in the wash.

BE BRAVE FOR TRUTH

Paul told his friends in Corinth to "be alert, stand firm in the faith, be brave, be strong" (1 Corinthians 16:13 GNT). This was a call to stand for truth.

How can you be brave and stand for truth?

By not believing everything you hear from so-called Christian teachers, authors, bloggers or social media friends, or even from your friends.

By making a habit of testing what they have to say. And by holding firm to the Word of God and saying no to doctrinal creeps.

This paraphrase of Paul's words to the Galatians puts it so well:

> I can't believe your fickleness—how easily you have turned traitor to him who called you by the grace of Christ by embracing a variant message! It is not a minor variation, you know; it is completely other, an alien message, a no-message, a lie about God. Those who are provoking this agitation among you are turning the Message of Christ on its head. Let me be blunt: If one of us—even if an angel from heaven!—were to preach something other than what we preached originally, let him be cursed. I said it once; I'll say it again: If anyone, regardless of reputation or credentials, preaches something other than what you received originally, let him be cursed. (Galatians 1:6–9 THE MESSAGE)

Paul welcomed his friends to test and check that what he was saying was true. He was thrilled when the Bereans "received the word with all eagerness, examining the Scriptures daily to see if these things were so" (Acts 17:11).

So test what you hear. Make a habit of this.

Test everything. Including what you hear from me. If it is true, it will stand up to scrutiny.

"Beloved, do not believe every spirit, but test the spirits to see whether they are from God, for many false prophets have gone out into the world" (1 John 4:1). "Test everything; hold fast what is good" (1 Thessalonians 5:21).

The church needs more strong women—women who hold fast to

sound doctrine and teach what accords with sound doctrine, regardless of how politically incorrect and unpopular that might be.

Women with soft hearts, sharp minds, and backbones of steel. Women who speak truth with a spirit of grace and love and humility. Who have a rock-solid conviction that the Bible is true. Who stand on guard, holding Scripture on the right and the sword of the Spirit on the left.

Strong women who pledge themselves to defend truth to their dying breath.

"Masada will not fall. Not on my watch. I swear. I swear. I swear."

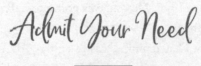

True strength is a paradox, because it
occurs when you reject the wrong kind of
strong and embrace the right kind of weak.

I was once in a fight. And it wasn't just a mild skirmish. It was an all-out, fist-swinging, shin-kicking, arm-twisting, knockdown, WWE-type brawl.

The altercation was on a Thursday night. I know that because the rhythm of life in my childhood home followed a predictable pattern: Friday night was youth group. Saturday was chores, baths, hot dogs for supper. Sunday was church, company, more church. Monday night was deacon's meeting. Tuesday night was boys' and girls' clubs. Wednesday night was prayer meeting. On Thursday nights, my parents left me and my five brothers at home and went out grocery shopping. Or so they said.

That Thursday I was assigned to do the dishes with my older brother, Gordon. (No electric dishwasher in our house.) He washed. I dried. We started squabbling about something, as middle-school siblings will do. I can't remember what we were bickering about. But I do remember the wisecrack that roused my furor and pushed me over the edge: "What do you know? You're just a weak, sissy girl!" he sneered.

That was it. I threw down the dish towel, raised up my fists, and challenged him to a fight. No one was going to call me a weak girl! It was the ultimate insult.

I hated dresses. I hated pink. I wasn't a girly-girl. Anything remotely feminine made me want to hurl. And I certainly wasn't weak! I could climb a tree. I could balance on the train track all the way across the trestle over the ravine. I could hit a baseball. I could swing a hammer.

Anything the boys could do, I could do better.

At first my brother ignored the gauntlet I'd thrown down. Being three years older, he was confident he'd wallop me. But when I didn't relent and goaded him with a few shoves, he finally accepted my proposition.

Since the kitchen was too small, we went into the living room and pushed all the furniture to the side. The smug, amused look on his face infuriated me. I was going to school him. No one was going to get away with calling me weak. Hadn't he been convinced by the Girl Power anthem of my day? I certainly had. "I am strong! I am invincible! I am woman!"[1]

I will tell you how that turned out later, in the conclusion of this book.

WRONG KIND OF STRONG

No woman likes to be called weak, and especially not by a man. I suspect that the women in Timothy's congregation were miffed that Paul had called them weak. They likely didn't view themselves that way. As

I noted earlier, evidence suggests that many of them were successful, independent, and self-sufficient. By contemporary Roman standards (and probably by our standards too) they would have been extolled as models of strength.

But these women weren't nearly as strong and capable as they thought. On the contrary, their habits indicated that they were small, under-developed, and stunted versions of the women they could have been.

They were just wee little women.

The reason they were weak was that they had embraced the wrong kind of strong. As we have been discussing throughout this book, they had accepted the Greco-Roman ideal rather than God's ideal of what it means to be a truly strong woman.

Our society also promotes an ideal for women.

For more than half a century, we've been inundated with femi-nist ideology. Billions and billions of dollars have been invested into promoting this view of female equality and empowerment. From the time a girl is born, she hears messages about how incredibly amazing and capable and strong she is simply by virtue of her sex.

You only need to peruse a girl's clothing section to see endless silkscreened Girl Power slogans like:

Girls Rule
Girls Run the World
I am pretty . . . pretty smart. Pretty tough. Pretty awesome.
Pretty fierce.
Strong. Brave. Bold.
Girl PWR
I'm not strong for a girl—I'm just strong.
Strong Girls Rule

These aren't playful, benign messages. They promote a specific ideology. (Ever see a T-shirt with the slogan Strong Boys Rule?) Like an IV drip into the vein of an unconscious patient, contemporary culture has pumped ideas about what it means to be a strong woman into our subconscious minds. By the time a girl reaches womanhood, she knows that it's vitally important for her to be strong, and she also has some deeply rooted opinions about what that means (though she generally has little awareness of where she even got those notions).

Countless websites, blogs, and news articles tell us how to claim and assert our Girl Power. In sum, here's what they tout as the top ten characteristics of a strong woman.

1. She always believes in herself.
2. She makes her own rules.
3. She puts herself first.
4. She doesn't depend on anybody else.
5. She does what she wants, regardless of what others think.
6. She loves herself no matter what.
7. She takes charge. She is the boss of her body, sexuality, finances, relationships (especially with men), and career (which ought to be a high-powered one; her aim is to be CEO).
8. She speaks her mind and never shrinks back.
9. She is brave and bold. She can do anything.
10. She fights patriarchy and helps other women become strong.

What do you think of when you hear the phrase "strong woman"? Based on current cultural messages, here are the adjectives I came up with:

confident
competent
self-sufficient
self-reliant

self-directed
fearless
independent
opinionated

decisive

assertive

in charge

insistent

tough

ambitious

relentless

powerful

fierce

bold

aggressive

unstoppable

unyielding

smart

resilient

Would you agree that this is the definition of woman's strength our culture admires and promotes?

If I were true to Hollywood, I might include that she bends like a pretzel and is a ninja warrior able to singlehandedly thrash and humiliate several skilled male assassins at a time. (Oh, and being sexy, rich, famous, and a powerful professional doesn't hurt either.)

Compare that with the popular conception of the traits of a weak woman:

inadequate

insecure

uncertain

indecisive

powerless

insubstantial

incapable

unable

spineless

quiet

meek

fearful

fragile

vulnerable

forceless

tender

delicate

submissive

docile

yielding

compliant

modest

soft

feeble

reserved

wimpy

Which type of woman would you rather be?

You're probably thinking, *Do you even need to ask? The strong woman, Captain Obvious.*

When I was younger I'd have thrown down the towel to anyone who suggested I possessed any traits on that weak list.

But wait a minute. Let's take another look. The lists certainly reflect what our culture promotes, but do they line up with what the Bible promotes? Can you spot any traits on the *weak* list that might in fact make a woman strong? And any traits on the *strong* list that might in fact make her weak?

Might not softness, compliance, tenderness, and quietness be positive traits? And might not self-reliance, aggressiveness, and an unyielding spirit be negative ones?

Who is the stronger woman, the woman who clings to her own self-interest or the one who sacrificially sets it aside?

My point here is not to suggest that women should aspire to be weak. On the contrary. The aim of this book is help you overcome weakness to become strong . . . but strong in the right kind of way. The Bible teaches that a woman with a gentle, quiet spirit is a strong woman. The problem is, culture feeds us a deceptive vision of what it means to be strong. And it also feeds us a deceptive vision of what it means to be a woman.

Now, please don't accuse me of promoting a fluffy, frilly, girly-girl 1950s ideal. (Did I tell you I once got in a fight, can swing a hammer, and can climb a tree? Okay, maybe not the tree-climbing part so much anymore, but I did just singlehandedly renovate my entire kitchen, including the plumbing and electrical.) I'm not into stereotypes. And the Bible isn't either. However, it does teach that, although male and female are created in the image of God equally, the sexes are different, and not just in our plumbing systems. We are *ontologically* different, which means we are uniquely male or female in the essence of our beings.

Throughout this book I've reminded you that Satan is the Über-creep who is a master at deception. (*Sssneaky* snake!) I've also reminded you that his modus operandi is to twist the truth ever so slightly. His lies always contain enough truth to make his arguments sound legitimate and believable. Otherwise we wouldn't fall for them.

When I read through our culture's top ten characteristics of a strong woman, I can see that each point contains a partial truth. For example, the first characteristic is "a strong woman always believes in herself."

It's undeniable that the Lord wants us to be confident and not to cower in fear or timidity. He has said, "Your strength will lie in quiet confidence" (Isaiah 30:15 HCSB).

Does God want his girls to be confident? You bet he does! But here's the twist. The world encourages a woman to be confident in herself. According to the Bible, a woman who is merely self-confident is a weak woman. She needs to put her confidence in the Lord in order to be truly strong (Proverbs 3:26; 14:26).

And therein lies the problem. The world encourages you to be strong on your own terms, in your own way, and in your own power.

One HuffPost writer maintained, "Being a strong woman means being unapologetically, fiercely, and wholeheartedly *you*."[2]

Being strong means you do you. You love yourself and put yourself first. You are your own god.

The Bible has a radically different perspective.

Jesus said, "If anyone wants to come with Me, he must deny himself, take up his cross daily, and follow Me" (Luke 9:23 HCSB). Unfortunately, the way the world encourages us to be strong subtly nudges us to adopt the characteristics of a creep: to be a lover of self, lover of money, self-promoting, disdainful, critical, cynical, resentful, defiant, not a lover of good, headstrong, self-important, a lover of pleasure rather than a lover of God (2 Timothy 3:2–4).

Remember, when Paul disparagingly called that group of women in Ephesus weak, his point was that they ought not to have been. He wanted them to be strong women. The irony is they likely thought they were. Unfortunately, their concept of what truly made a woman strong was not in line with the Lord's.

They had embraced the wrong kind of strong.

It comes as no surprise, really, that our culture encourages us to make the same mistake.

THE RIGHT KIND OF STRONG

The world tells us to rely on our own strength and to find strength within. But the Bible tells us to look to an infinitely more powerful and reliable source. It categorically warns us *not* to trust in our own strength. "For a man does not prevail by his own strength" (1 Samuel 2:9 HCSB).

Human strength is puny, flimsy, and anemic when compared with God's strength. It's like comparing the power of a dollar-store firecracker to that of a hundred nuclear bombs. Even "the weakness of God is stronger than men" (1 Corinthians 1:25). That's why self-reliance is the wrong kind of strong. We are to rely on God's divine strength instead.

"Be strong in the Lord and in the strength of his might" (Ephesians 6:10). "May you be strengthened with all power, according to His glorious might" (Colossians 1:11 HCSB). "Seek the LORD and his strength; seek his presence continually!" (1 Chronicles 16:11).

A strong woman doesn't rely on her own strength; she relies on the strength of the Lord.

Paul prayed for his friends in Ephesus, "I pray that the eyes of your heart may be enlightened in order that you may know . . . his incomparably great power for us who believe. That power is the same as the mighty strength he exerted when he raised Christ from the dead and seated him at his right hand in the heavenly realms" (Ephesians 1:18–20 NIV).

I am awestruck every time I meditate on this verse. It contains a truth that is simply jaw-dropping. Eyebrow-raising. Mind-blowing.

Just think: If you believe in Jesus, the incomparably great power of God—the *same power* that raised Jesus from the dead—is accessible to you! It's the immeasurable, great, and vast power of the Lord God Almighty, Creator of the Universe. He is "robed with strength" (Psalm 65:6 HCSB). "He has put on strength as his belt" (93:1). "Awesome is God from his sanctuary; . . . he is the one who gives power and strength to his people" (68:35).

I am overwhelmed when I consider that the power that formed the mountains, waterfalls, oceans, stars, and galaxies, the power that can bring the dead to life, is the same power that is at work in me. The thought is stunning. Staggering. Breathtaking. It's a truth that's difficult to grasp. No wonder Paul prayed that the light bulb might turn on so that believers would truly get it.

I don't think we can even begin to comprehend the magnitude of the strength we have in God. He "is able to do far more abundantly than all that we ask or think, according to the power at work within us" (Ephesians 3:20).

Can you imagine how different your life would be if you grasped that *his* power is at work in you? That *his* strength is at your disposal? And that you will become stronger and stronger as you increasingly lean on *him*, and not on your own capabilities?

Everything we have—all our talents and gifts and abilities—comes from God. Every breath we draw and every ounce of strength we possess comes from God. It's inappropriate for us to think that we can credit even the smallest accomplishment to our own strength. "Beware lest you say in your heart, 'My power and the might of my hand have gotten me this wealth.' You shall remember the LORD your God, for it is he who gives you power" (Deuteronomy 8:17–18).

I am simply a steward of what God has entrusted to me. I owe it to him to submit all my talents and strengths to his direction and control, and to give credit where credit is due.

"If anyone speaks, it should be as one who speaks God's words; if anyone serves, it should be from the strength God provides, so that God may be glorified through Jesus Christ in everything. To Him belong the glory and the power forever and ever" (1 Peter 4:11 HCSB).

In the Corinthian church, some people were self-importantly strutting their own strength and know-how. Paul asked them, "Who makes you so superior? What do you have that you didn't receive? If, in fact, you did receive it, why do you boast as if you hadn't received it?" (1 Corinthians 4:7 HCSB).

The rebuke that King Nebuchadnezzar got from the Lord several hundred years earlier wasn't nearly so gentle. Nebuchadnezzar had pridefully gushed, "Is not this great Babylon, which I have built by my mighty power as a royal residence and for the glory of my majesty?" (Daniel 4:30).

While the words were still in his mouth, God took him down a few notches. Nebuchadnezzar was struck with a debilitating mental illness. His sanity did not return until he looked up to heaven and acknowledged that God was God and he was not. Even though Nebuchadnezzar was king, he needed to learn that he was weak and insignificant in comparison to the almighty King, and that any ability and power he had actually came from God (vv. 31–37).

The Lord doesn't want us to forget that everything we are and have comes from him. Even when we're good at something. Even when we're operating out of the sweet spot of our personal strengths, talents, and gifts. *Even then* we are to rely on the Lord.

God told his people, "Woe to those who go down to Egypt for help and rely on horses, who trust in chariots because they are many and in horsemen because they are very strong, but do not look to the Holy One of Israel or consult the LORD!" (Isaiah 31:1). Going down to Egypt for help meant relying on worldly strategies and solutions, on human power and strength. You "go down to Egypt for help" whenever you rely on yourself.

King David's attitude was much more in line with the attitude God looks for. David said, "Some trust in chariots and some in horses, but we trust in the name of the LORD our God" (Psalm 20:7). That's not to say that David's army didn't use chariots and horses, but David relied on God, not on his own strength and capability, to give him the victory.

Did he give it his best effort? Yup. One hundred percent.

He also relied on God. One hundred percent.

The two mind-sets aren't incompatible. Not when we acknowledge that everything we have ultimately comes from God. He wants us to give it all we've got *and* totally rely on his strength. "Not by might, nor by power, but by my Spirit, says the LORD of hosts" (Zechariah 4:6).

Leaning on the strength of the Lord is a recurrent theme throughout Scripture. "In the 264 times the Hebrew word for 'strength' is used in the Old Testament, the majority of time the word refers to spiritual strength—to the strength of the Lord."[3] The word can mean to be strong, resolute, powerful, courageous, or firm in conviction that leads to action.[4]

Strength is possessing the inner resolve necessary to follow God's commands (Deuteronomy 11:8; 1 Chronicles 28:7).[5] That's an important point. So important that I'm going to repeat it. What is true strength? Strength is possessing the inner resolve necessary to follow God's commands.

God doesn't make us strong so that we have the power to do whatever we want. He makes us strong so that we have the power to do what *he wants*.

This is totally different from the world's perspective on strength.

Our culture says that a strong woman does whatever she sets her mind to. The Bible says that a strong woman has the power to do what

God says she should do. She has the power to be steadfast in doing what is right in God's eyes.

"Blessed are those whose strength is in you, in whose heart are the highways to Zion" (Psalm 84:5). A strong woman makes it her goal to get to Zion, the city of God. In other words, she sets her heart on following the path that God has for her. She boldly and courageously makes that journey her life's goal.

Her strength is in God and her goal is to follow him. This brings her great joy. Blessed—happy—are those whose strength is in God and in whose hearts are the highways to Zion!

Godly strength doesn't always look strong in the world's eyes. Take Jesus, for example. "He was oppressed, and he was afflicted, yet he opened not his mouth; like a lamb that is led to the slaughter, and like a sheep that before its shearers is silent, so he opened not his mouth" (Isaiah 53:7). Now, that doesn't sound very strong, does it?

Paul explained that Christ's apparent weakness wasn't actually weakness at all; it was a demonstration of strength because he was being obedient to God. He emptied himself. He assumed the form of a servant. He became "obedient to the point of death, even death on a cross" (Philippians 2:7–8).

By willingly making himself "weak" in this way, he victoriously crushed and conquered the power of sin. What the world viewed as weakness was actually an act of incalculable strength. Christ wasn't crucified because he was weak—because he wasn't strong enough to escape so unpleasant a fate. The crucifixion was the supreme expression of his strength.

Paul upheld this apparent contradiction as the model for his own behavior. He explained, "[Christ] is not weak in dealing with you, but is powerful among you. For he was crucified in weakness, but lives by the power of God. For we also are weak in him, but in dealing with you we will live with him by the power of God" (2 Corinthians 13:3–4).

The Corinthians were grumbling against Paul, saying that he was weak compared with the superapostles. Paul warned them not to be fooled by his weak bodily presence and his meek and gentle demeanor. In God's economy behavior that appears weak can be teeming with strength. Gentleness and meekness aren't weakness. These traits pack a stronger punch than harshness and impertinence. Though Paul appeared weak to the Corinthians, he knew that he was empowered with the strength of God. He knew that God would use him to crush the sin in their midst powerfully.

The Bible's Faith Hall of Fame talks about men and women who were mighty for God, though they appeared weak by the world's standards:

> Time would fail me to tell of [those] who through faith conquered kingdoms, enforced justice, obtained promises, stopped the mouths of lions, quenched the power of fire, escaped the edge of the sword, were made strong out of weakness, became mighty in war, put foreign armies to flight. Women received back their dead by resurrection. Some were tortured, refusing to accept release, so that they might rise again to a better life. Others suffered mocking and flogging, and even chains and imprisonment. They were stoned, they were sawn in two, they were killed with the sword. They went about in skins of sheep and goats, destitute, afflicted, mistreated—of whom the world was not worthy—wandering about in deserts and mountains, and in dens and caves of the earth. (Hebrews 11:32–38)

The world was not worthy of these strong individuals. People viewed them as weaklings, but they were mistaken. These faith-filled men and women had the right kind of strong!

In this section, we've noted that the right kind of strong humbly relies on God's strength. It is weak and dependent in the right kind of way. We've also established that the right kind of strong gives us the power to do what God wants us to do, even though doing the right thing can make us look weak in the eyes of the world. The next thing I want to talk about is the thing that makes the right kind of strong so incredibly phenomenal—we can be strong even when we are weak.

God's strength is made *perfect* through weakness.

WHEN I AM WEAK, THEN I AM STRONG

Human strength is a fragile illusion. It often fails when we encounter difficult circumstances. Suddenly, out of the blue, life can fall apart. An accident. A grim diagnosis. The loss of a job. Calamity. Betrayal. Relationship breakdown. These are the times when we see how weak we really are.

The slogans on our T-shirts may advertise that we have Girl Power, or that we are Pretty Smart. Pretty Tough. Pretty Awesome. Pretty Fierce. That Girls Can Do Anything, or that Strong Looks Good on Me. But deep down, we know it's not true. Our own strength is woefully inadequate. The slogans are hollow. No amount of personal empowerment can silence the nagging realization that we don't have what it takes.

We just don't.

Our strength and our sense of control are only figments of our imagination, illusions that disappear as quickly as a vapor in a puff of wind. "Surely all mankind stands as a mere breath! . . . Those of low estate are but a breath; those of high estate are a delusion; in the balances they go up; they are together lighter than a breath" (Psalm 39:5; 62:9).

Have you ever felt that way? I have.

When I have reached the end of my capability and don't have an ounce of strength left to draw on, that's when the power of God becomes exceedingly precious to me. It's then that I cling to him to receive what he has promised. "He gives strength to the weary and strengthens the powerless. Youths may faint and grow weary, and young men stumble and fall, but those who trust in the LORD will renew their strength; they will soar on wings like eagles; they will run and not grow weary; they will walk and not faint" (Isaiah 40:29–31 HCSB).

When I have no strength, there's nothing I can do but fall into the arms of my strong heavenly Father. And find strength there.

The apostle Paul often reached that point. He told his friends about the many times he'd felt weak, including his imprisonments and beatings that often left him near death.

> Five times I received at the hands of the Jews the forty lashes less one. Three times I was beaten with rods. Once I was stoned. Three times I was shipwrecked; a night and a day I was adrift at sea; on frequent journeys, in danger from rivers, danger from robbers, danger from my own people, danger from Gentiles, danger in the city, danger in the wilderness, danger at sea, danger from false brothers; in toil and hardship, through many a sleepless night, in hunger and thirst, often without food, in cold and exposure. And, apart from other things, there is the daily pressure on me of my anxiety for all the churches. Who is weak, and I am not weak? (2 Corinthians 11:24–29)

Paul said the affliction he experienced in Asia was so extreme that he and his ministry companions were utterly burdened beyond their strength and despaired of life itself.

They were sure they were going to die.

"But that was to make us rely not on ourselves," he explained, "but on God who raises the dead" (1:9).

While Paul experienced a lot of difficult things, he had one weakness that particularly irked him. He called it his "thorn in the flesh" (12:7 NASB). We don't know exactly what this weakness was, but we do know that Paul felt harassed and tormented by it. Three times he pleaded with God to take it away.

The Lord told him, "My grace is sufficient for you, for my power is made perfect in weakness" (v. 9). As a result of this answer, Paul stopped asking the Lord to get rid of it. Instead, he began to view the weakness as an opportunity for God to showcase his divine strength.

"Therefore I will boast all the more gladly of my weaknesses, so that the power of Christ may rest upon me. For the sake of Christ, then, I am content with weaknesses, insults, hardships, persecutions, and calamities. For when I am weak, then I am strong" (vv. 9–10).

The right kind of strong is "made perfect in weakness."

In other words, weakness presents the perfect occasion—the clearest, most conspicuous opportunity—to showcase God's power. God's ability shines with spectacular brilliance when it is etched against the backdrop of human inability.

God works through every human ability that is surrendered to him. But working through weakness proves that he can also work in the absence of any ability whatsoever on our part. Where it is especially obvious that we didn't have the capacity to prevail, he gets the greater glory. That's why God's strength is made perfect in weakness.

I don't know about you, but I take great comfort in the fact that *I don't need to be strong.*

It's okay to be weak.

In fact, my weakness gives God the perfect opportunity to show me that he doesn't need my strength or ability. He just needs me to lean on him.

And he'll do the rest.

Paul didn't say he liked being weak. Nor did he say he intentionally tried to be weak. No. What he said was that he was "content with weaknesses" for the sake of Christ.

He understood the value of it.

He understood that human inability is the perfect showcase to display God's ability. "We have this treasure in jars of clay, to show that the surpassing power belongs to God and not to us" (4:7).

Paul's weakness increased his dependence on Jesus. It forced him to lean in to that relationship. That's why he concluded, "When I am weak, then I am strong." As theologian J. I. Packer once said, "God uses chronic pain and weakness, along with other sorts of affliction, as his chisel for sculpting our souls. Weakness deepens dependence on Christ for strength each day. The weaker we feel, the harder we lean. And the harder we lean, the stronger we grow spiritually, even while our bodies waste away."[6]

This brings to mind the life story of Joni Eareckson Tada. In a split second on a hot July afternoon in 1967, a diving accident transformed her life forever. She went from being an active young woman to being paralyzed from the shoulders down and facing every day in a wheelchair. Joni is a quadriplegic. Today, more than fifty years after her accident, it's astonishing to see what she has accomplished. No one could have imagined it.

She is an internationally known artist who paints by mouth, a talented vocalist who has released several albums, a TV and radio host, an author of more than fifty books, and an advocate for disabled persons worldwide. She founded Joni and Friends, an international ministry to the disabled, which hosts conferences, refurbishes wheelchairs and mobility devices, encourages the disabled, and speaks up for their rights. Her story was published in an award-winning book and movie. She has received six honorary doctorates, has been honored with dozens of awards, and serves on the Disability Advisory committee of the US State Department.

Against devastating odds Joni has touched millions of lives around the world with the healing message of salvation, hope, and strength in Jesus Christ. Though she is confined to a wheelchair, she has been a ministry powerhouse for the kingdom of God. And not only has Joni done all this while living with quadriplegia, she's also battled breast cancer and chronic, excruciating lifelong pain. Every day has been a struggle.

Joni has claimed that her weakness, that is, her quadriplegia, is her greatest asset because it forces her into the arms of Jesus every single morning when she awakes.[7]

Every morning it is a challenge to get up. It is so hard living with quadriplegia and pushing 65 years old. When I wake up in the morning, my eyes are still closed, my head is on the pillow, and I can hear my girlfriend in the kitchen running water for coffee. I know she's going to come into the bedroom in a moment. She's going to give me a bed bath, do my toileting routines, exercise my legs, strap on my corset, pull up my slacks, put on my blouse, sling me into a wheelchair. Then she will push me to the bathroom, brush my teeth, brush my hair, and blow my nose. I haven't even opened my eyes yet and I'm already exhausted. I'm thinking, "I have no strength for this. God I am so tired of being a quadriplegic. I'm so tired of this. I have no ability to do this today, but I can do all things through you if you strengthen me. So would you please empower me today? Infuse within me today the grace needed to help me to open my eyes and face the day with a bright attitude, your attitude." I tell you what, when I pray that way—and it happens almost every morning—by the time my girlfriend does come into the bedroom with that cup of coffee, I've got a smile sent straight from heaven.[8]

I've met Joni. Her face absolutely glows. She is a powerful, living example of what God can do through weakness.

"Deny your weakness," wrote Joni, "and you will never realize God's strength in you. . . . The weaker I am, the harder I must lean on God's grace; the harder I lean on him, the stronger I discover him to be, and the bolder my testimony to his grace."[9]

We tend to think of weakness and strength as opposites. To be strong is a positive trait; it means to be without weakness. To be weak is a negative trait; it means to be without strength. But I hope you can see that the Bible doesn't adhere to this definition.

It redraws the lines.

Scripture teaches that everyone who relies on God is strong and that everyone who relies on self is weak. Your personal ability or inability doesn't indicate whether you are weak or strong; your dependence on God does.

We are strong whenever we depend on God. When we depend on him, he works powerfully through our strengths *and* our weaknesses. Our strengths put God's strength on display. But guess what? Our weaknesses also put God's strength on display.

You can be a strong woman regardless of what mix of strengths and weaknesses you bring to the table. Are you strong and gifted? Great! Understand that everything you have comes from God and rely on him for the wisdom and strength to use your talents for his glory.

Do you feel weak and incapable? That's great too! Because your inability is the perfect showcase for God's ability. It gives him the opportunity to prove how powerful and strong he is. It's a great paradox that, regardless of your inherent capability, embracing the right kind of weak will make you strong, and embracing the wrong kind of strong will make you weak.

Do you ever feel weak?

Contrary to what the world tells you, that feeling isn't something you should deny or be ashamed of. You are simply sensing the truth and reality of your situation. You *are* weak. We all are! A woman of strength recognizes she is weak and in need of a Savior.

She admits her need.

She knows that it's only the good kind of weak—the humble, soft, teachable kind—that will truly make her strong.

The Lord lets us feel weakness from time to time (or often, or even constantly), so we will learn to lean on his strength. He wants you to know that his grace is sufficient for you. Your weakness is the perfect showcase for his power. Leaning on him is what will make you strong. As you do, you will discover, as Joni and countless other women have, that you *can* do all things through him who gives you strength (Philippians 4:13).

CONCLUSION

Stronger and Stronger

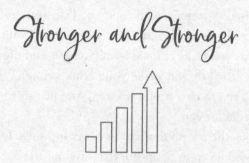

Among them are those who creep into
households and capture weak women,
burdened with sins and led astray by
various passions, always learning and never
able to arrive at a knowledge of the truth.

—2 Timothy 3:6–7

In this book we've studied the passage in which Paul called a group of women in Timothy's church weak. It's sad to think that history has immortalized them this way. In the pages of Scripture they will always be #LittleWomen—small, underdeveloped, diminished versions of the women they could have been.

I wonder whether they continued in their weak ways. Or if perhaps Paul's letter was a wake-up call. Perhaps some of them came to their senses and gave up the negative habits that were sapping them of strength.

Maybe they started to practice some positive, strength-building habits instead. A few may have grown to be as strong as Paul's friend Priscilla.

I hope so. In fact, I like to think this was the case.

Because we've all been there. All of us have walked in their shoes. All of us know what it's like to be weak in the wrong kind of way.

And even though we fail miserably at times, Scripture does not leave us without hope. We have a Champion who died for us, but even more, was raised victorious; who conquered sin and death; who even now is at the right hand of God interceding for us (Romans 8:34).

God wants you to be clothed with strength and dignity, to dress yourself with strength and make your arms strong (Proverbs 31:17, 25). He wants you to be a strong woman. And just think: to this end, Christ intercedes for you.

Remember, there is no shortcut or secret formula. There's just the time-tested wisdom from Scripture that lays out the habits necessary for building spiritual strength in your core. As I said at the start, the strength-building habits in this book aren't difficult tasks you'll need to add to your daily to-do list. They're simple, little things you can do *all the time*. If you do these things consistently you will grow stronger, but if you only think about doing them, or only do them from time to time, you won't.

Let's do a quick review of what we've learned from 2 Timothy 3:6–7 and discussed in previous chapters.

HABIT 1: CATCH THE CREEPS

A weak woman tolerates creeps ("creep into households"). She doesn't know how to spot them, nor does she have the strength to resist their advances. A strong woman remains on the lookout. She knows that sin does not advance by leaps; it advances by creeps—one tiny compromise at a time.

HABIT 2: MASTER YOUR MIND

A weak woman fails to guard her mind ("capture"). She is captivated and ensnared by patterns of thinking that are not in line with truth. A strong woman aligns her thinking with truth. She seeks to take every thought captive for Christ.

HABIT 3: DITCH THE BAGGAGE

A weak woman is loaded down with sin, guilt, and shame ("burdened with sins"). She doesn't deal with her accumulating baggage. A strong woman makes a habit of confessing quickly, honestly, openly, and with godly sorrow. She delights in the freedom and joy of Christ's forgiveness.

HABIT 4: ENGAGE YOUR EMOTIONS

A weak woman is governed by emotions ("led astray by various passions"). She suppresses her emotions, or she puts her brain in park and lets her emotions drive her around. A strong woman gets a grip on her emotions. She doesn't let Satan use them against her. Instead, she offers them up to God as weapons for righteousness.

HABIT 5: WALK THE TALK

A weak woman doesn't apply what she learns ("always learning and never able to arrive"). A strong woman understands that nothing is learned until it is applied. She examines her heart for signs of hypocrisy and consistently takes small steps of obedience.

HABIT 6: STAND YOUR GROUND

A weak woman doesn't have solid convictions ("knowledge of the truth"). She is swayed easily by new, popular ideas pushed by religious celebrities and Facebook friends. A strong woman exercises discernment. She holds fast to sound doctrine even when it is unpopular or seems old-fashioned.

HABIT 7: ADMIT YOUR NEED

A weak woman embraces the wrong kind of strong ("weak women"). A strong woman knows that constantly leaning on Jesus is what will make her strong. She acknowledges that all she is and has comes from him. She is strong even when she is weak, for God's power is made perfect in her weakness.

STRONG AND COURAGEOUS
EVERY STEP OF THE WAY

I introduced the previous chapter by telling you the story of getting into a fight with my brother Gordon because he called me a weak, sissy girl. I need to tell you the rest of the story.

With my fists raised, I slowly circled around the ring we had created, staring my opponent down. I knew that was the proper way to start a fight based on what I had seen in after-school dustups.

I circled a couple of times, then I started to swing.

At first my brother simply took evasive maneuvers. He was amused.

I was miffed that he wouldn't wipe that infuriating smile off his face. I swung harder. Somehow I managed to smack him full force in the nose. And the cocky smile disappeared.

That's when he started to fight.

And that's when I started to lose.

His blows hurt. It wasn't long before I was a sobbing, enraged, out-of-control mess, clawing and screaming and kicking as best as I could. Even though he was clearly winning, there was no way I would quit or admit defeat.

It was clear he was substantially stronger. There was no way I could ever win a fight with him.

Our brother Bert, who was a year older than Gordon, heard the commotion from downstairs and came up to investigate. He walked into the living room just as Gordon pinned me down face-first on the carpet. Grabbing Gordon by the scruff of the neck, Bert pulled him off me and shouted, "How dare you hit your sister!"

Snuffling, I explained that Gordon had called me a weak, sissy girl.

Annoyed, Bert retorted, "You better figure out that you *are* a girl, and that if you get into fights with him, you're going to get beat up." He continued, "Next time you have an issue, call me. And I'll deal with it."

I smile when I consider how accurately this childhood encounter reflects some deep spiritual truths about strength and weakness.

I don't like being called weak. I don't particularly like that Paul called women in the church in Ephesus weak.

But the truth is, all of us *are* weak.

In the battle against sin and deceit, our own strength is woefully inadequate. We think that we're strong enough to handle things, but we're not. Without help, we'll get walloped.

Every time.

Here's the irony: A weak woman tries to act strong. But a woman of strength recognizes that she's weak and in need of a Savior.

With Jesus Christ as our mighty Savior, we are able to win the battle. Not because we are so strong and invincible, but because he is.

Moses felt weak. When God commanded him to lead the children of Israel out of Egypt and into the promised land, he tried to talk his way out of the assignment. But the Lord wouldn't let him off the

THE RIGHT KIND OF *Strong*

hook. Every time the eighty-year-old came up with an objection about his weakness and lack of ability, the Lord nixed it. In essence, he told Moses, "The fact that you are weak is inconsequential. I am strong. I will be with you. I will help you. I will teach you. I am the one who will make it all happen" (Exodus 3:11; 4:10–17).

Moses must have learned a thing or two over the years, because when he addressed the people of Israel shortly before his death, as they were on the verge of entering the promised land, he urged them to be strong and courageous. He assured them that the Lord would go with them and fight on their behalf.

That's why they could be strong.

That's why they could be courageous.

> Be strong and courageous; don't be terrified or afraid of them. For it is the LORD your God who goes with you; He will not leave you or forsake you." Moses then summoned Joshua and said to him in the sight of all Israel, "Be strong and courageous, for you will go with this people into the land the LORD swore to give to their fathers. You will enable them to take possession of it. The LORD is the One who will go before you. He will be with you; He will not leave you or forsake you. Do not be afraid or discouraged. (Deuteronomy 31:6–8 HCSB)

The charge to be strong and courageous is repeated numerous times throughout the Bible. And each time, the reason for this bold attitude didn't rest on the ability of the individuals who were being commissioned. It rested on the fact that God would be with them. "Haven't I commanded you? Strength! Courage! Don't be timid; don't get discouraged. GOD, your God, is with you every step you take" (Joshua 1:9 THE MESSAGE).

God, your God, is with you *every step you take.*

It's a great reminder. Because becoming a strong woman doesn't just happen overnight. There are many steps on this journey. It takes years of consistent habits; thousands of small, seemingly insignificant steps of obedience. These small steps, taken consistently over time, will make a radical difference in your life. Godly habits are what will turn you into a strong godly woman. And at the end of your life, you will have the satisfaction of looking back and knowing that you were strong in the Lord.

The right kind of strong.

The only strong that really matters.

So, in closing, let me commission you with this charge: "Be strong in the Lord and in the strength of his might" (Ephesians 6:10). You *can* do all things through him who gives you strength. So be strong and very courageous.

"Don't be timid. Don't get discouraged. GOD, your God, will be with you every step of the way."

Looking for discussion questions and leader
helps? Visit www.marykassian.com

SEVEN STRENGTH-
BUILDING HABITS

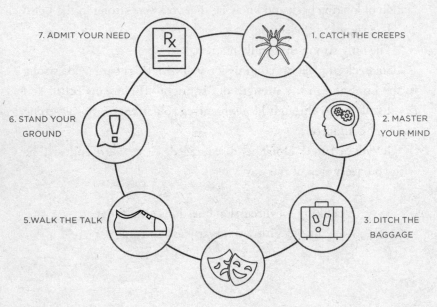

7. ADMIT YOUR NEED

1. CATCH THE CREEPS

6. STAND YOUR
GROUND

2. MASTER
YOUR MIND

5.WALK THE TALK

3. DITCH THE
BAGGAGE

4. ENGAGE YOUR EMOTIONS

NOTES

NO WEAK GIRLS HERE

1. "These Boots Are Made for Walkin'," performed by Nancy Sinatra, written by Lee Hazlewood, 1966. "Respect," performed by Aretha Franklin, written by Otis Redding, 1967. "I Am Woman," performed by Helen Reddy, written by Helen Reddy and Ray Burton, 1971.

2. I am indebted for much of my information about ancient Ephesus to Steven Baugh and his extensive study of Ephesian inscriptions. See Steven Baugh, "A Foreign World: Ephesus in the First Century," in *Women in the Church: A Fresh Analysis of 1 Timothy 2:9–15*, eds. Andreas J. Köstenberger, Thomas R. Schreiner, and H. Scott Baldwin (Grand Rapids, MI: Baker Books, 1995), 46–47. See also G. L. Borchert, "Ephesus," in *The International Standard Bible Encyclopedia*, vol. 2, ed. Geoffrey W. Bromiley, rev. ed. (Chicago, IL: Howard-Severence Company, 1915; Grand Rapids, MI: Eerdmans, 1982), 115–17.

3. Matthew G. Easton, *Easton's Bible Dictionary* (New York: Harper & Brothers, 1893).

4. Steven Baugh, "Cult Prostitution in New Testament Ephesus: A Reappraisal," *Journal of the Evangelical Theological Society* 42, no. 3 (September 1999): 452, http://www.etsjets.org/files/JETS-PDFs/42/42 -3/42-3-pp443–460_JETS.pdf.

5. Mark Cartwright, "Temple of Artemis at Ephesus," *Ancient History Encyclopedia*, accessed December 6, 2018, https://www.ancient.eu /Temple_of_Artemis_at_Ephesus/.

6. Steven Baugh, "A Foreign World," 46–47.

7. "Run the World (Girls)," performed by Beyoncé, written by Terius "The Dream" Nash and Beyoncé, 2011. "Independent Women," performed by Destiny's Child, written by Beyoncé, Cory Rooney, Samuel Barnes, and Jean-Claude Olivier, 2000. "Confident," performed by Demi Lovato, written by Demi Lovato and Savan Kotecha, 2015. "Fight Song," performed by Rachel Platten, written by Rachel Platten and Dave Bassett, 2015. "Brave," performed by Sara Bareilles, written by Sara Bareilles and Jack Antonoff, 2013. "Stronger," performed by Britney Spears, written by Max Martin and Rami Yacoub, 2000.

HABIT1 : CATCH THE CREEPS

1. Corey Charlton, "This Thai Woman Holds the Guinness World Record for Holding a Deadly Scorpion in Her Mouth for More Than Three Minutes," *The Sun*, June 5, 2017, https://www.thesun.co.uk /news/3728554/thai-woman-guinness-world-record-held-scorpion-in -mouth-three-minutes/.

2. "Phobia List—The Ultimate List of Phobias and Fears," FearOf.net, retrieved December 13, 2018, https://www.fearof.net/.

3. Johannes P. Louw and Eugene Albert Nida, *Greek-English Lexicon of the New Testament: Based on Semantic Domains* (New York: United Bible Societies, 1996), 194. Also, Barclay M. Newman Jr., *A Concise Greek-English Dictionary of the New Testament* (Stuttgart, Germany: Deutsche Bibelgesellschaft; United Bible Societies, 1993), 60.

4. C. S. Lewis, *The Screwtape Letters*, rev. ed. (London: Geoffrey Bles, 1942; San Francisco: HarperOne, 2015), ix.

5. *Autobiography of Charles Darwin*, rev. ed. (London: John Murray, 1887; New York: Barnes and Noble Publishing, 2005), 156.

6. "How Much Time Do We Spend on Social Media?" Mediakix, December 15, 2016.

HABIT 2: MASTER YOUR MIND

1. Soren Billing, "Four Decades of Stockholm Syndrome," *The Local*, August 21, 2013, available at: https://www.thelocal.se/20130821/49754, accessed December 13, 2018.

2. Christopher Klein, "The Birth of 'Stockholm Syndrome,' 40 Years Ago," *History*, August 23, 2013, https://www.history.com/news /stockholm-syndrome.

3. "Patty Hearst," Biography, updated November 28, 2017, https://www .biography.com/people/patty-hearst-9332960.

4. Johannes P. Louw and Eugene. A. Nida, *Greek-English Lexicon of the New Testament: Based on Semantic Domains*, vol. 1, 2nd ed. (New York: United Bible Societies, 1989), 352.

5. Esther Landhuis, "Neuroscience: Big Brain, Big Data," *Scientific American*, January 26, 2017, https://www.scientificamerican.com /neuroscience-big-brain-big-data/.

6. The National Science Foundation, quoted in Fran Simone, "Negative Self-Talk: Don't Let It Overwhelm You," *Psychology Today*, December 4, 2017, https://www.psychologytoday.com/us/blog/family-affair/201712 /negative-self-talk-dont-let-it-overwhelm-you.

7. "What Would Jesus Do?: The Rise of a Slogan," *BBC News*, December 8, 2011, https://www.bbc.com/news/magazine-16068178.

8. R. C. Sproul, quoted in Nathan W. Bingham, "Renewing Your Mind: Celebrating 20 Years and Still Growing," Ligonier Ministries, October 8, 2014, https://www.ligonier.org/blog/renewing-your-mind-celebrating -20-years-and-still-growing/.

9. Tim Challies, "Renew Your Mind," Challies (website), May 26, 2017, https://www.challies.com/articles/renew-your-mind/.

10. Spiros Zodhiates, ed., *The Complete Word Study Dictionary: New Testament* (Chattanooga, TN: AMG Publishers, 2000).

HABIT 3: DITCH THE BAGGAGE

1. Terrence McCoy, "The Strange Saga of Now-Dead Billionaire South Korean Ferry Owner Yoo Byung-Un," *Washington Post*, accessed April 3, 2018, https://www.washingtonpost.com/news/morning-mix /wp/2014/07/22/the-strange-saga-of-now-dead-billionaire-south -korean-ferry-owner-yoo-byung-un/?utm_term=.bb941e8d7407; Choe Sang-Hun, Martin Fackler, Alison Leigh Cowan, and Scott Sayare, "In Ferry Deaths, a South Korean Tycoon's Downfall," Nytimes.com,

July 26, 2014, accessed April 3, 2018, https://www.nytimes.com/2014 /07/27/world/asia/in-ferry-deaths-a-south-korean-tycoons-downfall .html; "South Korea Ferry Disaster Suspect Hid as Cops Searched Cabin," *NBC News*, accessed April 3, 2018, https://www.nbcnews.com /storyline/south-korea-ferry-disaster/south-korea-ferry-disaster-suspect -hid-cops-searched-cabin-n162861; "Thousands March in South Korea Anti-Government Protest over Ferry Disaster," *CBC News*, accessed April 5, 2018, http://www.cbc.ca/news/world/south-korea-ferry-disaster -sparks-anti-government-protest-1.3048816, *The Times*, 2015, "Ferry Disaster in South Korea: a Year Later," Nytimes.com, accessed April 3, 2018, https://www.nytimes.com/interactive/2015/04/12/world/asia /12ferry-timeline.html#/#time367_10851.

2. Will L. Thompson, "Softly and Tenderly," 1880, https://library.timeless truths.org/music/Softly_and_Tenderly/.

3. "Sin," Urban Dictionary, February 1, 2018, https://www.urban dictionary.com/define.php?term=Sin.

4. "Billy Graham's Answer: What Is Sin? Are All Sins Equal in God's Eyes?" Billy Graham Evangelistic Association, March 26, 2014, https://billygraham.org/story/billy-grahams-answer-what-is-sin-are -all-sins-equal-in-gods-eyes/.

5. R. E. O. White, "Sin," in *Baker Encyclopedia of the Bible*, vol. 2, ed. Walter A. Elwell (Grand Rapids, MI: Baker Book House, 1988), 1968. See also Deuteronomy 5; Matthew 5:33–35; 6:1–6, 9–10, 25–33; 22:35–38; 23:2–4, 16–26; 25:41–46; Mark 3:28–30; Luke 12:16–21; 16:19–31; Romans 1:28–32; 1 Corinthians 5:11; 6:9–10; 2 Corinthians 12:20–21; Galatians 5:19–21; Ephesians 4:25–32; 5:1–4; Philippians 4:6; 2 Timothy 3:1–3.

6. Thompson, "Softly and Tenderly."

7. Simon J. Kistemaker and William Hendriksen, *Baker's New Testament Commentary*, vol. 16, *James and the Epistles of John* (Grand Rapids, MI: Baker Book House, 1986), 246. See also Colin G. Kruse, *The Letters of John*, The Pillar New Testament Commentary (Grand Rapids, MI: Eerdmans; Leicester, United Kingdom: Apollos, 2000), 68.

8. Kenneth S. Wuest, *Word Studies from the Greek New Testament*, vol. 1 (Grand Rapids, MI: Eerdmans, 1955), 177.

HABIT 4: ENGAGE YOUR EMOTIONS

1. Douglas J. Moo, *The Letter of James*, The Pillar New Testament Commentary (Grand Rapids, MI: Eerdmans; Leicester, United Kingdom: Apollos, 2000), 74.

2. Randy Alcorn, "Emotions: Part of Being Created in God's Image," Eternal Perspective Ministries, May 2, 2011, https://www.epm.org /blog/2011/May/2/emotions-part-being-created-gods-image.

3. D. Martyn Lloyd-Jones, *Spiritual Depression: Its Causes and Cures* (Grand Rapids, MI: Zondervan, 1965), 60.

4. G. Walter Hansen, "The Emotions of Jesus," *Christianity Today*, February 3, 1997, https://www.christianitytoday.com/ct/1997/february 3/7t2042.html.

5. Matthew Elliott, *Feel: The Power of Listening to Your Heart* (self-pub., Amazon CreateSpace, 2014), 36.

6. See Mary A. Kassian and Nancy Leigh DeMoss, *True Woman 101: Divine Design, An Eight-Week Study on Biblical Womanhood* (Chicago, IL: Moody Publishers, 2012), 102.

7. Os Guinness, *God in the Dark: The Assurance of Faith Beyond a Shadow of Doubt* (Wheaton, IL: Crossway, 1996), 128.

8. Carolyn Mahaney and Nicole Whitacre, *True Feelings: God's Gracious and Glorious Purpose for Our Emotions* (Wheaton, IL: Crossway, 2017), 51.

9. Lloyd-Jones, *Spiritual Depression*, 65.

10. Mahaney and Whitacre, *True Feelings*, 58.

11. Andrew Colman, *A Dictionary of Psychology*, 3rd ed. (Oxford, United Kingdom: Oxford University Press, 2015), 248.

12. Elliott, *Feel*, 52.

13. Jon Bloom, "Your Emotions Are a Gauge, Not a Guide," Desiring God, August 3, 2012, https://www.desiringgod.org/articles/your -emotions-are-a-gauge-not-a-guide.

14. Lloyd-Jones, *Spiritual Depression*, 20.

15. Blaise Pascal, *Thoughts*, tr. W. F. Trotter (New York: P. F. Collier & Son, 1910), 136.
16. C. S. Lewis, *The Weight of Glory: and Other Addresses*, rev. ed. (London: Geoffrey Bles, 1949; San Francisco: HarperOne, 2001), 26.

HABIT 5: WALK THE TALK

1. "Number of English Translations of the Bible," American Bible Society, December 2, 2009, http://news.americanbible.org/article /number-of-english-translations-of-the-bible.
2. "Faith Has a Limited Effect on Most People's Behavior," Barna Research, May 24, 2004, https://www.barna.com/resear ch/faith-has -a-limited-effect-on-most-peoples-behavior/; "Research: Only 17% of Christians Actually Have a Biblical Worldview," *Relevant*, May 11, 2017, https://relevantmagazine.com/slice/research-only-17-of-christians -actually-have-a-biblical-worldview/.
3. "Leaning Tower of Pisa Facts," Leaning Tower of Pisa, http://www .towerofpisa.org/leaning-tower-of-pisa-facts/. Philippe Ridet, "Leaning Tower of Pisa Straightens Up," *The Guardian*, September 24, 2013, https://www.theguardian.com/artanddesign/2013/sep/24/leaning -tower-pisa-restoration-architecture.
4. I previously talked about the signs of hypocrisy in another book: Mary A. Kassian, *Girls Gone Wise in a World Gone Wild* (Chicago, IL: Moody Publishers, 2010), 174–178.
5. "Standing in the Need of Prayer," African-American spiritual, https:// hymnary.org/text/not_my_brother_nor_my_sister_but_its_me.
6. *The Very Best of Malcolm Muggeridge*, ed. Ian Hunter, 2nd ed. (London: Hodder & Stoughton Ltd.; Vancouver, British Columbia: Regent College Publishing, 2003), 109.
7. Several commentators have weighed in on the question of Isaac's age at the time of this event. Most believe that he was more than eighteen years old. For a review of the literature and a summary of the arguments, see Dave Miller, "How Old Was Isaac When Abraham Was Told to Offer Him?" Apologetics Press, 2003, https://www .apologeticspress.org/APContent.aspx?category=11&article=1272.

HABIT 6: STAND YOUR GROUND

1. Andrew Knighton, "When Rome Crushed Israel: The Siege of Masada," *War History Online*, March 1, 2018, https://www.warhistoryonline.com /ancient-history/rome-crushed-israel-masada.html.

2. Anthony J. Saldarini, "Knowledge," in *The HarperCollins Bible Dictionary*, ed. Mark Allan Powell, 3rd ed. (San Francisco: HarperOne, 2011), 521–22.

3. A. H. Pierce, "Hellenistic Schools" in *The Lexham Bible Dictionary*, ed. John D. Barry et. al (Bellingham, WA: Lexham Press, 2016).

4. "10 Famous and Great Philosophers in Greek History," EnkiVillage, https://www.enkivillage.org/famous-greek-philosophers.html.

5. "Epicureanism," ReligionFacts, March 17, 2015, http://www.religion facts.com/epicureanism.

6. "10 Famous and Great Philosophers in Greek History."

7. "Epicureanism and Religion," The Basics of Philosophy, 2009, https:// www.philosophybasics.com/branch_epicureanism.html.

8. Chris Fisher, "The Stoic God—Episode 3," April 5, 2018, in *Stoicism on Fire*, podcast, MP3 audio, http://www.traditionalstoicism.com/the -stoic-god-episode-3/.

9. "Stoicism: Practical Philosophy You Can Actually Use," Ryan Holiday, Meditations on Strategy and Life (website), June 17, 2014, https://ryan holiday.net/stoicism-a-practical-philosophy-you-can-actually-use/.

10. W. D. Mounce, *Word Biblical Commentary*, vol. 46, *Pastoral Epistles* (Nashville, TN: Thomas Nelson, 2000), 549.

11. For an excellent overview of the doctrine of the Word of God and the authority of our canon of Scripture, I suggest you read Wayne Grudem, *Systematic Theology: An Introduction to Biblical Doctrine* (Leicester, England: Inter-Varsity Press; Grand Rapids, MI: Zondervan, 1994).

12. David Emery, "Did the 1938 Radio Broadcast of 'War of The Worlds' Cause a Nationwide Panic?" Snopes, October 28, 2016, https://www .snopes.com/fact-check/war-of-the-worlds/.

13. A. Brad Schwartz, "The Infamous 'War of The Worlds' Radio Broadcast Was a Magnificent Fluke," Smithsonian.com, May 6, 2015, https://www.smithsonianmag.com/history/infamous-war-worlds-radio -broadcast-was-magnificent-fluke-180955180/.

14. "Fake White House Bomb Report Causes Brief Stock Market Panic," *CBC News*, updated December 17, 2014, http://www.cbc.ca/news /business/fake-white-house-bomb-report-causes-brief-stock-market -panic-1.1352024.
15. Walter A. Elwell and Philip W. Comfort, eds., *Tyndale Bible Dictionary* (Wheaton, IL: Tyndale House Publishers, 2001), 535.
16. T. H. White, *The Book of Merlyn: The Conclusion to the Once and Future King* (Austin, TX: University of Texas Press, 1977), 132.
17. Knofel Staton, *Timothy–Philemon, Unlocking the Scriptures for You*, 2nd ed. (Cincinnati, OH: Standard, 1988; Eugene, OR: Wipf and Stock, 2001), 147.
18. Staton, *Timothy–Philemon*.
19. "Doctrine," *English Oxford Living Dictionaries*, https://en.oxford dictionaries .com/definition/doctrine; "Doctrine," *Collins Dictionary*, https://www.collinsdictionary.com/dictionary/english/doctrine.
20. Grudem, *Systematic Theology*, 83.
21. Grudem, *Systematic Theology*, 83.

HABIT 7: ADMIT YOUR NEED

1. "I Am Woman," Reddy and Burton.
2. Danielle Campoamor, "What It Means to Be a 'Strong' Woman," HuffPost, October 21, 2016, https://www.huffingtonpost.com /danielle-campoamor/what-it-means-to-be-a-strong-woman_b_83 41406.html.
3. Eugene E. Carpenter and Philip W. Comfort, *Holman Treasury of Key Bible Words: 200 Greek and 200 Hebrew Words Explained and Defined* (Nashville, TN: Broadman & Holman Publishers, 2000), 182.
4. Ingrid S. Faro, "Strength," in *Lexham Theological Wordbook*, eds. Douglas Mangum et al., Lexham Bible Reference Series (Bellingham, WA: Lexham Press, 2014).
5. Faro, "Strength."
6. J. I. Packer, *In God's Presence: Daily Devotions with J. I. Packer*, ed. Jean Watson (Colorado Springs, CO: Shaw Books, 2000), 19.
7. Joni Eareckson Tada, interview by Eryn Sun, "Joni Eareckson Tada on

Wilberforce Award, 'Better Off Dead than Disabled' Mentality," *The Christan Post*, 2011, https://www.christianpost.com/news/joni -eareckson-tada-on-wilberforce-award-better-off-dead-than-disabled -mentality-71536/.

8. Joni Eareckson Tada, interview by Warren Cole Smith, "Joni Eareckson Tada: Suffering Is Sacred," *World*, October 22, 2014, https:// world.wng.org/2014/10/joni_eareckson_tada_suffering_is_sacred.

9. Joni Eareckson Tada, *God's Hand in Our Hardship* (Peabody, MA: Rose Publishing, 2012).

ABOUT THE AUTHOR

Mary A. Kassian is an award-winning author and international speaker. She has published several books and Bible studies, including *Girls Gone Wise in a World Gone Wild* and *Conversation Peace: The Power of Transformed Speech*. She and her family reside in Canada.